W9-BYS-683

"Today Asia is of utmost importance to Americans. What happens there may make or mar us as a nation. We need to know what makes Asia tick. I had the good luck to travel to many towns and villages in Asia and to talk with the people about what worried them. I met rickshaw boys and millionaires, peasant farmers and heads of state. They told me about the religious problems, the economic questions and the social revolutions that disturb them today. I talked of America and of Russia; and, like people everywhere, they told me some very funny stories about their politicians. In *The Voice of Asia* I have tried to share with you what the people of Asia told me."

JAMES A. MICHENER

Gift of
Dr. Harriet Semke

THE

VOICE

OF

ASIA

THE
VOICE
OF
ASIA

87-1771

BY JAMES A. MICHENER

Random House · New York

To
Ted Patrick

CONTENTS

THE COWARD   1

JAPAN   9

The New Japanese Woman   13
The Japanese Soldier   17
Clichés in a Tool Factory   20
The Ashes of Empire   23
Reasonable Doubts at a Strip Tease   27
The Proconsul   30
Observations   40

KOREA   45

The Tides of War   47
The Bureaucrat   50
Boy-san   53
The Unforgettable Face   56
Old Papa-san   58
Observations   61

CONTENTS

FORMOSA   64

    Indian Summer in Formosa   65
    The Governor's Mansion   67
    The Hard Way   70
    The Tank Commanders   72
    Observations   74

HONG KONG   80

    No Panic in the Streets   82
    The Old China Hand   84
    The Hundred Visitors   87
    The American   89
    Observations   92

SINGAPORE   94

    The New Leader   97
    The New Intellectual   100
    The Multimillionaire   102
    The Marginal Man   105
    The Schoolteacher   107
    The Man Without a Country   110
    Observations   113

CONTENTS

INDONESIA   116

    A Grand Old Man at 36   118
    Hercules Would Have Shivered   121
    Irian, Irian!   123
    The Crying Dutchman   126
    Observations   129

THAILAND   134

    The Buddhist Monk   138
    And Just a Little Magic   141
    The Samlor Boy   144
    Observations   146

INDO-CHINA   150

    The Scourge of Empire   152
    The Commander's Letter   154

BURMA   158

    The Patriot   159
    Housewife in Asia   162
    Three Rupees, Sahib   165
    Observations   168

INDIA 171

The Great Debate 172
The Case Against the New Woman 175
In Defense of the New Woman 178
Marriage for Love 181
Breaking the Caste System 184
The Hungry Old Man 187
The Refugee 189
The Optimist 192
The Cynic 194
The Grace of Asia 197
At the Waterhole 203
The Fight for Food 207
The New Mem-sahibs 210
Observations 214

PAKISTAN 216

Quaid-i-Azam 220
The Sheikh's Women 223
Motamar 225
Observations 228

AMERICA AND ASIA 233

Basic Facts for Americans 237
We Will Have a Second Chance 241
A Few Rules 243
Perspective 245

THE

VOICE

OF

ASIA

THE COWARD

I AM NO BRAVER THAN MOST MEN AND PROBABLY NO MORE CRAVEN, but once recently I was indeed a coward and I have regretted it ever since. On this particular subject of my cowardice, at least, I have determined never again to be afraid.

In 1945, after long months of rather silent speculation, I sat down in my hut on a tropical island and wrote an account of what it was actually like to serve in these waters. I called my narrative *Tales of the South Pacific* and discovered with pleased astonishment that several very good things would happen to it.

But one very bad thing happened too, and for that my cowardice was largely responsible. In the months prior to writing I had been reviewing the Pacific as I saw it and my thoughts were pretty well distilled in one story called "Lobeck, the Asiatic."

This Lobeck was a professor from the University of Virginia, an ineffectual sort of man who found himself thrust into the Navy because in Virginia it was traditional for men of good family to serve in that branch. He brought with him his interest in anthropology and a hankering suspicion that perhaps the white man, after all, had not been destined by God to rule all colored races. This heresy, of course, he had kept to himself as one of those peculiar and fantastic aberrations to which professors are prone.

But when he found himself in the Pacific he discovered that his mind kept thrusting ever westward to Asia and all he had ever read about this continent became additionally meaningful to him. He scoured the island libraries, reading all he could find. He talked with old Navy hands from the China station. And as sometimes happens to minds not otherwise occupied, he drifted into a monomania, out of which he developed the idea that America's destiny would not be determined by her relations with Europe, as he had always taken for granted, but rather in Asia, where the bulk of the world's population resided and from which no doubt would rise the bulk of the world's problems.

He used to bore his companions with these theories until one day they took him upon a safari through Bougainville, searching for a remittance man who had been sending radio messages concerning Japanese movements in the Slot. When Lobeck saw the utter filth of the jungle, when he saw old men with scrotums that had to be carried in wheelbarrows he became sick and his companions laughed: "You've been bleating about Asia. But at the first taste you throw up. Some Asiatic!" To this the queasy-stomached man replied, "What's important is that so far as Asia is concerned I'm still right."

When the manuscript was submitted, all but one critic said that the Lobeck story was no good. Had no humor, wasn't well written, and was based on a ridiculous idea. And since the book was overlong, and especially since Asia had nothing to do with stories about the South Pacific, it really ought to go.

I was new at these things and was grateful for having a book published at all; so against my better judgment I killed Lobeck and his Asiatic monomania. Well, it's not quite right to say I killed him, for like any venal author I quietly took the best parts of the story and tucked them back into other stories—from which they were lifted right onto a Broadway stage, where they didn't seem dull at all—and the final manuscript turned out to be almost as long as it was in the first place. I achieved this legerdemain by numbering page 327 twenty-four times, from 327a through 327w.

But when that most perceptive critic Granville Hicks reread the manuscript he took the trouble to come right into New York and say, "When you cut the part about Asia you cut the heart out of your book."

I said, "I felt the same way, but I had to follow advice."

Hicks said, "Sometimes you can get the wrong advice."

I said, "This is my first book and I can't fight everybody. I've already accomplished a miracle in cutting."

Hicks said, "Yes, I noticed your miracle of numbering one page twenty-four times. But can't you fit in this Asia business somewhere?"

We studied the manuscript but I could find no place to do so. Ever since I have regretted the omission. I feel this the more since I did stand fast on one other story which was also labeled dull by the readers. This was "Wine for the Mess at Segi," a trivial little yarn about some Navy men trying to get a case of whiskey. I was warned that civilians would be bored by this, for nothing happened and the subject matter was too topical. This time I insisted that for me such a story really was the South Pacific, and almost every veteran from that area who has written to me about the book has said that this yarn was the one that rang true and partly excused some of the other silly nonsense I had made up.

It takes time for a writer to determine just what his rights and obligations are. Hardy and Dostoyevsky were persuaded to change the ends of their finest novels—for the worse—and I make no apologies; but now I know certain things I didn't know in 1945 and I offer belatedly the central portion of my deleted story, written while the war was at its height.

Lobeck, The Asiatic

. . . That night Lobeck began to rant. He was declaiming about Asia. At first I thought he was drunk but the clarity of his speech dispelled that idea, for as he explained his theories to us it became clear that he really believed what he said.

"I'm maintaining," he insisted, "that we'll lick Japan this time. But when we've done so we still face the problem of Asia."

"Nuts," Tony Fry grunted. "Asia is Japan and Japan is Asia. Knock Japan back in line and we'll have no more trouble."

"I don't think so!" Lobeck cried. "You know what I think?"

"Who cares?" an ensign growled.

Lobeck laughed nervously and said, "I think China and Japan will unite under some new slogan. Maybe right after this war ends. And all the trouble will start fresh."

"China and Japan!" the ensign shouted. "By God, Lobeck, you have gone Asiatic."

This was the first time this curious phrase had been used to describe Lobeck and we all stopped a moment to consider the strange fellow to whom it had been applied. The phrase was appropriate, for in island slang anyone who went off his rocker was labeled Asiatic. A soldier might grab his rifle and batter his way to the heart of some Jap position. Back home they gave him all sorts of medals but his companions dismissed him as the poor bastard who finally went Asiatic. The officer who brooded in his tent, perpetually drunk and screwing up his courage to bust the skipper in the nose—he was an Asiatic, too. We used the mysterious word to describe the mysteriousness of this life three years from home. By the simple application of the term we understood Lobeck. The poor bastard really had gone Asiatic.

A couple of officers reported to the captain that night and said Lobeck was beginning to jump his trolley: "Sir, the poor guy is talking about China and Japan uniting in a war against us."

The captain snorted and said, "He's feeling the heat." Then he called me in and said, "You know Lobeck. Keep an eye on him. Find out what's eating him and let me know."

I had a chance to talk with the professor the next afternoon and asked casually, "What's this about China going to war against us? Where'd you get that idea?"

The moody Virginian laughed and said, "Why should such an idea worry you? It's inevitable."

"I don't get it. China's a nation today principally because we backed her revolution."

"That doesn't matter. Do you remember when the Arabs of Western Asia tried to take things into their own hands? Spain finally defeated them. Then India had an abortive revolution, but England slapped her back into line. Now Japan is trying to organize Asia and it's us who beat her back into shape. But absolutely without question some other Asiatic country will make another try. I think it'll be a union of China and Japan."

"But they're mortal enemies! You ought to read history and lay off the opium."

"Enmities don't last long when something bigger is at stake. And Asia is pretty big."

"You think we'll have to fight all of Asia?"

"I don't know. But Asia is going to consolidate and probably they'll think they have to fight us."

"With China and Japan doing the fighting?"

"Unquestionably."

I went back to the captain and said, "Well, Lobeck really is in a pretty bad way. Says China and Japan are going to form an alliance as soon as the war is over. Then they'll fight us."

"Christ!" the skipper said. "He really has gone Asiatic."

He called his exec and said, "Relieve Lobeck of any important duties. Put him in charge of something safe like mess accounts. Poor guy's feeling the jungle."

Then he instructed me: "Keep an eye on him. He's probably harmless but you can never tell with these Asiatics."

I have been so haunted by my failure to insist that this story remain in my book that I have, as a sort of penance, adopted Lobeck's monomania on Asia. I have studied the continent with special interest since the war, building upon a permanent interest that goes far back to my childhood, fortified by brief visits to Western Asia a long time ago and rather longer visits to Eastern Asia more recently. Then, in late 1950, I decided to return to Asia and study it as directly as time and travel would permit. Fortunately, as I was about to sail, the New York *Herald Tribune* and *Life* Magazine worked up some assignments for me so that I could afford to fly to many more areas than I would have been able to visit on my own.

When I set out I vowed that I would report exactly what I thought about Asia, for I was more completely convinced than ever that the destiny of the United States will be determined in large part by decisions we make regarding our relations with Asia.

For Asia is an absolutely crucial land. It is more than five times as large as the United States (16,690,000 square miles to our 3,022,000). It has almost nine times as many people (1,300,000,000 to our 150,000,000). To ignore such a continent, wilfully to make it our implacable enemy, or stupidly to misunderstand the forces that motivate its nations would be extreme folly.

Asia is separated from Europe only by a name and some relatively low mountains. Indeed, Europe is merely a peninsula jutting out from Asia as Spain juts out from Europe. Furthermore Eurasia is separated from Africa only by the man-made Suez Canal and the Strait of Gibraltar. Americans should from now on think of Asia-Europe-Africa as one land mass; and if that tripartite continent ever consolidates against us we could possibly continue to live within our sea-protected walls, but American life as we know it would vanish.

It is no wild nightmare to speculate upon what might happen to us if Asia's present—and I am convinced temporary—enmity were to spread to Europe and Africa. If that ever happens then to the east the daggers of Scandinavia, Iberia and the British Isles are pointed at us. To the west we are threatened by Siberia, Kamchatka and the Kuriles. Directly athwart our Panama Canal lifeline would be the mighty menace of an aroused Africa.

Big as we are, we would then be surrounded. Rich as we are, we would then be cut off from many critical raw materials. Strong as we are, we would be doomed. Like metals that crystallize under pressure, our institutions and even our economic life would crystallize and shatter.

To think clearly about Asia, Americans must consider the problems of the six great nations that dominate the continent. On the mainland four wield the power: China (463,000,000 people), India (346,000,000), Pakistan (74,000,000), and Russia-in-Asia (50,000,000). Off the eastern coast stand the other two great nations: Japan (83,000,000) and Indonesia (80,000,000).

I tried to invent some striking statement to dramatize the importance of these nations, but simple facts are more dramatic than any comparison I could contrive. Little-known Pakistan is much larger in population and potential world importance than any nation in Europe save Russia or any nation in the Americas save the United States. And unknown Indonesia is the sixth largest nation on earth.

In Asia I talked with as many people as I possibly could. Since both *Life* and the *Herald Tribune* have very able political correspondents I was not interested in meeting big-shots. Nor did I attempt to do financial, parliamentary or economic reporting. Instead, I went into a nation, sat quiet, listened, and in time found that all sorts of people wanted to talk with me. For specific details of how this was accomplished see the opening section on Singapore.

I approached American embassies only once—although I was treated with appreciated courtesy by American officials—for I did not want American views nor did I want to talk with those Asians who were tied to American interests, however commendable. Similarly, I did not approach any Asiatic government, although the police in Burma made me do so, and government press agents in India and Pakistan very quickly got on my trail and were of immense help.

I talked with some 120 Asians. Of these I have reported on 53 individuals or groups. In three reports I compress into one composite character opinions delivered by many different individuals; but these composites are clearly indicated in text. No interview, except one in which I said hardly a word, lasted less than two hours. Many lasted eight or ten. I ate with so many Asians that I could never repay their hospitality, and I enlisted so many interpreters that I must have been a nuisance.

I asked almost any question that came to mind, apologizing if it was clearly intrusive, and only once was I refused an answer. I cannot swear that all I report is true, but I can swear that on the day I talked with these people they wanted me to believe that what they said was true. I have not edited their thoughts and have allowed obviously self-contradictory remarks and statistics to stand.

You will find little colorful dialect-English in this book. Innumerable Asians speak perfect English. Those who talked to me through an interpreter spoke grammatically in their own tongues. It is a serious mistake to imagine that all aliens talk hilarious pidgin, and even when they do so they are not being ridiculous, for they are trying to convey an idea, and it is ideas we are after, not cheap giggles.

When time permitted I started conversations far back in childhood days: How much did your father earn? Did your mother sew your clothes? Did the rich man on the hill ever speak to you? How many pounds of rice did this field produce? Who took it to market? If your bullock died, where did your father get another? What did your teacher tell you in school? Have you ever traveled as far as Delhi? Have you met American missionaries? That suit you are wearing, how much did it cost?

Sometimes these questions would continue for three hours. Then I would say, "Perhaps you have some questions you would like to ask me." Then I would tear up all that I had copied for the first three hours, for when the Asian started to ask me questions the things that were really eating him came out. I could never have gone bluntly to a stranger and asked him, "What problems trouble your soul?" But after he had built patiently a portrait of his childhood, his home, and his financial life he himself reached his soul. And from that point on we had some tremendous conversations. The proof is that since I have returned home at least half the Asians with whom I talked have written to me adding points I had overlooked or asking further about American problems.

I went anywhere I wanted to in Asia save China. I talked with people of almost every conceivable calling. And I can say that this overwhelming experience of friendship, understanding and brotherhood has left me changed. True, many of these Asians had interests directly opposed to mine; they said that their nations had interests opposed to the interests of my country, so that many of our conversations were far from goody-goody mutual congratulation societies.

But of one thing I am certain. The most meaningless cliché used to obscure our understanding of Asians is to label them yellow hordes. They are yellow, many of them, but they are also individual human beings who can be approached by every single psychological avenue used to persuade Americans. The nation of Pakistan—as a group of such human beings—is motivated precisely by the same social, economic, political and nationalistic drives that motivate the sovereign state of Texas or the regal city of New York.

At the conclusion of the interviews from each given country I attach a brief summary of what informed Americans should know about that nation. Perhaps I am foolhardy in attempting to generalize at all about Asia, but remembering the cowardly way in which I killed Lobeck, a fellow-Asiatic, I am determined that henceforth I shall state exactly what I think about this enormous and important continent.

JAPAN

O N THE NIGHT OF NOVEMBER 30, 1944, THERE WAS UNUSUAL ACTIVITY on the equatorial island of Emirau. On the airstrip, poised a few miles above Rabaul, 320 allied airplanes had been assembled for what was to be the greatest smash of the war against the Japanese entrenched on Rabaul.

But at midnight we were summoned to a steaming hut and told that the strike was off. Instead, we were to fly north to Leyte Gulf in the Philippines, where General MacArthur had run into compelling trouble.

Then an unmilitary-looking major in a baggy uniform rose and said, "Admiral Nimitz directed me to fly down here to tell you men a few facts of life." He then proceeded to give the most chilling lecture I have ever heard. The steaming tropical hut suddenly became an ice box and I doubt if there was an American in that room who was not scared silly.

For the major said, "You know the ordinary rules of war. If captured you give only your name, rank, and serial number. If you report anything else that might aid the enemy, and if we recapture you, we try you for being a traitor. Those are the rules.

"Tonight you are flying north on a long and dangerous flight over enemy-held islands. Some of you will probably go down. Some of you will be captured. And if you are so stubborn that you give the Japs only your name, rank and number you will be shot within ten minutes of your capture—if you're lucky. If you're unlucky, you'll be tortured to death."

He described the unspeakably barbarous treatment Japanese officers handed out to downed American flyers. He told of American aviators who had escaped from Japanese captors and of how they had been beaten up regularly. Then he told us the tricks whereby we could escape death or torture. If we were smart.

He put it right on the line. He said, "If you quote me as having told you this, I'll have to say you were liars. But Admiral Nimitz has decided that in dealing with the Japs we must throw the book away. Therefore, if you are captured you are first to give your name, rank and number as the law demands. But as soon as they start to muss you up, make believe that you've turned yellow. Give them little bits of news. Cry a little. Tremble. Then give them a little more. When they see you're a coward they won't shoot you. They'll prefer to get a little glory by turning in a real spy. Do anything in your power to get past that first gang. They're the ones who shoot you or slice your head off.

"When you get back to civilian interrogators, continue to betray small things, niggardly, one by one. Above all, tell the truth, because they can check on you. Stay alive that first night. If you can do that, they may send you to a rear area where your chances of living are 50-50.

"Is this being a traitor? If you are caught betraying your country you'll be tried and there'll be no good shouting for Uncle Chester. You've got to sweat that part out yourself. But just between us, Nimitz wants you to stay alive."

There was a horrible chill in the room. On the airstrip, mechanics started revving up the planes for their perilous flight. Then the major added, "Besides, Nimitz says that right now it doesn't matter how much the Japs know. They're licked and they can't do anything about it. We have the unspeakable bastards licked."

We flew north fully aware that if we landed on the intervening islands we would be eaten, tortured and perhaps beheaded. This was not a hypothetical war-mongering story we had been told. This was not barbarity manufactured to keep the troops alert. This was the way the Japanese fought.

In November of 1949 my wife and I were on the northern coast of New Guinea when a native living near Finschafen reported to a district officer that something had long been preying upon his conscience. He led the officer to a hidden grave where Australian workmen uncovered the remains of six allied airmen. Their hands had been tied behind their backs and for five days they had been subjected to terrible and public torture. Then they were beheaded.

This was not some concocted story. This was not atrocity-mongering. Nor was it even a token of some terrible momentary bitterness. These atrocities had been planned. New Guinea natives had been marched to the parade grounds to witness them. This was how the Japanese had fought. They were the most cruel and barbarous enemy of modern times.

Exactly a year after I had stood beside this exhumed grave in New Guinea I was wandering about the northern island of Japan. I was alone. I had no American soldiers with me. I was accompanied by no Japanese police. In fact, the part of Japan I was in was so remote that if I did get into trouble it might be several days before any kind of substantial protection could be given me.

I knocked about Hokkaido for several days, wandering into small towns, talking with people I met, using sign language when necessary, but most often finding some eager young person fluent in English who took pride in serving as my interpreter. One young man stayed with me for the better part of a day. He was kind, attractive, intelligent. He enjoyed my company and at the end of our trek I offered him some money, but he would not take it.

"I like Americans," he said.

"Were you in the army during the war?" I asked.

"Yes," he replied. "I fight against your men. In New Guinea."

He was a measure of the miraculous change that had taken place in Japan. Five years ago he might have used me for bayonet practice. Today he was one of the best friends I met in Asia and after two days of the most intelligent service he finally accepted a small fee, adding in embarrassment, "Money is not necessary. I like to exercise my English."

When General MacArthur landed in Japan in late 1945 the islands were protected by more than 2,000,000 first-line troops not yet spent in battle. They were sworn to die to the last man protecting their homeland, yet our Americans marched ashore without a single major instance of sabotage, without a single retaliatory murder, except the usual man-to-man brawls over women or liquor.

The occupation of Japan is without parallel in history. It was so amicable that it remains a mystery. But four apparent reasons can be given: First, our inspired decision whereby the Emperor was kept alive and unbombed preserved a unique symbol around which the Japanese could mobilize their emotions and from which they would accept directives. If one American was responsible for this decision, which I doubt, he surely deserves recognition as one of the sublime citizens of our generation. His simple act of intelligence preserved a million lives and established the bases for harmonious relations between two of the world's great nations. His was a military and moral victory of incalculable importance. He demonstrated vividly how much wiser it is to know Asia than to ignore Asiatic structures.

Second, the personal qualities of General MacArthur determined the firmness, the wisdom and the justice of most American actions in Japan. It can scarcely be denied that this austere and symbolic figure captured the imagination of the Japanese people, as he no doubt intended to do. It is false to say that the Japanese transferred their worship of the Emperor to MacArthur. Evidence proves the contrary. But the Japanese, faced by total military, economic and religious collapse, recognized and appreciated a real man when they saw one. It is quite possible that they might have accepted the leadership of some indecisive and puling governor; but the fact is that in MacArthur they found a leader to their liking. They prospered under his regime.

Third, the high ability of the civil administrators brought by MacArthur to Japan helped in the stabilization of the nation. Military men surrounding MacArthur have often been dreadfully second-rate stuff, so it is the more commendable that he sought out only the best civilian assistants. Excellent brains were applied to the job of organizing Japan and the solid work they did in reconstructing Japanese economy, administration and civil life will last a long time after the candy icing of the supposedly democratic reforms has been forgotten. On questions of food supply, land reform, freedom of expression and social reform the MacArthur team has accomplished much.

Fourth, the reconstruction of Japan was made easier because the majority of Americans who served in the occupation positively liked the country and the people. Probably 75 per cent of the pre-Korea forces—military or civilian—enjoyed living in Japan as much as they did living in the United States. This applied particularly to the wives of American occupation personnel and is not based on the unearthly charm of romances between unmarried American soldiers and Japanese girls. My work in Tokyo took me repeatedly to the Provost Marshal's office, and I was never there without seeing at least four G.I.'s with their Japanese girls applying for marriage licenses. I asked several of them what they were going to do when their wives had to go back to America to live and they said, "We aren't planning to go back. We intend to live here."

I do not know what happened to the Japanese soldiers between that icy night on Emirau in 1944 and the sunny days of 1950. I can only say that I wandered about Japan totally unprotected, that I poked my nose into any problem or any home or any business that attracted me, and I have never had so generous a welcome. I believe that most Americans who have visited Japan since the end of the war feel exactly as I did. I think we had better put it down as a modern miracle.

If you had to select one aspect of Japanese life revolutionized by the Americans and say, "This is the change that will last longest," what aspect would you take?

I would choose one of the most beautiful, shy and modest young women I have ever known. There is only one word to describe twenty-two-year-old Ryuko Ozawa. She is delectable. Tiny, slim, with jet-black hair in loose curls, perfect teeth, a winsome smile and lively wit, she is fortunately lovely.

It seems strange, therefore, to select this delicate beauty as the incorruptible and steel-willed symbol of the new Japanese revolution. But that's what she is.

"When I was a little girl in school," she says, "army officers came and taught us military drill. They told us of Japan's great destiny. They said we Japanese girls would have to work hard to be worthy of that destiny. I believed the army officers because at home my papa talked the same way. He instructed me how a girl should behave and why I must always bow to the superior judgment of my brother. My mama, of course, had nothing to say.

"In those days when a girl reached twenty her papa would meet with other men and decide upon a good husband for her. That was how my mama married. And in those days my husband—if he were good like Papa—would have been kind to me but I would rarely leave the house. I would never argue back. And if I had girl babies I would have expected my husband to instruct them how they must always obey the wishes of their men.

"But my pattern of life was broken by the war. In the early days it was even worse for girls than before. Officers appeared in our school many times. They told us Japan would conquer all of Asia and that America would never be able to attack us. These officers said that all patriotic Japanese women would bear many sons who would be needed to rule all this part of the world. I was a young girl, properly brought up, so I believed everything the army men said.

"Then the army leaders said I must stop school and work in a radio factory. I went to a small house where I made condensers which were taken to some other small house where they were added to something else. I worked eight hours a day and got 14 cents a month, which the army officers told us we ought to save to help the Emperor.

"I never doubted that Japan would win the war. But then bombs began to fall on Tokyo. Fire bombs, and they struck many small factories and burned them down. But on one terrible raid they burned more than that. At dusk a fire started in a high wind. The flames raged all that night, the next day and the next night. Whole sections of Tokyo were caught up in the flames. All oxygen was burned away and people dropped dead. The canals were choked with bodies. In that fire 88,000 people burned to death.

"My home was destroyed and flames were all around us. There was nowhere to run. But we were lucky. Nobody in my family was killed.

"After that we knew the war was lost, and although I love my papa very much I was glad to see that now my mama took charge. She was quiet and gentle and warned me that when the American troops arrived they would rape and murder girls like me and that I must hide and not let myself be seen.

"But when your men arrived they were just the opposite. My papa almost died with shame when I announced that since I had learned English I would take a job working with the American Army. He started to shout that I could never do such a thing, but Mama was firm and said it was all right but I mustn't fall in love with any of them, for she still didn't trust them completely."

It is quite impossible to describe the soft melodic voice of this Japanese girl. It is not sing-song, not at all, yet it is a song. She has difficulty with certain sounds, as when I asked her if her father would permit her to date Americans. Shocked, she cried, "Absorutery not! Nebber, nebber!" Later when I asked her if she liked to dance she said, "Berry much indeed." And when I asked her how she had learned she replied, "G.I.'s teach me." I said I thought there was an internal contradiction in these three statements. She laughed musically and said, "What I mean is that Papa would nebber, nebber give me permission." That contradiction I let pass, as apparently her father had been forced to do before me.

Ryuko flung her curls back from her shoulder and said, "But you understand that I like the G.I.'s. All Japanese girls do, because the G.I.'s are very courteous with us. Very pleasant. But I also remember what my mama said, 'Yellow girl and white man is no good.' Yet three of my best girl friends, all college graduates like me, married Americans and they are very happy. I think you find that most Japanese girls who have G.I.

babies without being married would have had Japanese babies the same way if the Americans had not come. I do not know a single friend who has had such a baby. If my friends loved G.I.'s they married. If not, they left the Americans completely alone."

Seeing this attractive young woman you feel instinctively that those Americans who married girls like her are fortunate. To complete the record she adds, "I myself am getting married next October. To a wonderful young man who teaches astronomy at Tokyo University. Like my older brother and sister I chose the man I wanted to marry. Papa's pride was badly hurt that I didn't ask him to find me a husband, but he can't say anything because he knows he couldn't have done any better than I've done.

"I am sure my husband will prove to be a man of modern ideas about women. How can I be sure? Well, I refused to marry two other men who wanted wives in the old pattern. My husband is very gentle, he is well educated, and he was never a soldier. Anyway, I wouldn't let him order me around if he did want to. There are many American families in Tokyo and girls have seen that American wives don't stand being ordered about. Not one of my friends has married a Japanese man of the old type.

"Yet in many things I prefer the old Japanese ways. I like homes where people still take off their shoes. I like politeness and especially I like girls to wear the brocaded kimono. You have to admit that Japanese women don't look good in Western clothes. Legs too short. If you will be in Tokyo long I should like to appear in my Japanese dress."

One afternoon she arrived in an exquisite gold-and-blue embroidered kimono. She was half-embarrassed at the dazzling figure she made and laughed. "The G.I.'s call this my double-breasted gabardine. It takes me forty minutes at least to get into it."

I said that I knew girls who took that long to get into a sweater, and she said, "That's the kind of thing Papa says when he is waiting for me. The kimono is very tight around the middle, so that one day when I wore it to do my typing in, I fainted. It's also very expensive. Costs four months' salary to buy this. Papa always looks pleased when I wear my kimono, but even so he complains. Why? Because I don't also put my hair up in the old style. But that takes two hours more and I think I can get by with my curls."

Her fine black hair reached well toward the middle of her back in big loose curls that framed her delicate face in lovely patterns. Her eyes glowed as she said, "I like it best at New Year's, to see a banquet room filled with girls in rich kimonos. That is very lovely."

She asked me if I would go back in my notes to where we started. "I don't want you to think that my papa opposes everything modern," she explained. "It was Papa who sent my brother to the University of Cincinnati to study science. It's just that Papa has had to change his ideas so very fast. It hasn't been so difficult for Mama, for she was always gentle and kind. But Papa can be fun, too. He jokes that if Americans are so rich, why don't they pay me more than $21 a month? But mostly he thinks back to the old days. Only a little while ago he caught me reading *The Return of the Native* and commanded me to stop. Then he remembered that the Army no longer forbids us to read English books and he said, 'Well, go ahead and read.' I think that Papa will never be completely modern. But it doesn't seem to pain him so much any more to accept the idea that I will be.

"In one way the change from old to new has not been successful. Neither I nor my brother nor my sister nor any of my friends has any religion. We simply cannot believe in Shinto. And Christianity holds nothing for us. Definitely I would never marry a Shinto boy because sooner or later he would go back to the old ideas about women. Would I marry a Japanese Christian boy? Perhaps, but you don't find many of them and the boys don't seem to be very attractive. I have heard of one religious group I might like to join. The Quakers. I read about them in one of the army magazines and I think without knowing it my mama has always been a Quaker.

"How do I feel about America? Very mixed up. If you had not won the war Japan would now be rich with many possessions. But if you had lost I would be living as girls lived five hundred years ago. I shall never forget the instructions the Japanese officers shouted to us when I was a little girl.

"But I will say one thing about America. Even Papa has to admit that your troops have behaved very well. I do not know one girl who was offended. Another thing, too. America must not leave Japan too soon. But even if you should I know that the girls who have tasted freedom would never go back to the old ways."

Ryuko Ozawa, the adorable little revolutionist, has a most curious name. Ryu- means dragon, and -ko is the traditional suffix for female. A female dragon! I have never known a human being with a more misleading name.

Masao Watanabe has quite a different kind of name. In English it would mean Pretty Boy Smith, but there is nothing Pretty Boy about him. He's rugged, lean, tight-lipped and steel-eyed. I think that, of all the faces I saw in Asia, I remember his most unforgettably. He was a tough, competent, incorruptible man.

For eighteen years he had been a professional soldier fighting for his Emperor in many parts of the world. Defeat and forced return to civilian life had brought hard days and he clung to his ragged army uniform and peaked cloth cap drawn tight about his bullet head.

I found Masao in the north of Japan and he typified the demobilized soldier bewildered by civilian life, perplexed by the occupation, but grimly holding on until that day when he would again be needed in the Army. The great question in my mind, and indeed all the world's, is whether defeat and civilian life have changed him. I submit his words without interruptions by me, for they are terribly important words to weigh.

"I was born on a small farm. My parents raised rice and at times we had as many as fifty peasants working our fields, yet in a way we ourselves were peasants, too. I was the fifth of six children and went as far as the agricultural college. But I quit agriculture because I discovered something else that I really wanted to do.

"It happened at nineteen. I had to report for military training. All Japanese boys did. I was a tough specimen. No teeth missing. I could march for a whole day. The training was hard and I liked it. You ask if it was brutal? Yes. If I did wrong an officer might knock me down or beat me. In those days I feared officers to the point of trembling. Many years later I came to know your American Army, where the officers were gentlemen. Well, I still think our way was best. In brains your army was as good as ours, without queston. But not in endurance. How you say it? Guts. That we had. If not, the officers beat it into us.

"Even so, I liked the life and I decided to join the regular army. My career began at a fortunate time, just as Japan was starting to rule Asia. In Manchuria we used to march many days in freezing weather and I became head of twelve light machine guns. My unit never lost a battle in Manchuria.

"Then we were sent to China and I was present at the fall of Nanking. Yes, I knew you would ask about that. I'll tell you all I know about Japanese troops in Nanking. To begin with, I'm a married man and understand both why troops sometimes run wild and why they shouldn't be allowed to do so. But all I myself saw at Nanking was one terrible incident at the river. Our soldiers herded many Chinese onto ferryboats and cut the boats loose down the river. Then our men raked them with machine guns. Did my machine guns take part in this? No, for by this time I had been promoted from machine guns to something else. I can honestly tell you I saw nothing more than that of the rape of Nanking. Did more take place? I can only tell you what I myself saw.

"About this time we began to hear of the Greater East Asia Co-prosperity Sphere and we thought it a fine thing. Japan needed more food. True, in Manchuria we had found both land and food but in North China we saw what Japan could accomplish in building a better Asia. I now decided to stay in the Army for good and I was returned to Japan for officer training.

"I was sitting in tactics class when we heard of Pearl Harbor. It was tremendously exciting. Our instructor grew inflamed and cried, 'Now you see a superb tactic for starting a war. The American fleet cannot oppose us and we will capture all of this.' His hand swept across all of East Asia. He added, 'By this simple tactic Japan has become totally united, America totally disrupted. If any of you are afraid, remember that Japan has no history of defeat.'

"Because we were like all students we whispered, 'That's right, but he doesn't know that America hasn't any history of defeat either.' Then a brilliant student told me, 'I can see exactly what will happen. We'll capture all of East Asia and threaten Australia. Then our leaders will offer peace and the enemy will be so frightened they'll agree and Japan will have all she needs.' This sounded so reasonable that I was sure it would happen.

"So as a lieutenant I returned to the northern border of Manchuria with our very best army waiting to smash Russia. We have always hated Russia and have always known that sooner or later we would have to fight the communists. I patrolled the border and we had lots of little wars but no big one.

"Now we began to hear quiet rumors about Japanese defeats at Guadalcanal and Saipan. Nobody I knew even dreamed that Japan could lose the war and we disciplined very harshly any enlisted man who asked questions. The worst I thought might happen was that when we offered the Americans a peace treaty we wouldn't get quite as much as we could have had earlier.

"Then came the sickening news of Iwo Jima. You cannot understand how we felt. We knew, of course, that Japan itself would never be invaded but we also knew that the wonderful peace we might have forced upon you was lost. We had no more illusions about holding all of Asia.

"The sick feeling continued, and after Okinawa we were rushed down to Kyushu, our southern island. When we landed we were told straight out, 'You are our finest army. You must prepare to die here.' We dug immense fortifications. I truly believe your troops would never have driven us off that beach—alive. Myself? I was quite prepared to die.

"At the front trenches we heard nothing of the atom bomb but one morning the Emperor spoke on the radio. Reception was bad and we thought it was all an American trick, some Americans talking like the Emperor. Anyway, none of us knew how the Emperor talked. We would have killed any American we caught that day. Then a printed paper arrived and we read that the Emperor himself wanted us to surrender.

"You ask why a powerful army that had never been defeated gave up? Because the Emperor told us to. When I was a boy I played tennis. When you lost. Game, set, match. Now this contest was over. Game, set, match. Why should we fight? The Emperor had declared the match.

"When your troops arrived we were pleased. I mean that they were not at all the barbarians we had been led to expect. They were a surprise pleasure."

With the peace, Masao Watanabe had lost his occupation and now worked for a miserable wage in a miserable hut filling out forms. In order to discover what his conditions would have been had he stayed in the Army I asked him what he would be had Japan won. Coolly and sensibly he replied, "I'd be a full colonel in New York, asking you these same questions." Then he laughed and added, "Seriously, I'd still be a professional soldier, possibly a colonel. Who knows? Maybe I'll get to be a colonel one of these days.

"Because I believe that sooner or later you'll have to rearm Japan. It is in your interest as well as ours. Did you ever hear of the German Emperor who liked cherries? He found that sparrows ate them too, so he commanded all the sparrows to be killed. Next year the beetles destroyed the cherries completely. So the Emperor had to bring the sparrows back.

"For example, we Japanese would never have been kicked around in Korea the way you have been. We know how to fight in such terrain. We understand the Chinese, too. We could be doing your fighting for you.

"But if we ever do get our army, please see to it that it's not a national army, like the stupid national police we now have. To be any good it must be the Emperor's army, as before. Then we would fight to the death. Better still, we might have an Emperor's army serving under control of the United Nations. That would be a strong army, too.

"You have expressed surprise that I am not bitter about my fortunes. I'm a soldier, but on one point I am angry. You Americans have ruined our Japanese women. Now they meddle in politics. They try to be a force in the community. They misunderstand their new freedom and their conduct is foolish. Now I'll admit they deserve equal rights, but why must they prove they have them? For example, why so many divorces? Why so much money spent on clothes? And tell me honestly, have you ever seen anything so ridiculous as Japanese women in slacks?

"But we can forgive you for such little mistakes. As a matter of fact, I hope Americans will not leave Japan for at least ten more years. Not until we have our army. Otherwise there will be chaos and Russia will take over. Then if you lose Japan you lose the Philippines. When they are gone Australia and all the Pacific is gone. And when the Pacific is lost you are doomed."

I said bluntly, "You talk about an army. If you had one, could we trust you?"

Watanabe replied with equal bluntness, "Probably not. But you can trust that our interests are your interests. It comes down to this: You'll have to give us an army and hope that we use it wisely."

The demobilized soldier, pecking away at a minor job in civilian life, never once refused to answer a question, never once tried to butter me up. He was a rock, an absolute rock. He was still as lean and hard as he had been in uniform. When he talked he leaned forward as if waiting for a bugle to summon him to more important business, long delayed. As we parted he said, "To prevent a flood you must build dikes. Sooner or later you'll have to let us have an army. You'll have to trust us."

CLICHÉS

IN A

TOOL

FACTORY

Like most Americans I was reared on clichés about Asia. I firmly believed: (1) "Asia can never develop a modern civilization because its people are too backward." (2) "India will never develop into a first-rate country because of her religious differences." (3) "Japanese militarists need not be feared because Japanese factories cannot produce modern armament." (4) "The Japanese aviator is a dud because his peculiar eye structure prevents him from flying planes the way we do."

The last cliché had many variations, according to the branch of service involved. I knew many Americans who seriously believed that the Jap Navy would capsize in battle when taking sharp turns to starboard because they had stolen their blueprints from us and we, knowing of their intentions, had cleverly withheld one essential trick that kept our ships upright in a tight turn. As far as the Army was concerned, it too could be ignored because Japanese soldiers, while brave, were nevertheless peasants who could not be taught how to break down their guns if they jammed in battle.

And even after I had exploded for my own satisfaction each of these clichés, I still believed as late as June of 1945 that no American invader would set foot on Japanese soil until at least 60 per cent of the population had been destroyed or had committed hara-kiri. At that somber point I used to shudder, taking refuge in the greatest cliché of all: "After all, Asiatics aren't like us. There is no approach to them."

Responsible and knowledgeable Americans had disseminated these clichés and I had swallowed them hook, line and sinker. Then I went to Morioka.

It is a small manufacturing city in Northern Japan, an overnight trip from Tokyo. I arrived there in winter, when gloomy night fell toward five in the afternoon. Only a meager detachment of American troops remained in the city, so I was pretty much on my own, and every evening I used to wander aimlessly among the alleys of the city.

I say alleys advisedly, for there are only a few paved streets in Morioka, and from them lead narrow, mud-filled alleys along which much of the secondary industry of Morioka takes place. These alleys were always the scene of intense activity.

As dusk fell innumerable Japanese hurried from one small shop to the next. Here I could see the greatest variety of dress I had ever seen in one place. Old women came by on platformed wooden shoes, dressed in burlap bags wrapped about them until they were indeed as wide as they were high. Old men trudged by wearing medieval costumes that must have remained unchanged for well onto a thousand years. Working girls passed in heavy slacks, their bottoms enormously rounded. Army uniforms, tattered Chinese dress and modern sack suits that could have come from New York appeared in the parade. And everywhere there were children with the brightest chapped cheeks you have ever seen.

No description of the varied dress can altogether convey the beauty of a Japanese provincial city, for at least one-third of the population perches on their wooden platform shoes to keep out of the mud, and these shoes permit only an eight-inch step, so that the parade which goes up the alleys is a mincing, dancing rhythm of bowing heads, smiles, nods in the darkness.

However, it was not this gracious ballet that attracted me to Morioka but rather the grubby factories in which modern commercial products were being made; and along one alley, drenched in mud, I came upon my tool maker.

His hovel was ten feet wide and ran back through two rooms, above which were two other rooms. The front of his shop was open. There was no fire to warm him, so he worked completely bundled up in tattered clothes, for Morioka winters are just like Philadelphia's.

I judged the tool maker to be about fifty, but his face was so seamed and dirty that he could have been seventy. He sat on a rickety chair, on a rickety floor, working at a jerry-built bandsaw. A single unshaded forty-watt bulb hung directly in his face and the belt which conveyed power from a grimy motor was unprotected. There was one spigot in the room, but no washbasin, so that the water ran onto the floor and into an open drain.

If you had stood in this dismal, unsanitary and unimproved factory you could understand how Americans had accepted the cliché that Asia could never develop a modern civilization.

But as I talked with the bundled-up tool maker I could recall other experiences with Japanese industry. In late 1942 their Navy rushed out of the darkness at Savo Island and with uncanny skill practically wiped out our fleet protecting Guadalcanal. It seemed a miracle that they could penetrate those waters and spot our night-shrouded ships. Later we discovered that Japanese oculists, working in exactly the same kind of factories that I saw in Morioka, had developed a light-gathering binocular of revolutionary efficiency.

At another time I was on a carrier when American airmen returned cursing purple. They had risked their necks by leveling off on Jap ships only to have their torpedoes fail to explode. This experience was so common that the failure of our armament to operate was something of a national disgrace. Japanese torpedoes, whipped together in dismal factories, consistently ran true and destroyed their targets.

Once I talked with airmen who had to tangle with Jap planes and they told me of their instructions: "If you are alone and meet a Jap Zero, run like hell because you're outnumbered." These planes had been manufactured in pathetic factories completely lacking in bright chrome surfaces.

Finally I saw the Nippon Kogaku optical works from which came camera lenses which equaled or surpassed any now being made in the world. The factory was so ramshackle, the machinery so wretched that no American board of health would have permitted even broom handles to be made there.

I spoke to the tool maker in Morioka about these things and he laughed. "This machine all right. It runs. Costs little keep it going. We get along."

He told me of the American colonel fresh from Detroit whom our army had sent to inspect cities like Morioka in 1946 to discover how Japan had acquired the industrial might to destroy us at Pearl Harbor and practically drive us from the Pacific before we got rolling.

"This colonel came to Morioka," the bundled-up man said. "Studied our factories and cried, 'My God! How did you men dare to wage war against the United States?' We replied, 'We saw pictures of your big new factories. We weren't afraid. We don't need big machines. We got lots of men. We work like this.'" And he slapped the dangerous, unguarded power belt that whirred under the single unshaded lamp.

I wish every American who believes the old clichés about Asia could visit the alleys of Morioka. It is folly to believe any longer that Asia is doomed to a second-class status in any given respect. It took Japan only from 1860 to 1940 to catch up with the rest of the world. There is no logical hindrance that I can see—raw materials, natural skill, will power, intelligence—that will keep the rest of Asia from making the same spectacular advances. Indeed, the pace of learning and communication having been so speeded up, I should expect India, China, Indonesia and Pakistan to move rather more rapidly than Japan did.

At any rate, let's never revive the consoling cliché that Asiatic battleships will turn turtle when they make a sharp right turn.

THE

ASHES

OF

EMPIRE

There was another man in Morioka who remains for me a tragic symbol of what Japan tried to accomplish but what was wrested from her at the last minute. Shigeru Kyoko is a fifty-year-old banker, a slight man with a bald head and exceptionally pleasing manner. He bows sharply from the waist in the old custom and sucks in his breath as a prelude to almost every statement. He is extremely intelligent and now works at some menial job for the Americans.

"When I was a young man," he says, "I worked hard in college and left Tokyo University with honors in law. I studied the world about me and decided that Japan would need men to run its foreign possessions. I landed a good job with the Oriental Development Company, which had a monopoly in the exploitation of colonial territory. I was sent to Korea, where I handled small loans.

"I gave Koreans money for only one purpose. Increase rice production. Japan had to have more food and Korea was a fine place to grow it. We charged only 11 per cent interest and I handed out money right and left. Anyone who could plow up a square of land could get money from me. We sank artesian wells, built great dams, laid sewers for small villages and really made Korea over. Not heavy industry, you understand. Just rice. Always more rice.

"I was not happy in Korea. It was really a stupid place. The Koreans never understood us. When we made them plow under fifteen farms to build a reservoir all they could see was the destroyed farms, not the wonderful new water and the increased rice production. I would call the average Korean shiftless and lazy. We even lost many loans to these shiftless people. Far too many.

"But even more disgusting were the Japanese peasants they sent us. Naturally we didn't get the best stock in Korea, but we were totally unprepared for the dregs we did get. Eighty per cent of them turned out to be completely worthless. Wouldn't work. Got homesick. Complained about the cold. If we didn't guard them they'd run right back to Japan, loan or no loan. In their defense I must admit that our Government often did allocate them impossible land. Can you imagine asking men to grow rice on rocky soil? No wonder the peasants said to the devil with it. Besides, Japan needed rice so badly the peasants were forbidden to grow anything else. Well, most of them sneaked back to Japan and became public nuisances and scrounged off city dumps.

"Actually I had little to do with Koreans because I always lived in government barracks. But it would take a strange man to like a Korean. They were uneducated, uncultured. In a thousand years they had done nothing to improve their land and they hated us for having done so much in ten. I was really overjoyed when the company moved me out of Korea."

Now Mr. Kyoko grows excited and in beautiful, fluent English describes the high point of his empire-building life. "Ah, Manchuria!

There was a wonderland. There was a glorious land for young men with energy! In Manchuria I discovered a way of life that I had never before dreamed existed. In Japan my father was very conservative. Very old men ruled Japan. Even in Korea I was never really free in making loans. Always some old man looking over my shoulder. But in Manchuria young men ruled! We were daring. We accomplished immense things. We made that cold land flourish like a garden.

"They put me in charge of fiscal policy for one of the northern areas. Life was dangerous with bandits and Russians about. Even the climate was hostile. An inferno in summer, a freezing terror in winter. But we had great work to do and solid houses to protect us from the storms.

"I felt in those years as if I were helping to determine the future of Japan. We had a phrase in those days, 'Manchuria is the life line of Japan.' We made it that. We grew food in the productive soil. We gathered the rich resources. Manchuria became a symbol of our inevitable war with Russia. And all about us was the terrible excitement of an expanding world.

"Anyone would have been thrilled by what we accomplished. I alone spent millions, built many establishments. I helped my unit produce more than forty per cent of the world's soybean crop.

"In Manchuria I was deeply happy. I lived with a big free spirit. In Manchuria I found the coronation of my youth."

Mr. Kyoko's voice loses a little of its fervor and assumes a more relaxed and stately accent as he says, "Well, we must all surrender the excitement of our youth. The Army needed me to help them in North China and with extreme regret I said good-bye to Manchuria and reported for work in Tientsin, where I helped establish an invasion currency. To my astonishment I found that I loved China. Its gentle manner of life soon made me forget Manchuria. My wife joined me and we watched our children grow up with Chinese friends. I learned the Chinese language, a fact which later saved my life, and I came to have many Chinese acquaintances. They were gentle, moderate people of great culture.

"I was content to live out my life in China. I had what you call an abundant life. Electricity, a refrigerator, a radio, a German player piano. I became head of a stamp collectors' society and my sons were enrolled in a fine school. To put it in a phrase, 'My wife wore silk.'

"Even my work was gratifying. I helped maintain a currency that was fair to all and a spur to business. I will not say that we were loved by the Chinese, but many of them admitted to me that under our supervision they lived more securely than ever before. It was with a sense of horror, therefore, that I watched the Japanese empire crumble.

"It began, I have always held, with our South China adventure. What had we to gain there that we didn't already enjoy in North China? I remember a story we whispered at the time. A Japanese general reports to the Emperor, 'Three days ago a glorious victory. We killed 40,000 Chinese, losing only 2,000. Two days ago a glorious victory. We killed 50,000 Chinese, losing only 3,000. Yesterday the most glorious victory of all. We killed 60,000 Chinese, losing only 5,000.' The Emperor grew very sad and replied, 'What terrible victories! Pretty soon no more Japanese.'

"But I will tell you the truth. When we destroyed Pearl Harbor and conquered Java I felt a surge of patriotic fury. I realized with enormous excitement that the generals were right after all. We could conquer all of Southeast Asia. Then came Iwo Jima and the darkness.

"When we surrendered, Tientsin was filled with infuriated Chinese raging through the streets to murder every Japanese. But I could speak perfect Chinese and escaped to the home of the Chinese friend with whom I had often traded stamps. At considerable risk to himself he smuggled me into an American concentration camp, where a wonderful Marine sergeant named O'Brien from Detroit said he would let me hide if I would teach him Japanese. He didn't learn my language but I did learn his, as you can see."

I talked with many Japanese whose fortunes had been wrecked by the war, and never once did I hear complaints or self-pity. Friends who conducted the same kinds of interviews in Germany said the tears of remorse almost washed away the papers. In Japan I heard time and again the old tennis phrase, "Well, it was game-set-match. I had to find some other kind of job."

Mr. Kyoko, the banker, was a good example of this fortitude. He took off his horn-rimmed glasses, managed a professional smile, and smoothed out the crease in his threadbare trousers.

"I'll have another cigarette, thanks. We've all come to like the American brands. You say you write fiction? Well, that's a fine occupation, I'm sure, but you mustn't think, 'Poor Kyoko. A tragic man. His life ruined.' My friend, believe me when I say that I do not lament the loss of my worldly possessions. Recently I have even had to sell some of my furniture. But we have a saying in Japan: 'He who climbs a great mountain must come down the other side.' Remember that. It may do you good some day. My good luck rose with Japanese conquests. What would be more likely than that my luck should collapse with army defeats? I paid a high fee for my airplane ride.

"Only one thing embitters me. Today I am ruled by petty, stupid men because the Americans have been afraid of intellectual Japanese who could rule well. Furthermore, my children are being reared with no reverence for the Emperor.

"I agree with the Americans that it was ridiculous for us to have made a living god of the Emperor. But the new type of Japanese is just as wrong not to recognize the Emperor as a symbol of all that is fine and good in Japanese life. It's better for a man to believe in something like that.

"What laws would I pass for Japan if I were put in power? I'd send 30,000,000 Japanese to countries in nearby Asia, especially to that wonderland Manchuria. I would increase the rice production in all Southeast Asia and exchange it for Japanese manufactures. With the last drop of my blood I'd keep Russia out of Korea and Formosa, for when the communists control those two points they have Japan criss-crossed with airplanes. And in time I would ask America to establish a Japanese army and depart. After that I would try to maintain a long-range friendship with your country."

Mr. Kyoko, the banker with no bank, wiped his glasses and laughed. "A big program I've laid out. America will help on much of it because it must be obvious to you that it is in your interest that Japan be saved."

REASONABLE

DOUBTS

AT A

STRIP TEASE

The American occupation of Japan has been so successful that any reasonable human being suspects it can't all be true. Inevitably one gets that sinking feeling in his stomach that the whole thing must be a gigantic farce played by clever antagonists.

What assurance have we that there has been any real change of heart in the Japanese? How do we know that the old Zaibatsu who ran Japan without ever taking office are not now running it without taking office? What proof have we that the Japanese are truly our friends? None. We have no proof at all.

Japan has her own historic destiny to work out. She is an Asiatic nation faced by Asiatic problems. It is unrealistic to expect her to remain permanently tied to our leadership. It is stupidity to demand that she kowtow indefinitely to our needs rather than to her own compulsions.

Neither our money nor our guns nor our friendship has bought the soul of Japan. She has her own way to go, and like all nations in all times she will go that way and not ours.

Yet we can accept as fact her willingness to have us occupy her in 1945. Her military leadership had been proved bankrupt. It had not only failed to win; its vaunted code of conduct had been betrayed. As a symbol of its abject disgrace, its very leader, Tojo, made a sorry hash of his honor-demanded hara-kiri. It is doubtful if any previous military dictatorship ever collapsed with quite the same sickening whoosh. Japan wanted new leadership. They liked the kind that General MacArthur gave them.

But many shrewd observers doubt that Japan took the United States very seriously after the first two years. An Englishwoman who knew Japan well has described our occupation as the imposition by young barbarians of a barren culture upon one of the oldest continuing cultures in the world. It is her opinion that our influence will be tolerated while necessary and then painlessly stowed away in historical memories when we will have gone.

I do not entirely agree with this. Certainly nine-tenths of the cultural hoop-la we introduced was unnecessary and a little ridiculous. But there were other contributions which may last: (1) Liberation of women. (2) A new concept of where the authority to govern rests. (3) Better land distribution. (4) Revision of the Emperor's status. (5) Rationalized manufacturing procedures. Such positive changes may help to modify all subsequent Japanese history, even though we should fully expect a virulent nationalism to revive after we have left.

What does seem wrong is to demand credit for other trivial changes which more often than not were either misguided or downright ridiculous. There is no inherent merit to popcorn, American candy bars, new-style movies or jitterbugging. I am thinking especially of that strip tease I saw at Christmas.

I have heard of men who have encountered varied experiences at a strip tease, but I believe I am the first who ever learned a political lesson at one. It happened in Tokyo.

Some friends insisted that I would never understand the Japanese until I saw their version of an American strip tease. Accordingly I climbed to the top of a very tall building where a theatre had been improvised, including a runway reaching out among the spectators. A tinny orchestra hammered out tired American jazz, and when the curtain rose a woefully bedraggled line of girls wearing practically nothing waved their hands back and forth across their faces and yelled American songs in baby English.

It was as unsexy as one could imagine for the girls were self-conscious, the audience was bored and the costumes were unspeakably dirty.

The whole affair would have been a dismal waste of time except for the dramatic interlude, *Gone with the Wind*. This playlet was so astonishing, so subversive and so clever that I want to report it in detail.

The curtain opened on a Southern plantation mansion, around which a chorus of girls in crinoline chanted, "Is It True What They Say About Dixie?" At each mention of Dixie they fluffed up their crinolines and showed their grimy pants. When they drifted offstage one of the most forlorn Negroes of all time staggered past the lights while a heartbroken baritone sobbed "Ol' Man River." Other Negroes appeared totin' and sweatin'. Then the main story began.

The owner of the plantation, dressed in gentlemen's purple clothes of the period, had a young wife and two lovely daughters. But he was involved with a no-good gambling woman who appeared almost naked. The hero chased her around for some time and finally caught her, whereupon the rest of her clothes fell off and there was a pretty torrid love scene while the chorus again wanted to know if it was true what they said about Dixie?

The no-good woman demanded extra gifts and the scene shifted to a gambling hell, where the plantation owner was bilked of his money, his wedding ring, his wife's dowry and the plantation itself.

The pitiful creature, sobbing in remorse, was next seen trudging homeward, taking his spite out on his slaves, beating up his wife, throwing his children into the storm, murdering the no-good woman, still naked, and ending in the sheriff's handcuffs.

It was an amazing show. All aspects of American life were ridiculed. There could have been no purpose other than to burlesque life in the South. Every cliché of the communists was dragged out, explained and posed for exhibition.

Halfway through the drama I stopped looking at the stage and started looking at the audience. I found to my surprise that they in turn were watching me. There were two men in the middle row who kept looking up at my box and laughing. They were not disrespectful. They were amused. I think they might have been amused that Americans should have been so stupid as to permit *Gone with the Wind* to be shown in an occupation theatre.

Finally the curtain fell on this dismal drama and the announcer appeared in super-unctuous style to say that as a special tribute to the Americans the management had devised an extraordinary number symbolic of Christmas day. The audience applauded politely.

Then appeared a fat and perfectly repulsive young woman who started to do a violent strip tease. I had difficulty associating this with Christmas, but suddenly the orchestra explained it all. They broke rapturously into "I'm Dreaming of a White Christmas." The announcer thought it was all very moving, for he stood ramrod straight, saluting.

I looked back at the two men in the middle row. They were laughing out loud this time, and I had the strange feeling that somebody in that audience was having hell kidded out of him.

For this reason I doubt that the British lady needs to worry much about young America having forced alien cultural patterns upon historic Japan. I imagine the Japanese are not too impressed by chewing gum on the Ginza. What has been good in our occupation they'll keep. What was bad they'll reject. All nations have done that in the past. Americans would be historically naive to think that our wishes will be any more sacred than those of past conquerors, or that Japan is one whit more stupid than nations which have previously lost wars. Things will work out pretty much as they have always done.

But beyond that we have one hope. When Japan finally does go her own way we can hope that she will remember her American guests as reasonably decent people. She may thus be inspired to retain a long-range friendship with us. It is upon that hope that we must gamble. Perhaps our letting the Japanese have a good belly laugh at our expense in *Gone with the Wind* will be one of those things that will be remembered in our favor.

THE

PROCONSUL

It was a dark wintry day in Tokyo and friends in the Press Club said, "If you've never seen General MacArthur leave the Dai Ichi building, today would be a good time."

We bundled up and walked down Shimbun Alley to a cross street which we followed to the Emperor's palace grounds. Then we walked briskly down to the Dai Ichi building, where a small crowd had already gathered.

It was a pregnant day, for the New York *Herald Tribune* had just run its famous editorial pointing out that General MacArthur should perhaps be displaced as military leader in Korea. Among the men at the Press Club it was generally known that the great debacle on the right flank near the Yalu River was somebody's fault and most of the up-front men felt that ultimately the blame would have to fall on MacArthur.

At the Dai Ichi building very tall and handsome military guards stood at brisk attention, symbols of our Pacific empire. At the curb a long automobile waited. In the streets traffic came to a halt. Japanese on bicycles were directed to place at least one foot on the ground. The crowd pressed forward.

Suddenly from the central doors a running guard appeared. Others leaped forward to hold open doors, and the erect guards snapped to an even more dramatic pose. The running guard hastened across the broad sidewalk and held the car door.

Then, from the Dai Ichi doors, the general appeared. He was erect, his stride was long, his large coat was tight about his waist, his belt ends hung sedately and his famous cap was precisely straight. He looked straight ahead and gave the appearance of a man not hurried but bearing a considerable burden.

In profound silence he entered the car and rapidly disappeared into the growing darkness. A Japanese policeman blew his whistle and traffic was allowed to resume. My guide said, "It's sort of pathetic to see a great general end his career in disgrace this way."

"What do you mean?" I asked.

"This Korea business. If the story is ever released back home it'll mean public disgrace."

We returned to the Press Club in deep gloom. These were the bad days. Our troops were getting kicked about in Korea and there was already talk that the Navy would have to pull some kind of miracle to save the right-flank army that had been so badly mauled. Many correspondents thought we might have to evacuate Pusan as well and surrender all Korea. There was serious talk of a Russian invasion of Japan. MacArthur had rarely been in a tougher spot.

I felt additionally sorry that these evil days had come upon the general, for I had known him—not personally—in many weathers, and I wondered what would be the effect on America of the stories coming out of Korea. Our men had done badly. One British correspondent who had seen a lot of fighting in lots of wars summarized it this way: "American troops are fleeing southward before untold hordes of Chinese barbarians—in company strength." We also knew that a tremendous and probably unjustified military gamble had been taken, without adequate preparation, for at times our Marines had marched into the teeth of a half-million Chinese, with no mechanical support, with our men spaced sometimes fifty yards apart. We hoped that Americans back home would not become panicky over the news, for of course we did not then know that Americans were not to be told the full gravity of the debacle.

When I got back to my room I thought of this great provocative character. Through a strange series of events I had developed a vast admiration for MacArthur's military genius. It happened in this round-about way.

On Espiritu Santo, south of Guadalcanal, I was with a squadron of Marine fighting planes when our pilots limped back to base after having plastered Jap shipping. The flyers were already jittery and bushed when they heard over the radio General MacArthur's latest flamboyant communiqué from Australia. He announced that his planes had sunk the Jap ships which had actually been destroyed by our Marines a thousand miles away.

There was a horrified silence, for this was the fourth or fifth time the general's flaming communiqués had stolen the show. That night his picture happened to appear in a newsreel, and the Marines wrecked the joint. Thereafter it was a rule that all newsreels had to be inspected before showing to the troops, so that any pictures of General MacArthur could be eliminated. Otherwise so many coconuts would be thrown through the screen that it would become impossible to continue showing films.

Later, in 1944, I happened to be traveling through all the islands from Manus through Bougainville and on down to Guadalcanal. The announcement had just been released that those islands were to be transferred from Admiral Halsey's old command to General MacArthur's enlarged area. Since I traveled on headquarters' business it was mistakenly assumed that I might have some pull with the admiral.

On every island, eleven of them, Army, Navy and Marine officers came to me and begged me, sometimes with tears in their eyes, to get them transferred either back to Noumea or right up to Iwo Jima—anywhere, so long as they would not have to serve under MacArthur. This was not a mass hysteria. It was the result of factual stories about the ridiculous military nonsense not only tolerated by MacArthur's command, but actually sponsored by it.

Men who had fought a free and honorable war in the South Pacific shuddered at the prospect of becoming a part of the MacArthur fancy-dress hoop-la and ballyhoo. I myself helped one young fellow escape a perfectly safe desk job with MacArthur. He volunteered to swim underwater to explode Jap mines at places like Okinawa.

For a short period after that I was in a position to compare the general's flamboyant communiqués with what appeared to be the sober truth, and in late 1944 I would rather have been assigned to a small-boat invasion of Truk than take a job in the MacArthur system. It is a matter of record that when I was threatened with such a transfer, I too volunteered for underwater demolition off the coast of Borneo. I believe that most of my fellow Navy and Marine officers felt the same way.

It was with these preconceptions that I went to Australia some time later, where I witnessed one of the most terrific fist fights of my life. An American Marine had observed, in a saloon, that he didn't think General MacArthur was so hot. A big, rangy Australian knocked him into the sawdust. "No bloody man livin' can speak that way about the general!" the Australian bellowed. And he proceeded, with the help of a few murdering bushrangers, to clean us all up.

The love for General MacArthur in Australia—up to 1949—was unbelievable. It makes any subsequent American professions of gratitude seem rather puny. For in 1942 Australia lay totally at the mercy of Japan. The finest Australian troops were in Africa and England. The British Navy, on which Australia obviously relied, was engaged elsewhere. There were no munitions. Already the Japs had penetrated almost to Port Moresby and their planes had started the reduction of Darwin. It was beyond compare the darkest day in Australia's history.

Into this terrifying void stepped General MacArthur. Resolutely he said that he would not only save Australia, but would recapture the Philippines, too. For three years he never once wavered in this determination. In ringing phrases he conveyed to the Australian people his iron confidence in his and their destiny.

Then, almost as if he were constructing the timetable, he moved from Melbourne to Brisbane to Hollandia to Manila to Tokyo. His long assault on the Japanese Empire was one of the most brilliant in military history, and I have heard Australian military men describe it as "the impeccable campaign." This is an opinion in which I concur. MacArthur's subjection of Japan was a campaign without blemish.

But when I returned to Australia in 1949 I did not find the same hushed reverence for MacArthur, the savior of the nation. Instead I encountered an embarrassed confusion. There were many Australians who muttered through their teeth, "Who in hell does he think he is, sitting up there in Tokyo? God?" There was a prevalent feeling that the one American who best understood Australia had failed her.

What accounted for this change? General MacArthur in 1949 was faced by the frightful problem that will ultimately face every American leader in the years to come: "Japan has 83,000,000 people; Australia has 8,000,000. Which country shall we make concessions to in order to have that nation as a strong ally?"

General MacArthur, facing this inevitable problem, had suggested that perhaps Japanese food and population pressures might be relieved by permitting Japanese emigrants to occupy New Guinea. It is difficult to convey the shudder that passed over Australia when this proposal was announced. The savior of the nation had somehow forgotten the nation. Henceforth the name of MacArthur would be linked with that of Woodrow Wilson. They were two well-meaning Americans who understood the Pacific so imperfectly that they had advocated placing Japanese on New Guinea, a scant 90 miles from Australia.

A very learned Australian asked me, "What can MacArthur mean? Suppose the Japs had held New Guinea on December 7, 1941? They could have invaded us with no trouble. That would have meant evil for Australia but it would have been disastrous for the United States. What bases would MacArthur have used for the reconquest of the Philippines? Where would he have staged his great drive north? Tell me, has MacArthur been so worshipped by the grinning Japs that he's gone balmy? Does he think he is the arbiter of the Pacific?"

I replied that the general had been forced to face one of the great problems of the Pacific—Japan or Australia—and without turning his back upon the latter had seen that he simply had to acknowledge the priority of the former. I added furthermore that no one else seems to have a solution to the question of New Guinea, this vast and wildly wealthy island. Australians can neither populate it nor develop it. Indonesia, which will soon own the western end of the island, can populate it but not develop it. America, which could develop it but not populate it, was in effect thrown out of the area by Australia's childish insistence that we abandon the great base of Manus in 1945. That leaves only Japan, which has the facilities both to populate and develop. "In fact," I concluded, "an Australian in New Guinea who knows the island better than either of us has come to just that conclusion. Bring the Japs in. Treat them decently. And pray that in time of trouble they will remain loyal."

The Australian wiped his lips and asked, "Then you agree with MacArthur?"

"Yes."

"May God help your nation on the day it happens."

"The decision was made a long time ago," I replied.

"What do you mean?"

"When you decided that no one but white people could settle your empty continent."

"That was one of those difficult national decisions that all countries have to make," the Australian replied.

"Our choice of supporting Japan or Australia is exactly the same kind of choice," I said.

"If MacArthur forces this through his name will live in infamy," the Australian cried. And he spoke for many of his countrymen.

Some time later I worked with a distinguished woman who was writing a book about Asia, and she told me of General MacArthur. Her story was so deeply moving that from time to time she had to pause to gain control of her tears. She said, "I was in Santo Tomas prison. For more than a year we heard nothing about the progress of the war except what the Japanese told us. Singapore had fallen. Australia was gone. Seattle had been invaded.

"My former houseboy used to smuggle food into the prison, although he risked his life doing so, and sometimes he added bits of news he had picked up from the outside. Hong Kong had fallen. New Zealand was gone. The Japs held Honolulu.

"In despair we thought of our future and the most we could hope for was that some kind of Japanese-dictated peace would permit us to work as their underlings.

"Then one day my houseboy smuggled in a bar of chocolate. I . . ."

She broke down completely. In prison she had lost fifty pounds and had been mortally shaken by her experience. Then she resumed. "This bar of candy bore a wrapper which read, 'I shall return. General Douglas MacArthur.' "

Again the woman broke down and it was some time before she could continue. Then she said, "We were famished for sweets but we could not break that wrapper. It passed from hand to hand, the first substantial news we had heard. From that day we never doubted."

For this woman General MacArthur was beyond reproach.

Yet at the time MacArthur was accomplishing these miracles it was reported that a young naval officer had been court-martialed and sent home in disgrace for merely writing on his hut where enlisted men could see it:

> "With the help of God
> And a few Marines,
> I have returned
> To the Philippines."

When I tried to track down this rumor I was told that it was not only true but that the charge against the young man was sacrilege.

It was with these conflicting emotions that I arrived in Tokyo in late

1950. I met at least 36 famous and reasonably honest correspondents, of whom 32 detested general MacArthur. Some of them had personal reasons. They had released the flash that the general had said the boys would be home by Christmas. Subsequently the story was denied and they were branded as liars. Others had been at the Yalu River and had witnessed what they called a wanton waste of American life on a precarious military gamble. Others, while supporting the gamble as one of those calculated risks which characterize all war, were nevertheless outraged at the militarily inept way it had been carried out. All of them said that MacArthur's conduct of the occupation of Japan was excellent, but that his own imperious aloofness from the Japanese people as well as from his own homeland was insufferably arrogant.

Only four correspondents would agree with me when I argued that his original conquest of Japan had been a military classic. In view of this 32-4 vote of "No Confidence" I was astonished at America's news reporting when General MacArthur returned to the United States in April, 1951. I happened to be traveling in an automobile through the West and was able to listen sixteen hours a day to the radio and read ten or twelve newspapers. Not once did I catch a hint that those Tokyo newspapermen who knew MacArthur best had grave doubts as to his divinity. I therefore concluded that one of three things had happened: (1) either all the newsmen I had met in Tokyo were liars; or (2) they had forgotten to send reports home; or (3) most unlikely of all, every report had been lost in the otherwise reliable mail. It was unthinkable that the Tokyo news reports had been suppressed.

In shivering disbelief I listened through those fateful days for one dispassionate review of the controversy. Instead, I heard a great network report that their man in Tokyo had come upon a sergeant on the Ginza with tears in his eyes who muttered between clenched teeth, "Why did they have to do this to my commander?" At this point I nearly threw up. The average enlisted man I knew on the Ginza usually called MacArthur just what the average enlisted man had called Halsey or Eisenhower: "Old fat mouth." And when the general did return I felt the old sick feeling all over again when I heard the breathless announcement that the first thing he had ordered was a chocolate milk shake and a hot dog; for in at least a dozen Japanese PX's and especially at Haneda Airport, they serve the best milk shakes in the world—and have for the past five years.

I have reported my varied and shifting attitudes toward this controversial figure in such detail for one reason only. MacArthur has become, understandably, the most listened-to American spokesman on Asia. It is critically urgent to evaluate what he and everyone else says about Asia, for so very few of us know anything about this enormous continent—and we must learn.

The first nineteen paragraphs of General MacArthur's speech to Congress on April 19, 1951, are among the soundest, clearest and most substantial words ever uttered by an American statesman regarding Asia. They constitute an epitome.

Nor can anyone reasonably doubt that his short-range policies in Japan were superb. His factual knowledge of Asia is enviable. I wish we were going to have, for the next two generations, men in charge of our Asia policies who know as much.

I do think, however, that several of General MacArthur's basic attitudes toward Asia warrant inquiry. We must remember that he is merely one human being. The policy of 150,000,000 other Americans toward the 1,300,000,000 people of Asia cannot possibly or properly be based upon the opinions of any one man.

First question: What does General MacArthur mean when he says to Clyde A. Lewis, Commander of the Veterans of Foreign Wars, in his letter released on August 28, 1950, ". . . it is in the pattern of the Oriental psychology to respect and follow aggressive, resolute and dynamic leadership"? Until Thanksgiving Day of 1950, General MacArthur consistently suggested that he knows Asiatics and that they will buckle down if white men show a little force. That idea is completely discredited and defunct. The French have shown a lot of force in Indo-China, and there are few signs of benighted Asians buckling down. In fact, it is the white men who duck when peasants hurl hand grenades among them. The Dutch mustered considerable force against the Indonesians and so frightened them that all the Indonesians did was throw the Dutch right out of every island. General MacArthur himself, shortly after his Formosa letter, threw at North Koreans and Chinese communists the greatest relative superiority of airplanes and naval gunfire in history, and the Asiatic peasants were so impressed they marched right on and tossed our best troops into the ocean at Hungnam. The fact is that General MacArthur wrote his letter in the palmy days when his troops were having easy pickings and seemed destined to attain the Yalu River. It must have seemed as if the old order in Asia was being restored; Asiatic forces were then wilting before a show of arms. Those old days are not coming back. We must absolutely erase from our national memory the ancient idea that a little show of force is going to scare hell out of quaking Asians, after which we can make them do what we want. That day is past. Anyone who tries to revive it is doing both America and Asia a disservice. I prefer to believe that General MacArthur meant that if Asia ran wild against us it was useless to counter such aggression without real force. Asians, led by Russians, ran wild in Korea and it was necessary to use substantial force to discipline such wilful aggression. But I dispute whether in the long run we could either dominate Asia by force or support our policies and our friends by war. And even if by a miracle we could do those things, I still don't think we should. I think that identifying the legitimate desires of Asians and helping them to attain those desires peacefully will be the far better policy.

Second question: What does General MacArthur mean when he says, in his address to the Congress, that from our Pacific islands chain extending in an arc from the Aleutians to the Marianas, "we can dominate with sea and air power every Asiatic port from Vladivostok to Singapore . . . and prevent any hostile movement into the Pacific"? Does he mean that we shall forever be at enmity with Asia? If he means that then he means that the United States is permanently at war for the next fifty years. We had better batten down the hatches and prepare for a long and terrible siege. For in such an implacable enmity we shall not be besieging Asia. Asia-Europe-Africa will be besieging us. If we are resolutely determined to oppose Asia's self-determination, then the Asia-Europe-Africa coalition will become a reality, possibly led by Russia but just as possibly led by some Asiatic power in the 1980's or 1990's. More likely General MacArthur meant that during the present impasse when China threatens to run wild, it is prudent to keep bases in Formosa and the Philippines from which to forestall aggression eastward, especially against Japan but also Australia. But the ultimate purpose of bases anywhere—Japan, Philippines, Formosa or Australia—must be to serve as bridges rather than as bastions. We must ultimately co-operate with Asia and Asia with us, otherwise island fortresses are of no use. In the last war when our relations with Asia deteriorated to the crumbling point, our bastions fell like overripe plums. Our great hope with Asia lies in our establishment of common interests and mutually respected aims.

Third question: What does General MacArthur mean when he says, "The Philippines stand as a mighty bulwark of Christianity in the Far East, and its capacity for high moral leadership in Asia is unlimited"? This is an alluring but dangerous idea. It takes us back to the 1850's when it was believed that time and missionary effort would convert all the world to Christianity. It perpetuates the belief, which arose before the other great religions of the world were studied comparatively, that only Christianity can solve the world's problems—and all other religions would then retire to the darkness from which they had sprung. That idea no longer bears inspection. I happen to believe strongly in the Christian faith and I think it one well suited to the spiritual leadership of our democracy; but I also suspect that in the long run it may well be some Oriental religion infinitely older than Christianity that will provide the spiritual leadership for that part of the world. No one can overlook the fact that Asians happen to be totally committed to their religions, which in certain respects serve them even better than Christianity serves us. (Care of the old would be an example.) But I am not attempting to compare and evaluate religions on a basis of merit. I am satisfied with the one I have and believe that in its finest manifestations it is a supreme expression of man's longings. In fact, if I had never known Asia I would be content to believe that my religion was incomparably the finest in the world. But having experienced the passionate devotion with which Asians are committed to their religions, having heard the anger that rises when Christianity tries to force its way into their lives, displacing a religion they prefer, I am no longer willing to stipulate that my religion is automatically bound to conquer the world. And as for finding in the insecure and confused Philippines a moral bastion from which to do the conquering, that seems ridiculous. In fact, I should rather think there was a danger that it might work the other way around, especially if Islam should become a great solidifying force in Asia pulling naturally toward the many Muslims in the Philippines. That is not likely, but what is likely is that each of the great religions of Asia will retain authority in its allotted geographic area and that in each religion the many good points will triumph over the obvious weaknesses: Christianity in the Philippines; Judaism in Israel; Buddhism in most of Southeast Asia; Islam in Indonesia, Pakistan, Iran and westward; Confucianism in China; and Shintoism in Japan. I would dread to see a religious war set aflame amid that collection of diverse faiths.

Final question: What do the supporters of General MacArthur mean when they insist that he knows Asia better than any other living American? Does he know Indonesia (population 80,000,000)? Not that I know of. He probably knew something of the Dutch East Indies, but I believe he has never been to Indonesia. Does he know India (population 346,-000,000)? He may have visited British India but I don't think he has ever been in free India, and there is a vast difference. Does he know Pakistan (population 74,000,000)? I don't know of any visits to Pakistan. Does he know at first hand modern Iran, free Burma, the dominion of Ceylon, French Indo-China, Thailand? I think that to establish his credentials we should be given a list of his visits to these places, and their dates, for a visit twenty years ago hardly warrants life-and-death modern generalizations. As a matter of fact, how well does General MacArthur

know modern China? How often has he traveled there? How far inland
and to what districts? Actually, there must be a great deal about Asia
that General MacArthur does not know at first hand. On the other hand,
his constant wartime briefings and postwar considerations of policy have
undoubtedly built up in his mind a fund of knowledge that is unequaled.
He has shown himself to be able to master an infinite amount of information supplied him by others. Furthermore, he probably knows the Philippines far better than most Filipinos. He knows Australia intimately, New
Guinea and the islands, and Japan (although many Americans in Japan
would deny that he knows much of Japan at first hand). I ask these
questions about his personal knowledge of Asia because great new nations have arisen in the postwar period. It worries me when leaders in
Congress repeat that he alone understands this new Asia. If we don't have
a half-dozen men who understand vast parts of Asia better than he does,
we are doomed.

I want to make it perfectly clear that General MacArthur knows ten
times more about this continent than I will ever know. But it is not the
knowledge of one man or a score of men which will bring us to a better
accord with Asia and the Asians. It is, rather, a new orientation of mind
and heart to a culture and a religious history and a political, social and
economic transformation to which all Americans will have to accommo-
date themselves.

OBSERVATIONS

The fundamental fact about Japan is that it cannot feed itself. It has
too many people and too little land. In an area the size of Montana it
packs in 83,000,000 people, 53 per cent as many as we have in all the
United States. We have 49 people to the square mile. Japan has 577.

What is worse, most Japanese land is not arable. Japan has a higher
percentage of steeply sloping land than any other major nation in the
world. By miracles of energy it has made land tillable that would elsewhere be waste, but even so, 45 Japanese must subsist on each acre of
arable land, whereas in America the same amount of land must support
only 0.28 people. In other words, landwise America is roughly 180 times
better off than Japan.

This startling fact is repeated in other portions of Asia. The continent
has barely enough food to feed everyone a minimum diet, if the food is
properly distributed. War, famine, political anarchy or unavailability of
shipping automatically mean that somewhere in Asia someone will have
to starve to death. (I have given the most hopeful interpretation of the

facts. Most specialists in this field, including some I respect, contend that even under perfect distribution Asia would not have quite enough food to prevent starvation. A few investigators, some of whom have convinced me, argue that Asia is not yet producing all the food she is able and that a minimum subsistence is possible.)

Rice is of course the key food. The three greatest nations of Asia—China, India, Japan—are rice-deficit areas. They cannot produce enough even under perfect conditions to feed everyone. Other areas, notably Pakistan, Thailand, Burma, Indo-China and in peacetime Korea and parts of Indonesia, produce surpluses.

The deficit areas are large and powerful; the surplus areas are weak and unorganized. Consequently the power politics of Asia consist of the deficit nations trying to gain control of the surplus nations.

In 1942 Japan held Malaya, Thailand, much of Burma, much of China, Korea, Indo-China and all of Indonesia. She had thus solved the problem of Asia. She had food sources and markets for her surplus manufactures. Arrogantly she announced the doctrine that "Southeast Asia is our rice paddy." Had she been able to force or trick the United States into an armistice in 1943, Japan would unquestionably have dominated Asia for generations to come. She would have lived well and the rest of Asia would have starved.

Well, we and our allies upset those plans. The German-Japanese attempt to organize Asia failed. But the basic problem remained and today we are right back where we were in 1941. This time the alliance is a Russian-Chinese one, but its purpose is the same: the organization of Asia. I believe without a shred of doubt—in fact I am more certain of this than of any other fact about modern Asia—that if we had not stepped into Korea, the Russian-Chinese alliance would today control Indo-China, Malaya, Thailand, Burma and possibly Indonesia and parts of India. At that point the Russian-Chinese alliance would be approaching the success which eluded the German-Japanese coalition.

Observe that each of these attempts is a Europe-Asia combination whose ultimate purpose must be the unification of this vast central land mass. (Africa obviously would have to get in line almost immediately after the union of Europe and Asia.) It is probable that in each instance the European partner has thought that once Europe and Asia are organized, the Asiatic partner can be controlled; but it is unquestionable that any such alliance to be effective must ultimately destroy the United States by monolithic pressures if not by actual war. Thus we have no choice when any combination such as Germany-Japan or Russia-China runs wild. We must challenge it or perish.

But when we defeated the former attempt in 1945 we were left with the same old Asiatic problem of rice-surplus areas and rice-deficit areas. And when we defeat the Russian-Chinese coalition we will once more be left with the perpetual problem. It is interesting therefore to speculate upon what might have been the one moral and supportable solution to this question. For three generations it seemed as if a British-Indian coalition might organize Asia. Steps were certainly being taken, politically and economically, but the arrogance of the British and the intransigence of the Indians—plus America's unwillingness to support such a balance-of-power statesmanship—caused this relatively palatable solution to fail.

There remains the alluring prospect of an American-Asiatic alliance that might succeed where the great Europe-Asia alliances failed. (I am assuming failure of the present menace.) Some Americans have been talking recently as if they were attracted by the possibilities of an American-Japanese coalition. I think such a combination very dangerous and impossible to offer as a serious solution to the problem, for these reasons: (1) Japan would be unwise to tie herself so completely to a non-Asiatic power. (2) America would be misguided to form an alliance with only 83,000,000 people when doing so would alienate 1,220,000,000 former Japanese enemies. (3) The coalition probably wouldn't succeed anyway.

Two other alternatives to this last prospect of an American-Asiatic alliance remain. It would have been good if we could have consolidated our friendship with China into a constructive and pacifying partnership. That we failed to accomplish this is one of the tragedies of our generation. I am not convinced that we are permanently denied this possibility, but chances look gloomy at present.

We seem equally determined to throw away the last alternative. Had we started five years ago in the first flush of Indian independence—for which we were in part spiritually responsible—we might have built an American-Indian coalition that would in time have embraced all nations between India and Indonesia. If there is even the remotest chance of reconstructing such friendships we should bend all of our energies and wealth in doing so; but I greatly fear our petulant anger at India and her childish retaliations have destroyed such possibilities.

Perhaps, in the long run, that is best. Perhaps we have reached the point when any Asiatic coalition with either Europe or America is untenable. I would like to think that Asia was growing to the age when she would stand alone, working out her own destiny and achieving her own strength. If Russia's avowed intention of subjugating the continent can be forestalled, we might witness an Asia strong enough to stand alone. Americans should want this, and should work to achieve it; for I doubt if we have anything to fear from a strong, secure and prosperous Asia. The dreaded Europe-Asia-Africa alliance will come when Asia is so weak that it will fall prey to some European adventurer.

What will be Japan's role in a strong Asia? To answer this we must consider England. Some historical analogies are misleading, but the identity between Japan and England is so striking as to be most illuminating. Each is an island kingdom. Each is placed strategically off the coast of a continent. Each has a non-continental tradition. Each is overpopulated. Each is underfed, if constricted to its own foodstuffs. Each lives by exporting manufactured goods to foreign markets. Each has been more enterprising, more energetic than continental rivals. And today each is faced by almost identical post-war problems, England working hers out in a socialistic pattern, Japan working hers out in a kind of super-socialism whereby a rich friend pours in enough wealth to postpone the dire decisions that have had to be taken in England.

Japan must return to her former position of trading manufactured goods for food. In the 1930's her bicycles, clocks, rubber-soled shoes and cotton goods flooded Asian markets, providing Asians with a standard of living they never enjoyed before or since. Prior to the actual outbreak of the Korean war Japan had resumed an important trade with Communist China. This was reasonable, for ultimately Japan must trade with China or starve. To forego this trade would be economic folly. As a matter of unpleasant fact, even during the Korean war a good deal of the much-decried Hong Kong-Red China trade consisted of transshipments of Japanese goods exported to Hong Kong. Japan should do everything she can to build up her Asiatic trade.

In this respect Japan is much like Australia. The United States needs each of these Asiatic nations as friends and bulwarks. But to expect either of them to integrate its economic policies with ours is ridiculous. We could easily absorb Japan's exports if we were willing to close down all our manufacturing plants in New England, Pennsylvania and Alabama. We could also absorb Australia's agricultural products by the simple trick of retiring every farmer between Ohio and Nebraska. Since either action is unlikely on our part, Japan and Australia will have to find what markets they can.

By any line of reasoning one comes to the conclusion that Japan has her own national destiny to achieve. For a transitory period after 1945 that destiny coincided with America's, but we must not expect it to remain so. If tomorrow we were to withdraw our economic support of Japan, she would be right back where she was in 1932. Actually, she would be much worse off now, for then she could rely upon Formosan and Korean food, and she controlled Chinese markets. She would again be tempted to solve her economic impasse by military adventures.

There are those who argue that Japan today is somewhat better off than in 1932 because of manufacturing and organizational improvements made under American supervision. These have indeed been considerable, but they are more than offset by a constantly increased population, which grows by nearly 2,000,000 a year. By some experts this population increase has been called Japan's major problem.

It was disturbing, therefore, to find that late in General MacArthur's regime, when an overdue analysis of Japan's status had been made by a team of skilled American researchers, a group of American housewives living in Japan forced MacArthur to tear out the final recommendations from every copy of the report. Those pages dealt with birth control.

This raises a terrifying moral problem. It was put to me bluntly by an American in India. He said, "Every time a Christian housewife in Omaha puts ten cents in the collection plate to help the medical missionaries in Asia, she is committing a grave moral sin unless at the same time she is taking steps so that one day we can cede all of Canada to surplus Asiatic populations—or all of the United States west of the Mississippi."

At present the death rate in much of Asia is so high that life expectancy is only 27 years as compared to 69 in America. If all who now die needlessly lived on to 69, the population of Asia would be more than doubled. If food supplies were not multiplied enormously Asia would either starve to death or overflow onto other continents. To encourage either of these alternatives is immoral, whether a Christian housewife in Omaha does it or a Japanese General Tojo. This is a major problem that America will have to face. It is absolutely inescapable. We will probably have to face it soon in Japan.

The brighter side of the picture is that since 1945 Japan has acquired technical and social skills. Her women have been set free. Her energies are greater than ever before. Her people understand at least the rudiments of democracy and personal responsibility.

The most we can hope for is that Japan will work out her destiny in Asia mindful of the fact that we wish to be her friend. I have no patience with Americans who think that by either our conquest or our wealth we have in some curious way purchased the soul of Japan. Nations cannot be bought that cheaply, and when by chance they are for sale, they are never worth the purchase price.

KOREA

FORTY MINUTES AFTER I LANDED IN KOREA TWO ENLISTED MEN WARNED me: "Sir, if you go home and write a musical and call it *South Korea*, and put in pretty girls and singing men, we're going to bash your brains in."

And they pointed to the ruins of this tragic land. We were at the edge of Seoul and it looked like a vast grave. More than a million people had once lived there, but now it bore a unique and horrible distinction: it had been captured and recaptured more than any major city in modern history. It was a foul ruin.

I flew over a good deal of Korea and I saw towns in which only a few chimney-roots remained. Not a roof, not a house, not a public building. The fiery hand of war had erased all habitations.

I believe you would have to go back to Carthage to find an equivalent to modern Korea. True, there was devastation in the Thirty Years' War, but not accompanied by total obliteration of communities by air and surface fire. True, cities like Lidice and Rabaul were totally destroyed in the last war, but they were not entire nations.

Korea is a horrible nightmare. Word of Korea has flashed all through Asia. Russian provocateurs have whispered that this is what America accomplishes when she sets foot in Asia. American propaganda has been tardy in refuting this claim, so that today Korea is more than a smoldering wasteland. It is a symbol of American intentions.

This perplexes and infuriates me. What has happened to our intelligence and our ability to talk with other people if we permit Korea to stand for us in a continent whose very liberties sprang in part from our honest good will?

Brutally, the facts are these. An American today in Asia had better not go out at night. He is likely to get shot. He cannot get into China at all. Siberia is closed to him. If he is caught in the jungles of Malaya or the back roads of Indonesia or the suburbs of Manila he is likely to be murdered. In India, Pakistan and Thailand he is welcomed, but he had better duck for cover in Indo-China. And he would be wise to stay indoors in Iran, too.

What has happened? When China revolted against her imperial masters we lent moral and even financial support to the fighters for freedom. When Indonesia revolted against the Dutch, the revolt would absolutely have failed had America not sided with the insurgents. We supported India, Burma and Ceylon in their struggle for independence. We lent moral backing to Pakistan. We sponsored Japan's liberalizing constitution, and we encouraged the Philippines to break away from our tutelage. How does a nation which has consistently supported freedom in Asia find itself degenerated into the symbol of reactionary intervention?

Surely, our mistake in keeping Syngman Rhee as our man or our understandable poor timing in backing Bao Dai should not erase the memory of what traditionally we have stood for. But our recent fumbles in Asia have accomplished just that. In five years we tumbled down from an impeccable position of friendly and generous adviser to the slime of actual hatred. And Korea has become, under communist manipulation, the symbol of that hatred.

America has lost enormous moral prestige in Asia because of Korea. This is the more astonishing because we were right in going into Korea. We were right in staying there when the odds were all against us. We were right in seeing the communists thrown out of the land they invaded.

It was shocking to me, therefore, to find that even our own men in Korea did not know why we were there. The morale of troops on this point was so low that six times I had an opportunity to address large groups on the simple A-B-C's of America's existence.

I had the tough job of trying to explain why the same Americans who had applauded our going into Korea were at that moment quivering with fear and bleating that we should get out. I tried to explain how if we had not gone into Korea all of Southeast Asia would have fallen to the Chinese communists. Finally I endeavored to assure these doubting men that morality and right were with us.

It is regrettable when either a nation or a man has a perfectly moral job to do but somehow fails to explain either to himself or to the world why the task is essential and upon what moral principles it is based. This is particularly true when the United States—a nation unjustly accused throughout the world as having no philosophical or moral foundations—operates in Asia.

Awarding cynical criticism every point I can, I still believe that we were completely justified in going into Korea and that we would have been negligent of our duty to ourselves and the rest of the free world had we failed to do so. It is now our job, belatedly, to explain this to the people of Asia. For the present all they understand is that American airplanes, American shells, American napalm is killing Asians. Frequently in Asia I saw newspaper headlines, "Americans Kill 4000 Asians."

It is cold in Korea. In fact, I had never before in my life been really cold until I got caught out one night and had to sleep on the ground. From Arctic Siberia the winds of winter howled down into canyons that funneled them into gales. A soldier and I tried to sleep but the cold tied our bellies into knots. It was fearfully cold and I wondered how our men even farther north toward the Yalu could stand such gales.

But if we had supinely watched Korea fall to communist aggression, if we had encouraged China and Russia to absorb all of Southeast Asia, then the Asia-Europe-Africa monolithic coalition would have been launched and in time every home and village in America would have experienced a real ice age.

THE

TIDES

OF

WAR

The first Korean I met was fifty-six-year-old Succhan Lee, a most intelligent man with a grave, handsome face. He had obviously known better days and was now a poorly paid interpreter for the American Army. His story was a deep and moving tragedy, but the last thing he told me was so astonishingly funny that whenever I recall his somber face I have to chuckle.

He began, "I was a boy when Korea was invaded by Japan. It was terrible to watch our country lose its freedom, and there were many suicides. My friends wept for three days and our bravest soldiers hid in the hills, where they fought for a long time.

"My father was a famous classic poet and ignored the whole affair.

He stayed home and reminded us that many things happen in a lifetime and the wise man accepts them all. But I was young and swore that I would spend my life for Korean freedom.

"It was not easy. The Japanese ruled our land with terrifying efficiency. Spies reported if families did not speak Japanese at home. In law courts, schools, business houses it was necessary to speak Japanese. No Korean could get a good job and the Japs always let us know they thought we were swine.

"So when I was still young I decided to flee the country and join some Korean freedom movement on the outside. But the police would issue passports only to stupid Koreans too dumb ever to be a threat. So one night I escaped across the Yalu River and ran away to Shanghai, where I studied with Presbyterians. I learned English and some devoted friends collected money to send me to Ohio State University. I was ready to sail at eleven o'clock one morning, but at eight the Japanese secret police caught me and I never got to America.

"I escaped from the police before they could drag me back to Korea and hid in a Baptist college, where I learned most of what I know. Then I crept back to Korea and for three years worked in the Independence Movement. We were deeply inspired by President Wilson's Fourteen Points and were ready to give Korea a good government. But nothing came of it, so one day I gave up my revolutionary ideas and took a job teaching at the Methodist school in Seoul. Among other things I coached baseball, and do you know why I would like to go to America? To see the Yankees play a double header on a Sunday afternoon.

"I was very happy at my job, but in 1939 the Japanese moved in. They made us stop teaching English. They made us bow each morning to the Emperor and worship his portrait as if it were an idol. On the train one day I was speaking in Korean and the guard slapped me and shouted, 'Speak in Japanese.' Next we were forbidden to teach the Bible, but some brave teachers held classes at night with lights out. Then chapel was outlawed. Finally we had to give up baseball. So I quit. It was no use trying to run a decent school.

"I sneaked over the border again, although it was more difficult now, and after a long wandering in Manchuria I reached Tientsin, where I passed as a Chinese. Then when it looked as if Japan might lose the war I came back in a small boat and worked with the freedom movement again. Now I had to hide in the hills and small villages, for the police knew I was in the country and they tracked me down from place to place. Once I watched from a distance while they burned my English books.

"They took my son and made him join the army, where one night he was beaten to death. Some people will say that Koreans entered the Japanese Army willingly. I never knew one who did. It was always beatings and threats.

"When Japan surrendered there was a surge of joy. In Seoul I met my former friends, and since I could speak English they got me a job with your Army. I also started to teach school again and felt great pride that in some small way I had helped my country gain its independence. What I had sworn to do as a little boy had been accomplished.

"We had great hopes for this country. Many fine men were in the government and we had your help. Things looked pretty good, and then the North Koreans invaded us.

"What did I do? Well, I have been running most of my life and I am not exactly afraid any longer. I knew I was marked for assassination as a responsible liberal, but I waited until pay day and then came south.

"I have no very great feelings about the present war. Maybe I'm getting a little like my father, the poet. Many things will happen to a man in his lifetime and he had better learn to accept them.

"But I do not fool myself. Deep in my heart I know that a terrible thing has happened. This was a good country. We had many brave men in this country. They kept their hope alive for generations. I knew them in their China exile. They had not a bowl of rice to eat, but still they worked for freedom. It is most tragic to see them win their freedom and then lose it so very soon. It is sad to see a nation starting slowly on the right path and then watch it being destroyed. Even so, I am not dismayed. Surely, we've suffered before without despair.

"But there is one thing about which I am very determined. You Americans must not brand all Koreans as thieves and lazy men. Now you must listen to what I say. Yesterday I saw an old man leaning on a post and the American driver of our jeep said, 'Look at that lazy bastard.' So we stopped the jeep and I asked the old man what he had eaten in the last three days and he had eaten two bowls of rice, that's all. We are thieves, yes, but some of us are thieves who are dying of starvation.

"What I want you to do is to read this story from *Stars and Stripes*. In America a father of three children steals money to get his girls a Christmas tree. And all over America people get sentimental and say here is a fine man willing to steal for his little girls, and they give him jobs and money and food. Because it's Christmas.

"But in Korea many fathers see their children almost starve every day in the year and it's never Christmas. No one gives them jobs. Now you've been to Japan. Are the Japs all thieves? Much as I hate them I must admit they aren't. Why not? They have food. They have their own government. They have pride. Korea has never had these things.

"Let me tell you a story. The manager of our army post had a fountain pen that cost $25. It was stolen. He screamed against the corrupt Koreans. So I called all the Koreans together and told them that one of them had stolen the pen and had done Korea great harm by doing so. We tracked the pen down and a workman had sold it for $3. But why had he sold it? Because he had five hungry children. Was he praised for being a good father? Not at all. He was a dirty Korean crook. Believe me, he was exactly the same man as the American who stole for his little girls. Sooner or later you Americans must recognize this fact."

In the pause that followed I asked the terrible question, "What will you do if we leave Korea?"

Succhan Lee, a fugitive much of his life, knew that he had now worked himself into the corner from which there was no exit. "On the day you leave I will be assassinated."

Then how is it that whenever I think of this fine old man I laugh? Well, after we had parted he came running back and said, "There is one thing I wish you to write down. You know Herb Pennock?"

The question bowled me over but I said yes, I knew the great Yankee left-hander. Succhan Lee smiled happily. "Pennock pitched against Korea in 1922. I batted cleanup, but our first three batters never saw the ball, Pennock had such sharp curves. So our coach asked him to throw straight balls. I was first man up in the second and Pennock threw me a hard one straight down the middle. I banged it over Meusel's head for a two bagger. I wish you would write that down."

THE

BUREAUCRAT

Sometimes you ask one question too many. Then everything is wrecked. I had just finished my interview with Han Chang Bock—not his real name—and had taken an interesting photograph of his lean, intelligent young face. But now I couldn't use my picture of this gifted thirty-year-old Korean.

For as I was about to leave I asked Han, "Have you anything you'd like to add?" A torrent erupted in the exact words that follow.

"May I speak frankly? I have wanted to talk with someone, and from the way you listen I think you will understand. For months now we have had to tell Americans what they want to hear, but if you really want the truth Korea was much better under the Japs. Then we had law and order. A person knew what he was supposed to do, and he did it. There was no brutality and many Koreans had good jobs working for the Japanese.

"In one sense we were not occupied territory. We were a true part of Japan. A second-rate part, yes, but in another forty years, if Japan had had the chance, Korea would have been totally Japanese. The old men who hated Japan were dying.

"For example, Japan made us use their alphabet, not to persecute us but because all of our commerce was with Japan. They also gave us Japanese names, not to humiliate us but because they wanted us to fit in with Japanese life.

"I have no complaint against the Japanese. Nor do my friends. Why should I? The Japanese gave me a fine education. At Waseda University. True, my father was a rich man who had worked with the Japanese, so it was easy for me to get a passport from the police. But I knew many poor boys who also got to Japanese universities.

"When I graduated—I had excellent marks—the Japanese gave me a good job on the Korean railroad. It's true that Japanese workers doing the same work got 67 per cent more pay, but they had to live away from home.

"I really had a responsible job and I performed it well. Before long I was promoted to the rice board. You understand that I could never have become head of the board, rice being so important. The top man was always a Japanese. But in lesser fields Koreans had already progressed to the position of vice-head of the board and I don't think it would have been many years before some Korean would have become actual head. I believe I was being considered.

"It is true that in Korea Japan followed a strictly colonial policy. But only at first. Have you been to Hamhung? No, of course not. The communists have driven you out of there. But if you could have seen the factories of the north you would realize that in addition to its colonial policy Japan had a very far-reaching industrial policy.

"Let me tell you how an educated Korean looks at it. My father was rich and held much land. Perhaps he was favored by the Japanese, but most Koreans had a good life. All of us. There was law and order. We were told what to do and there was no trouble. Not even the war hurt us. The big war, I mean. Korea was never bombed. There was no fighting on our soil. Our rice crop was good and we could always hide enough from the inspectors to live well. Only the uneducated or worthless were forced into the Japanese overseas labor corps. Educated people like me worked one day a month for the war effort, but otherwise we did not suffer.

"Let me prove that sensible Koreans really preferred Japan. There was a Korean brigade in the Japanese Army. Our young men enlisted willingly and at Manila fought very bravely and killed many Americans. Why did our men fight so well? Because they trusted Japan. Did I join the brigade? No, my eyes are not good.

"During the war we heard nothing of Japanese defeats, for no such news could be published in our newspapers. The Japanese knew that our peasants with no land hated them and they feared a revolt. But there would have been none, for educated Koreans like me knew that we would have to co-operate with the Japs. We did not even hear of the burning of Tokyo, but by the time of the atomic bomb we knew that Japan was defeated.

"Americans will not like this, for they believe very strongly in democracy and what President Wilson talked about. But there are some countries that are not ready to govern themselves. Korea was such a country. I watched the new government of South Korea very closely and it was one terrible corruption. Who was Syngman Rhee? Few Koreans had ever heard of him. He was nobody. And his government was all bribery and confusion. Its laws were marked by indecision. Its army was unspeakably venal; is that the word? I mean generals made fortunes in private graft through selling army stores. Korea was a tragic land, totally lost.

"There has always been great talk among the Americans about Koreans stealing from your warehouses. That was not known under the Japanese. Our girls didn't run up and down the streets, either. They stayed home. But under your democracy we demonstrated in every way that we were corrupt and immature. We were not ready for democracy.

"Americans will not like this, but I believe that if the Japanese Army had been in Korea—especially those crack Manchurian divisions—all of this disaster in Korea would have been avoided. The Japanese know how to fight the Chinese.

"But now my country is ruined. There is even talk of cutting up the big estates before the communists get here. What good will that do? I ask.

"It doesn't matter much who wins any more. Korea is ruined. There is going to be starvation soon because the rice paddies have been destroyed. The big cities are torn down by guns and everybody seems to be going crazy.

"If America is kicked out of Korea I think I will go back to Japan. My father has some money there and I'll go to work in some kind of commerce. I certainly won't be sorry to leave Korea."

I have reported Han Chang Bock's explosion verbatim. That night he came to my quarters and said, "I've been thinking about some of the things I said this afternoon. Perhaps I might not be able to go to Japan, so I think it would be better if you didn't use my real name."

I said, "I've already given you a new name—Han Chang Bock."

He repeated it and laughed. "Like the Japanese. You give me a new name. And I was thinking about that photograph, too. If I'm not able to get to Japan it might be better . . ."

I said, "I've already torn it up."

BOY-SAN

Most American military men serving in Korea despised the Koreans. I am sorry to report this but it is the truth. The causes of this feeling were many. Koreans are vengefully proud. In long years of Japanese occupation they kept their spirits alive solely by their intransigent will. They were subdued but they were never bought off. Furthermore, even though the Americans were their helpful allies the Koreans never kowtowed to them. Third, we met them in time of war when their old suspicions of the foreigner were revived. Fourth, being near starvation they stole much American food, and being impoverished they stole our equipment. Fifth, their untrained troops had the bad luck to be found out consistently by attacking communists, so that time and again the Korean front gave way and permitted attacks against the American flanks.

So the average Yank had little time for the Korean. The men of B-Company were good examples. They invented new profanity to describe Koreans, but at the same time they watched out for Boy-san.

Everywhere in the company you could hear the exasperated cry, "Boy-san! Where the hell are you?" The plaintive wail was usually followed by shattering oaths whereupon a ten-year-old Korean boy would appear dressed in a jet-black schoolboy's uniform with white buttons and a celluloid edging which formed a dummy collar.

His face was mostly round, his cheeks were russet red, and he was always smiling. There were several thousands like him with our troops and they presented a special problem.

It was rather difficult to talk with Boy-san because if the question was embarrassing he grinned apologetically and said, "No got English," while if he ever did reply he always lied. In what follows, the truth as I was able to discern it from the men of B-Company appears in parentheses.

"I born Chonju where my father he own large farm." (His old man was the town drunk.) "I go school do berry good." (He was always a juvenile delinquent.) "When dirty communist come Chonju I much scared. I run away and hide in hills." (He collaborated famously and ate lots of their rice.)

"Then American come back. Berry strong. Berry fine men, Americans. I get job in mess B-Company. All soldiers say I best mess boy they ever damn well see." (During the first week Boy-san copped every available fountain pen and sold them all to a Seoul hock shop.) "Americans like me berry much, put me in school." (The captain of B-Company said flatly Boy-san was to get out of camp and stay out. The sergeant finagled it for the kid to be accepted by a Presbyterian orphanage.)

"Presbyterians fine people. I like berry much." (He ducked out the second night and rejoined B-Company.) "Pretty soon sergeant come for me and say he need me right away B-Company. This time I work berry hard pick up all things for men." (That's true. He picked up everything and sold it. The captain personally had the kid put in reform school. Two weeks later he was back with B-Company.)

"I like war. Berry much fun ride in jeep, shoot gun. Best of all I like American men. They good to me, I good to them." (The little racketeer nosed out bottles of bootleg hooch for them, terrible stuff that led to courts-martial.)

"I help all soldiers. I do all things for them. Keep camp berry clean." (He became the best boy-san in Korea for going into a village and asking girls if they'd like to come out to camp.)

"These pants I got on. Sergeant make them for me." (This is correct and rather difficult to explain. The sergeant despises Koreans, can never speak of them without the vilest adjectives to describe their thievery, knavery and general worthlessness. His opinion is shared by ninety-five per cent of enlisted men and most officers. Yet this same sergeant risked a court-martial by stealing an officer's pants and cutting them down to Boy-san's size. At home the sergeant never even mended his socks, yet now he was a tailor.) "Pretty good pants, huh? He make me shirt, too." (Boy-san stole the shirt when he scrammed from the reform school.)

"Big days! We ride into Seoul. Into Pyongyang. B-Company say I good luck. They take me along to Yalu River." (Not quite true. At Pyongyang the captain tried once more to jam his problem case into a reform school. Boy-san didn't care for it. He went up to the Yalu on his own and overtook his company right before the debacle.)

"Then bad days. Dirty communist come out of mountains. B-Company fight berry hard. Four night we fight communist. I always right up front." (Boy-san wanted to stay up front but the sergeant kept him in the rear. Said he didn't want the kid to get hurt.)

"So we walk back the same road we ride up. Fight, fight, fight. One day we catch truck. Then everything pretty good. I ride in front." (The captain said they better keep the kid up front where they could watch him. He didn't want the kid to get hurt.)

"In Pyongyang I leave B-Company. I go back to school." (The company took up a purse and gave it to an LST skipper and told him to see to it that the kid was kept in the Presbyterian school down in Pusan.)

"But I not like school. Pretty soon I back with B-Company." (The captain told me, "One day I looked up and cripes, there was Boy-san. He'd run away from school again and had ridden north with a truck convoy.")

"Now everybody in B-Company berry good to me. I think they glad to see me back." (This is curiously true. Everyone in the defeated company looked with deep tenderness at their little crook. They talked with him at night, cursed him with real affection and taught him to wash his face. Something had happened at Pyongyang which had made Boy-san terribly important. In the long and humiliating retreat the kid became a symbol, a focal point of human love.)

"Each night the captain say, 'We hold here,' but each day we move farther back. Pretty soon we get on train and come all way back to Pusan. Now we can't go no more. But anyway we got to have one damn fine Christmas." (The men of B-Company spent a good deal of money to send home for a complete outfit of clothing for their boy-san. The stuff arrived in Christmas wrappings and two men went into the hills near Pusan and chopped down a tree. There was a terrific Christmas.)

"Now B-Company don't try no more to send me to school. I stay with them." (The captain of B-Company said, "That kid stays with us.")

"So I think that even maybe when Americans leave Korea I go along." (Yes, the captain of B-Company said, "I don't want to hear any more discussion. When we leave, he leaves. And if Truman and Acheson and Ridgway don't like it, they know what they can do.")

The same problem exists in almost every unit. If Americans ever do evacuate Korea there will have to be a rule that no boy-sans may accompany our troops, but since what happened at Pyongyang there will be a mutiny if the rule is enforced.

What has Pyongyang to do with Boy-san? At Pyongyang the communists caught some boy-sans who had helped the Americans. They broke their backs and shot them.

I looked up from the serpentine chow line and saw across the steaming mess hall this wonderful face. It belonged to a Korean woman perhaps thirty, perhaps forty. War changes faces very fast.

She was not exactly beautiful, but she was magnificently clean and strong, the way a tree is impressive when its branches have begun to take permanent shape. She was of slight build, wore her hair severely back and observed the strangeness about her with calm interest.

I decided at once that I must speak with this woman, but the Army shouted that I was to stay clear. These people had just been rescued from the reds. When I tried to slip in the back door the Army shouted again. But later, when the Army was shouting about something else, I met Lee Keisook.

"Since I speak English badly, please ask questions slowly. I have been always an enemy of communists. In Seoul I would soon have been murdered.

"It is difficult to explain why I am here. I am not a brave woman. When Japs occupied Korea I simply did not notice them. I knew they were a terrible scourge sent to persecute us. We would never be rid of them. Perhaps I was a coward, but I made believe I did not see them.

"They were harsh uncivil people. They were stupid, too. They made all Koreans take Japanese names. They gave me Matze Moto Keiko, but nobody ever called me that. I never used it. They insisted above all else that women remain slaves of men. They closed our schools. They took all good jobs. But I cannot explain why I did nothing.

"When war came I did not even listen to broadcasts. I said that if such people were to rule the world I wished to know nothing about it. When collapse came I was sick in bed and did not even hear of the atom bomb. I felt no revenge, no success. Stupid little men had lost. That was enough."

Lee Keisook wears a slight touch of rouge and now her cheeks flush with excitement. "When peace came I began to see there could be a new Korea. We would build a fine government and a new land. I became head of Korean Girl Scouts and on a small salary helped organize the young girls of my land into hopeful groups. We took girls who were not Christians, anyone who was willing to work.

"A surge of hope came to our country. We had many fine men who knew the world and who had worked bravely for freedom. Our rice crops were getting better. Laws were reorganized. We were planning to give land to all poor people. It was very good, very good. Then the communists struck!"

Her husband now joins her, a handsome man who speaks flawless English and who knows much history. As they sit together, laughing in their despair, you think, "These are the kind of people you pray to God you'll meet when you move your family into a new town."

Lee Keisook says, "Yes, I'm willing to speak about my marriage. We had a small home. I did the cooking and once a week we had a woman to do the cleaning. Korean diet is monotonous, so I tried to get fish or good meat. You could say our marriage was the new kind. My parents did not arrange it, although I did bring a small dowry, which every girl should. I am fortunate in having a husband who prefers the new life. We discuss things together and handle money problems, too. All of my friends have the new-style home and no one would go back to the old Japanese fashion. We have fine woman doctors in Korea now. Even men use them, although it is customary for the woman doctor's husband to be present when she treats a man patient. In our last cabinet there was a brilliant woman Minister of Commerce. Graduate of a university in California. The communists boast of their revolution. We had a much better one growing up in South Korea. Men like my husband were leading it. But we were not spared the time."

Lee Keisook and her husband sit in a dirty quonset surrounded by all they own in the world—a battered suitcase, three bundles tied in shawls, two brief cases. But that morning Lee had borrowed some lighter fluid to clean her husband's suit and he looked quite neat.

"When the communists took Seoul the first time, I fled into the hills. They were after me because of what I had done with the Girl Scouts. For five months it was one meal in two days. Sleep always ready to run. Listen for the hammer on the door. They came at dawn and caught my brother. We've never heard of him since.

"Then the Americans came back to Seoul and we had enormous hopes. Plans were speeded for deep reforms, more schools, a united country. Our hopes made us forget the destruction our land had suffered. Whole towns wiped out and many people murdered. But we thought that with American help we could go ahead.

"If peace had lasted Korea would have been a splendid land. But now it is totally destroyed. When armies swing back and forth across the land so many times there can be nothing left.

"There were some things about North Korea that were better than South Korea. The differences between very rich and very poor were not so great. Their land reform? It was mostly on paper, but it was fine propaganda. But do not be fooled by their claims. Always remember Pyongyang. Why did so many people insist to come south when you retreated? People who have tasted both North Korean and South Korean life always prefer our freedom. I have to admit, though, that most North Korean women came south because it is a better climate here and more rice."

Then, with every Korean who speaks English comes the tragic, terrible, bleeding question: "What will you do if the Americans are forced out of Korea?"

Lee Keisook did not lament. "If they catch us we will be killed. But we do not think about that.

"What do we think about? We think about the United Nations. We think that sooner or later all the world must come together in one body. To cling to hatred of Japanese is wrong. To hate North Koreans is wrong. There must be one law, one brotherhood."

I think Lee Keisook uses lipstick, for now when she becomes excited over the future she seems radiantly lovely. She has worked hard to help her country. She has worked just as hard to keep her husband looking neat, to cook fine meals. And as she sits here almost at the edge of the sea into which she is being relentlessly pushed, she presents the unforgettable face of a woman who still dares to hope.

OLD

PAPA-SAN

When you speak of the hordes of Asia I wish you would always think of old Papa-san, for he, multiplied by a billion, is those hordes.

I met him in Korea, a scrawny old man of sixty-seven with a face lined by a thousand wrinkles. He seemed barely able to stand erect at the loading shed, but as younger men started to pile enormous burdens upon the wooden platform strapped to his back he underwent a metamorphosis. The heavier the load the straighter he became until at last he had three hundred pounds weighing him down. Then he strode off down the street.

I had real difficulty talking with Papa-san, as such old men are called in Korea, for he either answered in grunts, whereupon the interpreter would improvise what he thought the old man should have replied, or he broke into a torrent of words which the interpreter would dismiss with a contemptuous monosyllable. After persistent questioning I gather that this is what the old man meant to say.

"My father carried loads in the city and so did my grandfather, but my father was better off because he rented a small rice paddy, which I now rent too. I work at the railroad every day in the week from six in the morning till six at night and on three evenings each week I work nights too.

"On these evenings I go to all the toilets along one street in our village and collect fertilizer for my rice paddy and those of our neighbors. My paddy is eighteen feet long and ten feet wide.

"My wife plants the rice and cares for it, doing all the weeding by herself. After we pay our rent in rice we have none left over for sale and often do not have enough for ourselves. My wife also cuts the rice and threshes it and washes clothes for a rich family and takes care of my son's children and does the cooking. She also goes to the hills for wood.

"We live in a village five miles from the city. I walk to work each morning and walk home at night. My wife has been to the city several times but she doesn't like it and stays home.

"I carry things for people, but there isn't as much work as there used to be because of the trucks, so I also sell wood that my wife cuts in the hills. If it was just my wife and me we would have enough to eat, but I must care for my son's babies. My son was killed in the war."

Old Papa-san is not certain which war it was, but the interpreter, who wears store clothes, is sure it must have been the present war in Korea. Old Papa-san wears the ancient costume of rags and tattered sandals. He has never worn anything else, except that his son managed to draw an extra army blouse and gave it to his father, so that now the old man keeps warmer than he used to.

"We sleep on the floor and have some blankets. It is very cold but we are used to it.

"I make $29 a year and pay $9 in taxes, but of course that includes the tax on the rice we grow.

"The Japanese never bothered me. For me it was no different then. They gave me a new name and made me speak Japanese but they caused me no trouble. They did take away some of my rice but the Government now does the same.

"During the war the Japanese made me work four days a week, no pay, building the airfield, but we ate from their kitchen, so it wasn't bad. They took my son, too, but they gave him warm clothes, so that wasn't bad either."

Like most Koreans, Papa-san loves gambling, which he plays for pitifully small stakes, about 1/1000th of a cent wagered on various Chinese gambling games. He has also bought his granddaughters jumping rope with which they play a delightful game of skip-rope-and-run-around-a-tree. Or they play matching fingers so as to dispatch a partner running to a base and back again according to the number of points won.

"We have been to the movies but we have to walk so far at night it isn't fun for the children. The movies are Japanese, which are better than the American ones the city people see.

"I have no religion. Yes, it is true I used to believe in spirits and my wife still does, but we were told that was foolish. Now I don't bother. The Japanese did not try to make us believe in Shinto. One of the men who works with me is a Christian, but I don't know anything about it.

"We have meat two or three times a year and sometimes fish. There are men in our village who grow vegetables, but they are rich men with land. We have never been to the doctor or dentist. We wait until our teeth fall out. Nobody in our village has false teeth except the rich men with land. I work at the train but I have never been on one."

You listen to this dull recital and conclude that here is indeed a human clod, one meaningless unit in the hordes of Asia. But then you recall that once or twice this old Papa-san had shown much excitement and you decide to discover why. So you find another interpreter and seek out the old laborer again.

At first old Papa-san offers you the same desultory comments. "This year is pretty good. I can carry four bags of cement. Most of the men carry only three." Then suddenly the old man becomes vividly excited.

Reports the new interpreter, "The old man says there has been too much war. His son is dead. The children have no one to care for them, and where is he going to get clothes? He says that people ought to stop burning down cities and grow more rice."

You ask, "Where did he learn about burned cities? He said himself he's never been away from home."

The old man replies, "In our village we talk about what happens. I have three other sons in the Army, too. They tell us about the war. They used to say, 'Soon Korea be all one country.' Now they run away from the enemy and say, 'Soon Korea be all destroyed.' And then the new Government will give land to everyone."

You ask, "Who told you that?"

"I hear."

"Where?"

"My village. Man come and say pretty soon we get land."

"What did he say about the American soldiers?"

"He say American soldiers go home pretty soon. Then we get land."

"What will you do then?"

"Work, like always."

"But you'll have land. The man said so."

"Everybody always tell me I get land. Japanese say so long time ago. Korea Government say so little while ago. Americans say so when they come. Now new government say I get land. I don't know. I don't think so."

"What do you think will happen if American soldiers go home?"

"I think maybe later on my sons get land."

So when you think of the hordes of Asia it's all right to think of utterly stupid old men bent double with age and hunger and burdens. They're so dumb they hardly know what day it is. But, brother, they can get excited about some things.

OBSERVATIONS

Korea is a test of our maturity as a nation, for sometimes nations must exercise both determination and patience. We must be determined to win the ultimate victory and patient in avoiding side issues.

For example, we were right in entering the Korean war. Communist cells in many Asiatic countries were waiting for Chinese victories to release conflagrations which would have served as excuses for Chinese and Russian intervention and occupation. We were right in preventing this.

But we were also right, after having denied China a cheap victory, to avoid deep involvement which would have obscured sight of the main enemy. For the ultimate enemy is Russia. If she continues to bully her way toward a major world war, she will get it. Since 1942 we have made substantial efforts to be Russia's friend and she has consistently rebuffed us. She is the inescapable enemy.

Consequently we are faced with the extremely delicate and unpopular job of saving Asia with a comparatively small war while we conserve our major strength to defeat Russia if she wants a great war. This places us in a uniquely trying position. But I am convinced that difficult as such a position is, it tests the maturity of our nation.

Morally, our involvement in Korea is frustrating to the point of despair. While we work to do right we get blamed for all wrongs. Across Asia you never hear of United Nations aggression in Korea. It's always American aggression. Thus we have been inhibited militarily by our United

Nations partnership without gaining therefrom the moral approval th
we had a right to expect. We are in the unenviable position of the villa
humanitarian who enters a family fight to protect the wife from bei
bruised, only to find both husband and wife upon him. It is easy to ri
cule such a misadventure, but the world is a better place because h
bands have been forcibly restrained from beating their wives. And eve
time wilful national aggression is halted, the world becomes a little saf
for those who abide by the law.

The present low state of America's reputation in Asia is due to ma
factors. (1) The Russians provide Asiatic newspapers with excelle
propaganda proving that Americans are power-mad imperialists. (2) T
newspapers enjoy printing banner headlines against us because peop
the world around like taking irresponsible potshots at the top dog,
position we have been temporarily accorded. (3) Asians have a natu
tendency to transfer to us the accumulated abuse they used to hurl at t
now-absent British. (4) Our own information services haven't fur
tioned adequately.

All this provides a second test of our maturity. We must not g
angry because people don't like us. There seems to be a law of natio
that no country beyond a certain size can be loved. We have passed th
point and it is childish to demand affection. If we behave honorab
we will be respected and honest respect is better than condescendi
affection.

There remains the question of whether we should have entered t
Korean war at all. Some critics feel we should have stayed out and sav
our Sunday punch for Russia. I can respect this reasoning.

But I believe it is wrong. For if we had let Korea fall, Asia would ha
fallen too. Possibly even Japan would have been invaded. We wou
have had no foothold in Asia, and that would have been disastrous. R
call how valuable Australia and New Zealand were in the last war. Th
were our anchors of strength. Today Japan and Southeast Asia serve t
same purpose.

But I am unwilling to justify our occupation of Korea solely by clai
ing it was necessary to save our necks. Primarily it saved free Asia and t
entire free world. We should therefore do everything possible to tell t
people of Asia why we acted as we did. I am glad to say that after init
defeats in the war of truth, we are now making some substantial a
vances. Our free libraries, our cultural attachés, our Fulbright Fellov
and our Point Four program are doing a great deal of good. We are f
from having lost Asia.

But the ultimate test of our attitude toward Asia will come at the e of the Korean war, for then we must rebuild Korea. Even if it costs every American family 55 cash dollars—that would yield about two billions— we must rebuild Korea.

This nation has been completely destroyed by communist aggression, but the immediate instruments of that destruction have been our airplanes, our napalm, our barrages, and sometimes our wanton destructiveness. That we used these agencies to save the free world is a moral excuse but not an economic escape. Even if we apportioned our motives as 75 per cent to save the free people of Asia and 25 per cent to protect our own necks, that latter motive would be trumpeted against us as the only one.

We can silence such unjust accusations by rebuilding Korea, for we shall not only be building houses but a firm foundation for our Asiatic policies.

FORMOSA

FORMOSA IS ONE OF THE MOST COMPELLING COUNTRIES IN THE WORLD today. For here questions of international consequence come to focus. It is strange that this relatively unimportant island—less than half the size of South Carolina—should have become a major factor in American politics and a bone of contention between America and Britain.

Geographically the island poses little threat to Japan, because the Shanghai peninsula is much closer to Japanese targets than is Formosa. Nor does it constitute a major threat to the mainland of Communist China, from which it is some 110 miles distant. It does, however, pose a main threat to the Philippines and was indeed the base from which those islands were subdued in the last war. It also dominates Okinawa, and although it is not a major threat to Japan, if enemy planes were stationed on Sakhalin Island, Southern Korea, Shanghai and Formosa, they could whiplash Japan into surrender, although Formosa would be the least important of the four.

The island's importance obviously lies in its present visiting occupants, for here have fled the remnants of Chiang Kai-shek's Government, which only a few years ago controlled the most populous nation on earth. Somewhere between 250,000 and 600,000 troops defend the island, which would pretty surely have fallen to communist assaults had American military power not prevented this. Today Formosa remains a symbol of a once-free nation and a constant thorn in the flesh of the communists.

Its secondary importance lies in the fact that if the free world is forced by the Russian-Chinese block into a global war, Formosa would be one more base from which we could launch a counterattack. At that time the troops now on Formosa might give Communist China a great deal of trouble, and the Government now on the island might become the rallying point for an overthrow of the communists on the mainland.

Americans need to know a great deal more about Formosa than they now do, and as the following interviews are read, several questions should be kept in mind:

(1) Could Chiang's troops on Formosa, unsupported by full-scale American power, invade the China mainland?

(2) If Chiang's troops were put ashore with our support, is there any likelihood that the people of South China would rise to greet them?

(3) If we put Chiang's troops ashore, would they remain loyal or would they go over to the communists, as his preceding armies did?

(4) Is the Chiang Government now on Formosa a responsible one? Has it rectified the glaring weaknesses that were a major cause of its having lost the mainland?

(5) If Russia and China force a global war upon us, should we transport Chiang's troops to the mainland and support them as necessary?

(6) If in the prosecution of a global war we invade the mainland of China, should we reinstate Chiang's men as the government of the mainland?

(7) But fundamentally, can any nation ever defeat China, with its 463,000,000 people?

INDIAN

SUMMER

IN

FORMOSA

The way to see Formosa is from the cockpit of a C-47 flown by the Chinese pilot Y. P. Tom. You see below you a rich and beautiful island. To the east great mountains rise out of the sea to an altitude of nearly 13,000 feet. You see alluvial plains that produce an abundance of food, mines that yield gold and silver and coal, and factories that produce the products needed by a modern civilization. In fact, as you look at this prosperous island it seems to wear an Indian-summer complexion.

It is confusing, therefore, to discover that Formosa is perhaps the single country in the world that prays constantly for war. Everyone hopes it will be a general world war. And they want it now. Two years from now may be too late.

Y. P. Tom explains why. "On this island you find the bravest Chinese. They would not surrender to communism. Every man you meet here elected freedom. He could have stayed behind with the communists and maybe got himself a good job. Instead he ran away and crossed the ocean to be free.

"We call the island Taiwan now. It's Generalissimo Chiang Kai-shek's last stronghold. But from here, with the help of America, we shall storm back across the ocean and set Red China free. That is why we pray for war, because until you become involved we cannot hope to win.

"We are not ashamed of hoping for war, because unless we win China back, all of Asia will fall under Russian rule and then you are doomed.

"Why did I come to Taiwan? I could have stayed with the reds. They wanted me and they wanted my plane. I had a fine home, family, friends. But I had known freedom and I could not stay. Let me tell you how I learned freedom.

"My father was a wealthy merchant in the Philippines and when Japan stole Manchuria the Filipino kids teased me and called me 'The Manchuria Kid.' Right then I decided to fight for China and I went back home to study for the air force. The instructor in pursuit planes was a man I shall never forget. An American major. Very patient, very tough. He was the first white man I had met who loved China the way I did. Claire Chennault.

"When Chiang Kai-shek was kidnapped by communists I got the job of flying my plane over the red stronghold and dropping leaflets arranging for the surrender. Later I fought against Japan. Our entire group was destroyed by the superior Jap planes and those of us who escaped swore we'd get better planes.

"I was driven all over China by the Japs. For years I had no home. My wife died. Then I heard that Chennault was starting a volunteer group and I got myself appointed liaison officer. Later I served as pathfinder for the great raids on Canton, Hong Kong and Formosa.

"Then I spent a lot of time in America, flying B-24's from Pueblo, Colorado, to China. I loved those wonderful American bars. The other pilots, when they had time off, chased after pretty American girls, but I always headed for the bars. They used to say in Pueblo, 'Search the bars and get Y. P. back for his flight.'

"But I kept myself in good condition, and one day we lost 26 planes in one blizzard over the Hump. I was one of the few who walked out alive. I collected eight Americans from the wrecked planes and we hiked right through the head-hunter country. When we saw the plane come out of India to save us we all cried."

Y. P. Tom is whip lean, handsome and blessed with a huge grin. Above the roar of the engines he shouts, "See what I mean? I know what freedom is.

"That's why I'm absolutely certain we will win when we hit the mainland. I reason this way. When I fled China I left behind at least a hundred friends who wanted to come along. But their families were too big or their money was too small. They're still there waiting. I get letters from them, many letters smuggled out through Canton. The story is terribly sad.

"I had a friend in the Chinese Air Force who had communist sympathies. When the test came he flew his plane to the reds. Now he smuggles out word that he made a fearful mistake. But it's too late now.

"For millions of others it's not too late. They still have a chance. When we invade the mainland whole armies will rise to greet us. They have found that life with the communists is a bad and starving thing.

"Chiang Kai-shek? Every American asks about him. You can find the answer here in Taiwan. You see a new China. We are united. We are one family. Here even the rich and the poor get along together, something never before known in China. We've increased production so that we all have more to eat than ever before. We have a more common friendly life. Chiang is responsible for this. He is the only leader who can get us back to the mainland."

Then you look at Formosa. You see the food, the industry, the new life, the impatient army. "All we need," Y. P. says, "is the American Navy and supplies. We don't even ask for an army. The army is waiting for us. On the mainland."

As you land Y. P. Tom laughs and says, "That's why we pray for war. Because we know that if we don't take it to them this year, they'll bring it to us next."

THE

GOVERNOR'S

MANSION

When you first see Edith Wu you wonder, "Who's taking that girl to the dance tonight?" but later you find that she has two grown daughters studying at Northwestern University and you conclude, "She must be the most beautiful governor's wife in the world."

Her husband, K. C. Wu, was formerly mayor of Shanghai and before that deputy to T. V. Soong in foreign affairs. He also served as translator for Patrick Hurley and as negotiator with the communist leaders Mao Tse-tung and Chou En-lai. Casey, as he is known, is probably the outstanding civilian figure in Free China and it was natural that he should have been nominated Governor of Formosa, the last resistance point against the communists. He has governed spectacularly well and has caused outside observers to conclude that Free China would never have lost its hold on the people of China if all Kuomintang administrators had been like him.

His wife is even more remarkable than he. A dazzling beauty without a wrinkle, she is a petite woman with flashing smile and ready wit. She can also speak with fury.

"I know communists as few women do. Twice I have watched them totally destroy honorable negotiations. I have watched with what deviltry they play one idea off against another, how they obstruct every logical solution. They never intend to agree to anything. They are cruel, evil monsters.

"When Casey was mayor of Shanghai they deliberately set out to disrupt the civil life. They used diabolical trickery. When Casey attended a meeting at the University, communist students actually punched him in the nose, hoping that he would call the police, who would fire into the mob and kill somebody. Then they'd shout, 'Fascist aggressors.' But Casey commanded the police not to fire, so the communists punched him some more and called him a capitalist coward.

"I watched each step of the disaster. I could trace out the duplicity and am astonished that sensible people anywhere on earth should today even listen to communist invitations to any kind of discussion. They never intend discussing anything. They intend only to confuse issues, gain time, corrupt procedures."

In addition to her insight as a politician's wife, Madame Wu is one of China's leading artists. In an archaic style of the Sung Dynasty, she paints strong and yet delicately patterned landscapes on traditional scrolls. Her work is readily sold and is said to provide the income on which she and her husband live.

"I was educated in Christianity and freedom, but I've never been out of the Orient. It was easy to decide what I must do when the communists took over. Apart from the fact that Casey would have been shot, neither of us could tolerate communism. I have an aunt who committed suicide rather than live the indignities of such a life.

"There is absolutely no doubt in my mind but that we shall be living in Shanghai within five years. Because we represent what is good in the world. The democracies will have to help us in order to help themselves.

"Never forget that China has seen a mighty army collapse in less than eighteen months. True, it was our army and it collapsed because we had allowed the inner fire to go out. But millions of people who deserted us now want us back. They write and tell us what a bad bargain they bought, and I think China is going to see another great army collapse dramatically. This time the communist army.

"For communism is actively supported by very few people in China. Really, the present Government has fewer adherents than Chiang Kai-shek had when he was defeated.

"Then too we know that next year there is going to be a vast famine on the mainland, and then the nation will see that communists can cope with famine much less well than we did. From all across the nation we receive messages from people who await our return."

As if her accomplishments in beauty and wit and painting were not enough, Madame Wu is also a capable architect. The Governor's mansion in Formosa is a modest white house reached through an alley, but it is an almost perfect gem of planning.

"I built it. With my own money I built this house for Casey. He's one politician who never became rich. The house isn't large but it's what we want.

"It has a special significance. When we fled Shanghai our friends here asked, 'Where will you escape to when Formosa falls?' I replied that we wouldn't run any farther. They laughed and warned, 'But the communists will take Formosa very soon.' So I took what money I had and started to build this house. When anyone asked me what I was doing, I said I was building a house for the Governor until we went back to Shanghai.

"At first there was much derision that I should waste my money on a house we could live in for only a few months. Then slowly . . ."

Here Edith Wu's eyes flash and she speaks with fierce determination. "Slowly the doubters began to grant that maybe we weren't going to be pushed off Formosa, too. When the house was finished the entire island had hope. Now they said that when an army crossed the Formosa Strait it would be our army. Setting out for the liberation of China.

"You must believe that we will regain China. The gangsters that now

have it can't hold it. The people they rule are miserable and their freedom
can come only through the armies of Chiang Kai-shek."

As I left, Madame Wu apologized for some masonry still incomplete.
"We've omitted some of the little finishings. After all, we do not think of
this as our permanent home."

THE

HARD

WAY

During this year perhaps 200,000 American students will work their
way through college. If they ever feel sorry for themselves they should
consider Liu Ping, a bright, cocky student of political science at Taiwan
(Formosa) University.

"My father was a doctor and had thirteen sons. Ten of them died.
Don't ask me why. Before I could finish my degree at Chungking University the communists gained control of China. I was now faced with a
most difficult decision."

It's fun to talk with keen-eyed Liu Ping because in the classical Chinese manner he moves logically from point to point, introducing each
with a rhetorical question which he immediately answers, thus antici-
pating almost every query.

"Why was my decision difficult? I had to get my degree but I was
under suspicion of the communists. I had been a student of political
science, I spoke English, and my oldest brother was a major-general in
Chiang Kai-shek's armies. I was in a bad spot.

"What was I to do? I argued with myself for a long time and concluded
that what I had studied in political science was true. Man is supposed to
be free. A nation is supposed to have a decent government. I decided to
run away to Formosa where other people believed these things.

"How was I to get there? My father gave me two ounces of gold and I
walked through China for two months. When the gold gave out I went
four days without food. I arrived at the port of Amoy with nothing, no
clothes, no money, no friends. But there I met other students who had
made the same decision, and that gave me strength.

"What were we to do? We formed a committee and went to see a
ship's captain. We pointed out that since he was going to Formosa we
would go along.

"Did he agree? He did not. So we went anyway. We landed at last in
Free China. The first days were truly terrible. We starved and had no

place to sleep. Then the Kuomintang organized a shelter and the screening process began.

"We were so many and the university was so small that we were told most of us would have to go into the Army. But a few would be permitted to enter the university.

"How did they select us? By the classical method of examinations. For three weeks I lived on one bowl of rice a day and read every book I could find, memorizing whole passages. Then I asked a friend for a bowl of hot soup and took the examination.

"How did I stand? Very near the top. It was glorious. I was a student again. The Government said that as long as I did well I would get $4 a month and thirty katis of rice. That's enough. I have two shirts, two pairs of socks, one pair of shoes and one suit. I study very hard.

"Where do I live? I am shamed for to say I live nowhere. At night I sleep where I can. The shirts and socks come from my friends. I own no books, but this good American fountain pen is a help.

"Am I happy? I am very happy. For I study with excellent teachers and I know I am helping to build the new China. But one thing amuses me. I the student ran away from communism because my brother was a major-general for Chiang Kai-shek, but my brother the major-general stayed behind and joined the communists. Why I do not know. I have often had the idea that my brother is not very smart.

"My father and other brother stayed behind, too. In fact, I am the only one of all the friends I had in China who came to Formosa, but I hear that intellectuals are being killed when they can't be converted and I am glad I came.

"I hear from my family but they never write anything I want to know about. My younger brother works for the communists and I think he will be pretty happy because he was never interested in politics. I am sorry to say I am beginning to forget about my family. I may never see them again.

"Now what do I think of my new home? I see here in Formosa a new way of life. Things are healthy in Formosa. Justice prevails.

"Will there be war? Of course there will be. Very shortly. I shall be graduated by then and I'll take part. Everyone on Formosa is loyal to Chiang Kai-shek. Not long ago they shot four generals who weren't and one of them was a four-star job. They also investigated the Chinese who served as translators for American newspapermen. They were found to be communist spies, telling the Americans what Mao Tse-tung wanted them to believe. The translators were shot.

"But there is one thing perhaps you can explain. In American universities were many Chinese students. Why did more than 80 per cent choose to go back to Red China? What did they learn in your universities to make them do that? It is we, on this island, who stand for democracy and freedom."

When it came time to leave Liu Ping I did a regrettable thing. I have known many students in my time, the fine young men on whom the world depends, but I had never before known one who lived on a bowl of rice a day with only two shirts. So I offered Liu Ping some money, and in flashing anger he rejected it. "We need your ships and your tanks and your ammunition. But not your charity." And he stalked away in his worn and battered shoes.

THE

TANK

COMMANDERS

They were four young fellows, tough, straight and aching for a fight. They commanded tanks brought over from America and they were trained to a point of hardness that made even their faces seem metallic.

They narrated their formal histories with monotonous similarity. Major Fu had talked his entire Free China squadron into coming over to Formosa and the trip had been incredibly hazardous. Captain Liu had been pressing down on Harbin, Manchuria, when the American-forced armistice gave the reds time to regroup. He walked away on foot and smuggled his way to Formosa. Captain Chung had been a supply officer and had been pushed back and forth across the face of China for many years. "I was offered a good job with the communists, but even a total fool could see that Chinese communists had to do what Moscow said and I was ashamed of our men for being so stupid. I walked out of the office and expected to be shot in the back. Somehow I got away." Lieutenant Yao was the fire-eater type. He trembled as he spoke. "They shoot up my tank. They capture me. Five times I get away. I'm sentenced to be shot. I get away again. I make a sea captain bring me to Formosa."

Standing in a huddle about their tanks they looked like the backfield of a successful college football team, but when we left their formal histories they were not like college men at all. I asked each man three questions: "Where is your family?" "Are you ready to invade China?" "Will your army remain loyal this time?" These are pretty rugged questions to ask a group of young fellows.

When family was mentioned all stiffness and arrogance evaporated.

"I left behind my father and mother and seven brothers and sisters. They wanted to come. They blessed me for doing the right thing. They wanted to come along but they are so poor. None of them would listen to a communist."

"I do not hear from my family. It would be too dangerous to write. It's too dangerous to do anything in China now. But word slips out sometimes, and it's always bad."

One of the commanders speaks with great passion and says, "You must understand our Chinese family. We are very close together. At meals we don't eat like Americans, each sitting rigid in his own chair, apart from everyone else. We crowd over a common bowl and are quite close, the old people as well as the young. We love our families more than anything else in the world.

"Therefore it is very terrible to be lost from them. We worry about this a great deal. But we will never become communists in order to get back. I will never see my family again until I fight my way to their village. But when I arrive I know that whole armies will rise up from the soil to fight with us."

Lieutenant Yao, the fire-eater, says grimly, "I'm going back. My family sends a report of everything that happens. I'm going back."

When we get onto the subject of invasion, the toughness returns. Now the report is unanimous. "My tanks were never defeated in the field. We had many victories and were winning the war until you Americans forced a truce. What happened then? The Russians sent down fresh tanks, and when the truce was over we faced a completely new army.

"This time we won't be beaten by such tricks, unless some international truce stifles us again.

"All we ask of the United States is this: Ships to transport us to the mainland and supplies to feed the refugees that will flock to our lines.

"America should look at it this way. We are your natural allies. We are almost a branch of your Army. As you've found out in Korea, it's hard for America to protect itself in Asia without the help of many Asian troops. We are those troops."

There was such agreement on these points that I left the topic and asked whether the current army would behave any better than the earlier ones had. There was bitter comment.

"Out of a hundred men, one hundred will remain loyal. We have seen what communism does to a nation and we are vowed to destroy it.

"Why am I so sure we will remain loyal? Because we've shot the traitors. Yes, we even had to shoot a four-star general. And at the lake in the hills where Chinese girls served as prostitutes we found they were communist spies. We shot ten of them. There have also been cowards among us. They've been weeded out and we are a dedicated army."

Then, to my surprise, these tank commanders, sprung from peasant families, said, "We should like to ask you some questions too." I report them exactly as asked and leave the reader to guess what I replied.

1. "Do any Americans still believe the Chinese communists are agrarian reformers?"

2. "Is America so scared by the Korean war that she is going to turn isolationist?"

3. "Are you going to surrender Korea and Japan?"

4. "Is it true that because Red China has not declared formal war you will insist that Chiang Kai-shek surrender so as not to offend the communists?"

5. "If, against your advice, we open a second front in South China, will your Navy support us?"

6. "Is it true that you are afraid to rearm Japan?"

All four of the tank commanders, men who hated Japan bitterly, said that Japan should be rearmed. "In things that matter today she is an ally. She could help both China and America fight many battles."

But I kept coming back to that question of whether this new army would remain loyal and I asked bluntly, "Last time whole armies surrendered to the reds without fighting. Will it be different now?"

Captain Liu led me to a small room where the wall was covered with documents framed in glass. He translated one for me: "We who sign this pledge swear to restore China. We will drive the communists from the land. If necessary we will give our lives that China may be free."

It was a gloomy room and I thought it symbolic that already the ink on these pages had begun to fade. I pointed this out to Captain Liu, and he replied, "We did not sign in ink. That is our blood you see."

OBSERVATIONS

I should now like to report my answers to the questions appearing on page 65, because anyone who knows anything about Formosa these days ought to share his knowledge.

(1) Could Chiang alone invade the mainland? Certainly not. I was bowled over recently when I saw results of an American public-opinion poll in which 67 per cent of the citizens questioned thought we ought to take our battleships away from Formosa and let Chiang invade the mainland and recapture China.

I was not shocked by the wish that fathered the opinion, but I was astonished at the lack of simple information that would permit 67 per cent of our people to believe that Chiang could accomplish an impossible military miracle.

In the first place, he has at most 350,000 effective troops—best realistic guess is 250,000—with which to conquer a nation of 463,000,000.

In the second place, Formosa is 110 miles from China, more than five times the distance from France to England and the relatively trivial Straits of Dover have halted well-prepared invaders for many centuries.

In the third place, Chiang has no ships to cross the 110 miles, insufficient aircraft to protect him if he does get ashore, insufficient supplies to support an extensive campaign, inadequate munitions, and not enough trucks, tanks, half-tracks or the gasoline to run them for long.

If we want Chiang to invade the mainland we must supply American warships, American planes, American munitions, American supplies, American rolling stock and American officers to keep the offensive rolling.

No amount of wishful thinking can alter those facts. It is as fallacious to encourage Chiang alone to invade China as it would be to encourage Cuba to invade the United States.

In the same poll nearly 80 per cent of the people questioned thought we should use Chiang's troops in Korea. Here again we find an irresponsible opinion unless the results of such an action are foreseen and acceptable. It would be tempting to use Chiang's men in Korea, and they would be eager to go, for they would interpret our invitation as a promise that when they had finished helping us in Korea, we would help them recover the mainland.

For it would be totally immoral for us to use Chiang's homeless troops as mere mercenaries, only to turn them adrift when our troubles were past. In the first place, I doubt if Chiang's men would fight under such an understanding. In the second place, it would be an abandonment of our moral grounds in Asia and would forever damn us. We would be using Asian people as a means to our ends instead of recognizing their own legitimate ends. And that is what white imperialism has always done in Asia. We must not be trapped into playing that worn-out game.

Let us therefore reword those opinion-poll questions: "Should we lend our fleet, half our air force, thirty divisions of men, and corresponding equipment to Chiang Kai-shek for the reconquest of China?" "Should we invite Chiang's troops to help us in Korea on the clear understanding that immediately upon victory we will help them invade the mainland?" Those questions mean something, for they are related to facts. It doesn't matter if 150,000,000 Americans reply affirmatively to the other questions. The answers mean nothing but the expression of a wish.

(2) Would the people of South China welcome Chiang? There is a chance they might. Many of them would not be antagonistic. South China is almost a different nation from North China and has been so through much of Chinese history. A different language is spoken, rice predominates instead of wheat, and communism has a less secure hold than it has in North China. Therefore oppressions and mass killings seem to have been more frequent in South China. Resistance groups are reported to be stronger.

While on Formosa I saw dozens of letters smuggled out of China and even granting that I was shown only those which proved points Chiang's men wanted proved, the messages from South China were impressive. People there were fed up with communism. And when I was in Hong Kong I had opportunity to talk with many recent refugees and they repeated that resistance in South China could probably be depended upon. Significantly, this was before the harshest communist repressions were launched, so that uprisings to greet Chiang's men might be considered more likely now, offset by the fact that outstanding potential leaders of such revolts have no doubt been executed.

But each day invasion is delayed, chances for uprisings diminish, for the repressive nature of Chinese communism seems at least as terrible as that of the Russians. Any hope for spontaneous internal uprisings unsupported from without seems misguided and forlorn.

(3) Would Chiang's Formosa army remain loyal this time? If they were put ashore with our blessing, in our ships, backed up by our armament, and accompanied by our officers, there is a chance they would prove loyal. I know that the weight of evidence is against this, for never in recent history has a superior army collapsed the way Chiang's did in 1948–49. Many observers who know war much better than I say it will happen all over again.

I think that this time it will be different. First, every Chiang man on Formosa is there because he consciously willed to be there. Often he braved extreme danger. He did not merely vote in favor of democracy. He cast his ballot with his life at stake. Second, most men on Formosa have much to gain if they win the mainland. Third, the Formosa army is better trained, better staffed, and better indoctrinated than any previous Chiang army. Fourth, the Formosa army probably knows that if it surrenders this time most of its members will be executed. Fifth, there is such a thing in war as esprit de corps. Chiang's men now seem to have it.

I must immediately add that if Chiang's men were hauled up to Korea and launched into war without a clear promise of a mainland invasion, they would probably desert by the thousands. The men on Formosa are in no mood to be dealt with as mercenaries.

(4) Is the present Formosa Government responsible? It is probably the most efficient government in Asia today, not even excepting Japan's. It has solved the food problem. It has rationed goods so that everyone gets a fair break. It polices the island so that even white men can move about at night without risk of murder. It has launched an education program, prints liberal newspapers and insures just trials. Furthermore, in order to erase evil memories of initial Chinese occupation, the Government has specifically worked to protect the indigenous Taiwanese population.

In fact, if Chiang's men had given the mainland the same kind of efficient government they are now giving Formosa, it is doubtful if the communists could have won China. Chiang's men, shattered by the collapse of their mainland regime and humiliated by the defection of their supporters, have instituted profound reforms. In every sense this government is responsible.

(5) If global war comes should we use Chiang's men to invade the mainland? Certainly. If Russia starts war on Monday, we should transport Chiang's men to China by Tuesday morning at the latest. I am not promising that even with our help Chiang will accomplish much, but he will at least be a major irritation. And if we are forced into a global war we will be criminally negligent if we fail to use, within the definition of humanity, every weapon at our disposal. Chiang would tie down communist legions that would otherwise be used against us elsewhere. We would be that degree freer to engage Russia. And in the long run, if Russia loses, Red China will lose. Therefore if Chiang can help speed the fall of Russia, he is an asset.

But I would not think of taking Chiang ashore until such time as Russia were the avowed enemy. For remember that Chiang by himself can accomplish little and what he does achieve must be tied in with global strategy to have any meaning at all.

There remains one harrowing question. What if Russia never starts a war? What happens to Formosa then? I foresee a long and silent tragedy on Formosa. Thoughts of rewinning the homeland will have to be abandoned. Many troops will filter back to China and most of them will be shot. Formosa will prosper as a strange colony, half Chinese, half Taiwanese, existing under American-British protection. Other crises will arise elsewhere and Formosa will be forgotten. That is why men on Formosa pray for war. That is why Formosa is one of the worst places to build American foreign policy.

(6) If we invade China, should we reinstate Chiang's men? Yes. The

cadre of men Chiang now has on Formosa would give China a more efficient government than any similar group now available.

Two comments are necessary. When I say "give China a government" I wince inside. I am almost a maniac on the principle of self-determination and self-responsibility. I believe that until these principles are world applied we cannot escape trouble. Still I think that China must be given a government, and I cannot stop here to explain why I use such an oligarchical phrase. I discuss this later in the Indonesian section, but the reason briefly is this: Much of Asia is 90 per cent illiterate and for the time being such areas must be given a government. You find the best men you can, you back them up, and you pray that they will use their power wisely. If they don't, the illiterates assassinate them and try somebody else. It is under these circumstances that Chiang's Formosa group represents our best bet.

My second comment is that whereas I would back Chiang's men I would not reinstate by force Chiang himself. There comes a time in national politics when a symbol has lost its luster. On my trip I met many mainland Chinese, conservative men who had fled the communists. Not one of them ever said a bad word against Chiang. But none of them said a good word, either. When his name was mentioned these men laughed. He was a symbol that had worn thin. Only Westerners took him seriously. His devoted followers on Formosa revered him. But the people from the mainland just laughed. I rather believe that Chiang today is like Herbert Hoover in 1932. Hoover was still an excellent man. He was a fine administrator of unquestioned character. But it would have been a tragedy if some friendly nation like Great Britain had forced him back into the White House. The tenor of the times had changed and in 1933 he was no longer the right man for President. One might also compare Chiang with Churchill in 1945. Virtually every American wanted Churchill to continue as Prime Minister. In Australia and New Zealand even people who voted Labour wanted him retained back home. I suppose most Italians and Frenchmen wanted him, too. But the British didn't. That was what counted. If the wheel of history places us and Chiang's men back on the mainland, it must be the Chinese who ask for Chiang, not we who force Chiang upon them. I think this reasoning is not in conflict with my former willingness to have some kind of government given China. I am saying that unless it is a government they can accept, they won't take it.

(7) Can China ever be defeated? One of the most misleading historical clichés of all time is the one that says "China can never be defeated." Where this started I don't know, but it was responsible for the panic in

America in late 1950 when it seemed we would have to fight China. We were strangled with fear because we believed that no nation has ever conquered China.

How totally ridiculous! The Mongols conquered China. So did the Manchus, and for the first half of their 300-year rule gave China an excellent government. In this century the Japanese effectively conquered what parts of China they needed and could have gone on to subdue the rest had not their military leaders unwisely diverted Japan's energies into an attack upon the United States.

One should never make conclusive statements in the military field. Too much can intervene to upset certainties, but it surely seems likely that China can be defeated. If an American commander today were given the army that General MacArthur had in 1945, the navy that Nimitz had, and the air arm that General LeMay had on Okinawa, China could be subdued.

I apologize for such warlike talk. I am against war with China, but if it becomes inevitable I see no reason for panic. I should judge it to be somewhat less difficult to subdue China than it was to defeat Japan in 1941.

It is true that those nations which occupied China for long periods saw their personnel gradually submerged in the mass of Chinese population. The same thing happened to the Hessians who tried to occupy our Thirteen Colonies, and if our troops remain in Japan long enough thousands of babies that would have been born in America will be half-Japanese and their children will be lost in Japan's population.

But I have heard no serious proposal that America intends to absorb China. Anyone who contends that misunderstands both our intentions and our capabilities. We would be the ones who were absorbed. But what we can do, if the task is forced upon us, is to drive gangsters from China and help install a just government. Then we would have to retire and hope for the best.

HONG KONG

HONG KONG IS THE JEWEL OF ASIA, ONE OF THE LOVELIEST CITIES ON earth. Perched on a precarious island, overlooking a superb land-locked bay, this Oriental masterpiece alone is worth a trip around the world. From its heights you can look southward into the South China Sea and northward into the vast, red-colored, barren hills of China.

Actually there is no city of Hong Kong, for the name applies only to the island and to the mainland territory presently leased from China. Hong Kong is made up of several cities, the most spectacular one being Victoria, on the island. Here stately colonnaded buildings rise in grandeur symbolizing the enormous wealth of British corporations. Behind them climb incredibly steep narrow streets jammed to breathless over-flowing by the slums of Chinese workmen. To see these perpendicular alleys in midafternoon with sun streaming down them and sidewalk

markets swarming with endless crowds is to discover one of the overwhelming sights of Asia.

Across the bay from Victoria lies Kowloon, chief city of the New
Territory, where the water supply is collected, the vegetables are grown,
and the petty day-by-day business of life is carried on. Kowloon is more
spacious than Victoria, more Chinese.

Lumping these random segments together you have Hong Kong, but
actually you have nothing. For the wonder charm of Hong Kong is the
dazzling harbor where an ocean, a bay, a strait and a large river meet. In
this vital intersection you see every type of Asiatic craft, plus freighters
from all over the world, plus the sleekest luxury liners from New York
and London, plus the most whimsical ferryboats imaginable. Hong Kong
forms one of the world's great entrepots, those seaports to which the
produce of a thousand cities is brought for distribution throughout the
world. At night the harbor is like a gay dream with junks, sampans, out-
riggers, men-of-war and blazing cruise boats towering above the crazy
ferries. Even the names of the area recall the helter-skelter beauty of this
harbor. Hong Kong means "The Place of Sweet Lagoons," while Kowloon signifies "The Den of Nine Dragons."

Today Hong Kong is a mecca for everyone traveling in Asia. More
than a million freedom-loving Chinese from the mainland have fled to
this British colony. Japanese and Indian and Filipino businessmen in
search of markets come here. Americans and Russians and Chinese meet
here and do business. Exporters from London and Paris send their choic-
est goods to Hong Kong, where everything is sold duty free. And American men from all over the Pacific go A.W.O.L. from their jobs in order
to sneak down to Hong Kong for a weekend. It is not only the ravishingly
lovely dance-hall girls who lure them. It is especially those wonderful
British woolens.

In Hong Kong a man can go into a tailor shop on Friday at noon,
select suit materials from the most varied stocks in the world, have the
suit tailor-made exactly to his size, take the finished suit home on Saturday, and pay only $30 for the whole deal. The featherweight cashmere
I bought for $28 in Hong Kong costs $250 in America. I knew a fabu-
lous madcap Tennessee pilot employed by Chiang Kai-shek's commercial
airline who owned 35 of these suits. He was the best-dressed man in
Asia and when he introduced me to his 4-foot-11-inch tailor he tried to
convince me that I should order at least ten cashmeres. When I laughed
at the suggestion—an act I have often since regretted—the Tennessee
dandy ordered four more for himself. "To hold the tailor's respect," he
said.

Today Hong Kong is a breathless place. If war erupts in Asia generally, communist troops could probably overrun the city in a few days. There are defenses, true, and brave men to man them, but all the communists have to do is reach the mainland water supply and Hong Kong must fall. The city is also apprehensive about embargoes that might destroy the entrepot trade. And it is worried about the enormous influx of refugees from China. But it remains one of the sunniest, most evocative and memorable cities you can find today.

NO

PANIC

IN THE

STREETS

In the tradition of British colonial service Sir Alexander Grantham, Governor of Hong Kong, finds governing a hot-spot to his liking. The tall handsome Briton reports sharply, "I have heard of the rumors that Chinese communists will invade Hong Kong soon. Highly improbable. There is just one route for an invading army to attack our city. That route is a twelve-mile corridor through forbidding mountains. We have the greatest British force ever assembled in this part of the world ready to defend that corridor. The communists will not invade Hong Kong in the face of those odds. Rumors to the contrary."

Governor Grantham directs the destinies of his great city and its surrounding free territory from a magnificent mansion high on a hillside overlooking the bay which separates Hong Kong island from the mainland. Day and night busy European steamers, Chinese high-pooped junks and one of the best ferry systems in the world make the leading free port of Asia a teeming pattern of industry. Sir Alexander's mansion looks fine these days, for during the war it was thoughtfully rebuilt and polished by the Japanese.

In memory of that dismal time when Asian troops captured Hong Kong, many residents keep packed "one little bag" ready for flight. What plans has Sir Alexander for exodus? "Pure nonsense. We shall not be forced to leave Hong Kong. The little bags may be promptly unpacked."

Is there a possibility that Hong Kong might be retained by communists and free men alike as a kind of Pacific Switzerland for the interchange of goods and ideas? "Yes. That might be our purpose. At present we're alarmed over just one thing: The unemployment resulting from the American embargo on shipments through the port of Hong Kong. Of course, a close check ought to be kept on strategic goods which might slip through our city to the Chinese communists. But the present embargo instituted by the Americans works great hardship on the responsible Chinese who daily join the growing number of unemployed. This is the first time we have had unemployment in Hong Kong for many years. That's very good food for the communist propagandists. They cry that we British jump at the command of the Americans.

"I wish there were something we could do about the flood of Chinese refugees. They have moved into Hong Kong to escape the communist drive on South China. We have had to absorb a tremendous additional burden of population. Perhaps a million refugees before the tide ebbs. Many of them face unemployment and no doubt a large number, perhaps even half a million, will be forced to return to their homes around Canton. If this happens the half-million will be old folk. Young Chinese with education will not return to Red China for any price. They fear conscription into the red armies.

"But even in spite of the embargo and growing unemployment there is little danger of an economic collapse. True, one-third of our trade is normally with China, but the bigger two-thirds is with the South Seas, Africa and Indonesia. We can rely on that during the American embargo on shipments to China.

"The one grave fear and anxiety we in Hong Kong have is over the prospect of war between China and the United States. If that occurred, Hong Kong might be threatened."

Sir Alexander is a good man to study as the archetype of British colonial servant who has ridden out a dozen storms and who keeps calm in the face of the next one coming along. He has served in Asia on previous tours of duty. In Fiji during the last war he gave the Guadalcanal-Fiji area a superb administration that was marked by firmness in protecting British interests and wholehearted co-operation with American invading forces. I once had occasion to review a large batch of correspondence over an incident in which American troops had grievously infringed British law and rights in Sir Alexander's territory. He could have been very stuffy about the whole affair but reported briefly, "Let's get on with the war." He refused to press charges.

In recent months Sir Alexander has had terribly difficult decisions to make. When the reds captured China, seventy-two immensely valuable airplanes of the Chinese Government were stationed at Hong Kong. Chiang Kai-shek's Free China Government, of course, claimed them. But so did the new communist Government.

To many men the choice between the two would have been easy, but to Governor Grantham, steeped in the tradition that law must prevail, it was not so simple. Judicially the planes belonged to the communists. In spite of anguished cries across the world, including many from America, Sir Alexander refused to surrender the planes to the Free Government. The trial continued for many months and the planes rusted to death in the salty air. Finally the courts announced their decision: The planes belong to Red China. But by now they were no longer valuable. Governor Grantham's Hong Kong salt air had taken care of that.

"All in all," the Governor says, "I would rather be Governor here than anywhere I can name. I have a sentimental spot in my heart for Hong Kong. Twenty-five years ago I married a very beautiful American girl here." Now Lady Grantham, a diminutive and lovely Nebraska woman, serves as first lady of the island. She entertains Chinese, French, Singhalese, and if need be Russian dignitaries with rare grace.

But as you leave Lady Grantham's paneled dining room, as you say good-bye to the tall, self-possessed man who governs the hot-spot, you see on the bulletin board at the ferry building the warning: "Typhoon moving toward Hong Kong. Take Care." If Sir Alexander ever bothered to read the sign he would probably say, "Take prudent precautions, yes. But there's no need for panic. None at all."

THE

OLD

CHINA

HAND

For two reasons Bill Downs doesn't belong in this series. First, he's not a real person. He's eight people. He runs an airline, heads a major news bureau, is a world-famous writer, runs a big store, is an adviser to governments.

Second, Bill is not an Asian. He is a white American citizen and a registered Republican, a fact which is very important to remember as you listen to what Bill has to say.

For he is a real Asian. He was born in China, speaks the language, worked there for years. Educated in America, he went back willingly to a land he loves. And when he talks about Asia he really lays it on the line.

"Let's face it like men. The white sahib is through in Asia. Absolutely through. I don't mean he's going to be asked to leave. He's going to be kicked out. Out of Korea, Hong Kong, Indo-China, Singapore, Indonesia. And if he doesn't scram he's going to be murdered.

"The white man is absolutely through. He's done Asia a world of good, and much evil. But any careful balancing of good and evil is past. He's getting the bum's rush.

"And if he insists upon fighting his way back in he's going to be massacred. He's out and he's got to stay out for at least a dozen years while Asians rearrange the furniture in what we often forgot was their home.

"The compradore who encouraged serfdom while piling up profits is out. The missionary who did his pitiful best is out. The arrogant fools who lounged in the exclusive clubs and shouted to grown Chinese men with five children, 'Damn it, boy! Bring me that drink, you filthy dog!'—they're out. And the businessmen who were going to show the Orientals how to live and make 18 per cent profits a year. They're all out.

"Along the entire coast of Asia a KEEP OUT sign has been posted. And it's going to stay there for a generation. When some Admiral Perry's black ships come back this time to reopen Asia, they'll beg permission to land and there will be a lot of discussion about terms. And the discussion will be between equals."

Bill Downs is cautious about explaining how it all happened. "I don't go for this simple barefoot-boy, agrarian-reformer line. Of course every uprising is communist now. But it's a stubborn fact that all the trouble did start over land and general reform. The people wanted land and food. They wanted the insolent whites to get out. That's how it started.

"Then, by one of those lousy tricks of fate, their vague determination on reform happened to coincide with the rise of communism. The Asians had failed to make Englishmen or Frenchmen or Americans take them seriously. So they allied themselves with Russia, which made believe its heart bled for them.

"In the face of what's happening in Asia now, old clichés of thought are useless. Nobody out here admires General MacArthur more than I, but it's a fact that less than six weeks after his Formosa speech, when he said all you had to do with Asians was ruffle them with a show of force and they'd back down, he threw some of the mightiest air power ever seen in the Pacific at them in North Korea, and they kept right on coming at us. We've got to give up the old ideas.

"What should take their place? Humility. The honest-to-God acknowledgment of the fact that all men are brothers. An acceptance of the idea that there is no 'way to handle the Asian.' The Asian is a full-grown man with all of a man's aspirations and potentials. If we could honestly accept such a program we might some day get back into Asia."

Here Bill Downs disagrees with himself for the first time. Six of him are abjectly pessimistic. They say, "The simple reformers who could have been on our side are now hopelessly communistic. They will absorb all of Asia and then back up Russia as she absorbs all of Europe. Then America is totally cut off, for South America will wither on the vine and tag along with Russia. We'll hold Mexico and Canada but in fifty years of such a life we will subtly modify our nation into Russia's pattern. So in fifty years it won't matter much."

The other two Bill Downses say, "No need to commit suicide over this. It's merely a historical fact. We had a great chance in Asia and we muffed it. We're out in the cold for a dozen years while Asia adjusts itself to a communist life. But Asia needs what we have, our technical skill, our sense of brotherhood. We need what they have.

"Never believe that Asia is completely lost to Russia. We have many friends among the billion enemies. When they remember us, how we actually tried to treat them decently, they'll invite us back. I'll go. I like Asia, and I think I'd like it even better on their terms."

Then the eight Bill Downses join ranks in their opinions about what to do now. "Fight our way back to the mainland? Impossible. We haven't enough men. We haven't enough money.

"Use Chiang Kai-shek? Absolutely fatal. We lost Asia through this tactic. To try it again would merely mean losing Asia forever.

"Drop the atomic bomb? Completely useless. The first bomb would inflame Asia against us for as long as memory persisted. I've been telling you, Asians despise us today. Now you want to make them hate us, too. When you talk about the atomic bomb you're speaking of mechanical weapons. Long ago we won the war of mechanical ideas. We have superior planes, machinery, bombs, stores. What we lost was the moral war. We didn't have the idealism, the brotherhood, the sense of participation in actual daily life. Well, you can't win moral wars with atom bombs.

"What do you do? You retreat from Asia, leave it alone, allow it to stew in its own juices and then settle down. Then you come back in with a new program. A mature program of equals meeting to discuss mutual problems. And the first white man who shouts 'Damn your filthy hide, boy, bring me that drink,' you shoot him."

On one final point Bill Downs speaks with fervor. "As we leave we should bow out gracefully. Leave behind memories of a decent crowd of people. Remind everyone of our essential honor. There's going to be rotten days in Asia, and if they remember us as we were they'll want us back. What I mean is, let's sow a little love as we leave. We can never tell what it might grow into while we're gone."

This story is so contrary to what I anticipated and so contrary to what Americans believe that I offer it with hesitation. I vouch for every word that follows. I vouch for every fact alluded to. I ask only that the reader follow through to the last paragraph before reaching conclusions.

At Hong Kong I met an old Chinese friend who cried, "Tonight we'll not talk of war and communism. We'll have a friendship feast."

His Peking wife agreed and I was shortly served a memorable meal, consisting of eight main courses. Fish soup, cold delicacies, sweet and sour pork with white chestnuts, shrimp and green beans, fried chicken and toasted walnuts, pressed duck and dumplings Peking style, creamed vegetables with chopped nuts, ending with a curious dish of fish tripe and bean sprouts.

The banquet was spoiled, however, by the constant arrival at the door of strangers. They would knock quietly, speak in hushed whispers, then go away. Perhaps forty of them appeared during the dinner and finally the host explained, "Yesterday I placed a small ad in the Hong Kong paper. Wanted, a tutor to teach my children English. So far there have been ninety applicants."

I suggested that he must have offered a fancy salary, but he said, "I could afford to offer very little, but so many cultured Chinese have fled the communists that men have to work for any pay at all in Hong Kong. You understand that every caller tonight had at least an M.A. degree and many the Ph.D."

The next day I met the bright young scholar who had landed the job, and since he had just that week escaped from Shanghai I saw a chance to get an honest report of what life under communism was like. He said, "I'll answer your questions but you mustn't use my name. Too dangerous.

"I was a student at the university when the communists arrived. Nothing happened. I was allowed to graduate as planned. But at the start of the next quarter, English was dropped from the curriculum, Russian was made compulsory and everyone had to take a course called Political Lessons of Communism.

"There were no beatings or anything like that. Communists and non-communists got good food and had an even chance for good places to live. Only one thing affected me. I was placed on the list of suspected. They had three things against me. I was a Christian, I spoke English and I had studied economics.

"I was told I could not work anywhere at all in China until I came back to school for a year's indoctrination at no pay, with foul food and under police supervision. I refused and nothing happened to me except that I couldn't get a job.

"I want to explain that the communists were never numerous in the university or anywhere else. Out of a hundred students 5 might be communists, 10 Kuomintang, and 85 absolutely nothing. I was one of the 85. I never knew a communist, but after the successful revolution they disclosed themselves and I found that they had been the brightest, best and most hard-working people in the university. I myself had often voted for them. They had known what they wanted and were good politicians. I can honestly say that I never once suspected them.

"The Kuomintang 10 were just the opposite. Very bad marks but good dancers. I think that is why the Kuomintang lost China. No one could take them seriously. They were so inefficient and corrupt. All of my friends despised the Kuomintang. Not Chiang Kai-shek. We were willing to grant that he didn't know what his assistants were doing. In some ways he was a satisfactory leader, but no students took him seriously.

"I never did get a job in China and I wouldn't take the police course, so I left the country. How did I escape? I just left. Anyone can do so. What do you mean, how did I do it? I got on a train in Shanghai and got off in Hong Kong. Certainly they gave me a passport. Perhaps some day I'll go back. How do I get back in? I get on the same train and ride back.

"You want to know exactly why I left communist China? No job. I'd say that all China is now divided the way our university was. Five per cent communists, 10 per cent worthless Kuomintang, 85 per cent nothing. I understand Americans think the 85 per cent are gasping for Chiang Kai-shek to come back. Don't you believe it. If Chiang could make the Kuomintang revolution purify itself I think maybe some of the 85 per cent might join his army. But I'm afraid the communists are winning the 85 over forever. Jobs, food, good government. That's what the communists promise and that's what the people think they're getting.

"Furthermore, the communists have started to control the minds of China. Everyone must hate America. Every day we heard this. America is only trying to bring back white imperialism. America will restore the old way. Soon everyone will believe this and hate America very much.

"Would I have come to believe it? Well, I know how much America has done for China, but if every day I am told to hate America in time I would come to obey.

"Let me explain how it is. My group of students were being urged to join the Red Army. Now I know for a fact that none of us wanted to join, but they stuck three communists in with us and when the time came to volunteer these three said, 'Let's go fight for China,' and almost everyone in the group volunteered. That was when I decided to come south.

"Will I ever go back? Well, I have a good job here now, but if it looks as if Hong Kong is going to fall, I think I'll go back and take the police course and get a job there."

As he spoke the hundredth applicant arrived and I said, "Surely some of these scholars fled because they loved freedom," but the young man replied, "They divide in the same way. Five per cent are communists sent down to spy on the rest of us. Ten per cent are Kuomintangs who are running away. Eighty-five per cent are like me. They came down for jobs."

That was in January, 1951. My wife went to the Free Territory-Communist border and watched the interminable interchange of people between the two jurisdictions. Chinese came and went without trouble, just as the young scholar had said. But in March the mass executions in communist China began. Then the hundred visitors could no longer return to China. If they did, they were shot, for the communists very methodically take care of one thing at a time. Now the time had come to liquidate intellectuals who might be interested in America. So the guns were being heard all over China.

THE

AMERICAN

Linus Benniman was not his name. I understand from what he told me that he has a wife and kids somewhere near Chicago, so I would not like to use his name.

The waiter at the hotel said, "You ought to meet Mr. Benniman. He's an American, too."

The girl who tended the phone had the same idea and finally the bartender called me and said, "You two gentlemen live in the same hotel! You should know each other."

Mr. Benniman looked up. There was nothing shifty about him. He was a real, hard-working, average-looking man about five feet eight, possibly ten pounds overweight, but quite clean-cut. I seemed to have known thousands of Americans like him back home. Most of them were good fellows.

He held out his hand affably and said, "Matter of fact, I've been wanting to meet you. My wife sent me the records of your play. This Mary Martin must be terrific."

We talked about the States for a few minutes and he said, "You really must have seen something of the Pacific. How about a gimlet? A drink I discovered in Manila. I was doing some work there."

As we chatted it became apparent that he had seen twice as much of the Pacific as I had and ten times more of Asia. Once or twice he mentioned Shanghai.

"You been to Shanghai?" I asked.

"Sure," he replied. "Were you ever in Manus?"

This was a pretty startling question coming right out of the blue. Not many people have been to Manus and those who have try to forget it. I said, "I was there some months ago. When were you in Shanghai?"

"Like you. Some months ago. But this Manus. It must be one hell of a place. Millions of dollars of equipment lying around."

"There used to be," I replied. "But I understand our clean-up parties sold it all to some Hong Kong junk men."

"They did? When?"

"About four years ago."

"Oh." He twisted his gimlet about and we started to speak of Korea.

"That's a tough show up there," I said. "The fellows call it the police action where the robbers greet the cops with submachine guns."

He didn't seem much interested in Korea but asked, "You ever been in Bougainville?"

"Hell of a place," I said. "I didn't know Americans could get into Shanghai. Any chance of my making it?"

"Nope. No chance. Shanghai's really bottled up these days. This Bougainville. Is there a lot of old stuff still lying around there? In the jungle, I mean."

"Well, yes."

"Could a man dig it out? If he had the equipment?"

"Well, yes. Of course the Australians have given it a pretty thorough working over."

"But they haven't skimmed it clean? I mean the real back jungle parts. Inland from the beach."

"No, they haven't combed it out, if that's what you mean."

"That's interesting."

"But about this Shanghai business . . ."

Mr. Benniman put down his drink and asked, "Are you trying to cook up some headlines for a paper back home?"

"No. I wanted to get to Shanghai and couldn't. You say you've been there. I'm interested."

"It's not much of place," he said glumly. "Not any more."

That was all he would say, but next afternoon he came back at me pretty hard. He entertained me from four to seven and then ate dinner at my table. "You ever been to Hollandia?" he asked.

"I don't know much about Hollandia."

"How about Guadalcanal?"

"There's an army clean-up team there but there must be an enormous amount of stuff left on the beach."

"A person could go in there all right with a liberty ship?"

"No trouble. But the biggest collection of junk I've seen was at Leyte Gulf, in the Philippines."

"No luck. I know the Philippines like a book. That place has been currycombed."

"That's about the biggest collection I know of."

"You like baseball?" he asked abruptly. "Who you like in the National League?"

"I've always been a Giant rooter."

"There's a good ball club. I can never understand how they miss the pennant every year."

"Who's your team?"

"You'll laugh but here goes. The Chicago White Sox."

We had a long discussion of baseball. I also discovered that Linus Benniman was a Presbyterian, didn't think much of Roosevelt, was a graduate of a good university, and had once had his own business near Chicago. On most points he was a solid, safe conservative and reminded me of the good guys I used to know in the Kiwanis Club near Denver, Colorado.

"Shanghai's a queer place since the communists took over," he volunteered. "Police are everywhere. Last trip, a few months back, I was stopped at least fifty times for my pass. Look at the damn thing."

It looked like a quick job where the ink had spilled. "How do you get in to Shanghai these days?" I asked.

"I've been in and out there ever since the war. I was in the Air Corps."

"A fellow in Hong Kong told me the communists pretty much let people alone in the big cities. Is that so?"

"Up to now. But every time I've been back things were tighter. The way I notice is that my old-time Chinese friends have started shying away from me. And policemen tail me wherever I go." Then he laughed. "You ever been to a Chinese movie?"

For fifteen minutes he regaled me with stories of Chinese drama. He loved it. Said he really got a charge out of that tinny music. He said he thought Shanghai one of the great cities of the world.

"It must have done a terrific shipping business in the old days," I said.

"It will again," Benniman insisted. "You can't kill trade. At the first opportunity Jap ships will crowd Shanghai again, just as they always did."

"How do you get in? Fly in?"

"How would anybody fly in?" he asked.

That night he asked me about New Caledonia, the New Hebrides, Fiji and Samoa. Then he told me of his wife and two kids. I also found out that he liked Tschaikowsky and the University of Minnesota football team.

In fact, Linus Benniman was a good, solid, average American. He was selling scrap iron to the Shanghai communists because that was a quick way to make a buck. I knocked about the ports of Asia for some time and never met one shady international character plotting to betray his country. They kept to the alleys. But in the good hotels I met a lot of clean-shaven, eager men who were willing to sail their Panamanian liberty ships—the kind you used to see around Guadalcanal and Iwo Jima during the war—anywhere there was a fast buck. A good many of these business-men were Americans.

OBSERVATIONS

In the last war Hong Kong was defended by the British with ex-traordinary heroism. It seemed as if they understood the unusual merits of their island city and accorded it a defense worthy of its rare charm. Their bravery was repaid, for no Chinese in 1946 could point with scorn and say, "The British didn't defend their city. They have no claim to it." Consequently, there has been almost no anti-British feeling in postwar Hong Kong.

Actually, the British have a substantial claim to Hong Kong. It is an island off the coast of China. There is a legitimate lease on the Free Territory. Chinese living in Hong Kong have always received very just treatment. And Hong Kong has been operated almost as much for the benefit of inland China as for the benefit of homeland England. Jurid-ically, Hong Kong and Formosa could be considered parallel cases.

The fact remains, however, that Hong Kong can be captured almost any time that the communist leaders want it. Their counterclaims to it are strong. First, that an irresponsible Chinese government alienated the island from the homeland and that an even more irresponsible authority made the lease for the Free Territory. Second, that the day of any kind of foreign enclave in Asia is finished, no matter how good the original juridical claims. (This would also finish Portuguese Macao, a few miles down the coast from Hong Kong.) When I was in Hong Kong many residents wondered why the reds had not already moved in, and the great American business establishments were already starting to evacuate.

It is possible, however, that totally vulnerable Hong Kong might never fall. First, its very vulnerability protects it, because Red China knows it can take the city whenever it wants it. Therefore, there's no use to prove a point. Second, Red China gets just as much benefit from having Hong Kong remain free as do either the British or the Americans. Third, no matter how complete an iron curtain, some listening posts outside it are necessary. That accounts, basically, for the continued freedom of Swit-zerland and Sweden and the continued free operation of the United Nations. There is an outside chance that Hong Kong and Macao—with the latter enjoying much the better odds—will be kept as listening posts.

In this respect Hong Kong takes on an added meaning. Even the most powerful and monolithic states must preserve some contacts with the out-side world. Even when all the nations on earth are engaged in massive warfare, some enclaves of peace must be preserved so that when the war has worn out there will be some avenue by which peace can again be attained. Hong Kong may thus become a Switzerland of Asia.

SINGAPORE

FOUR TIMES ON MY JOURNEY I WAS INSULTED IN THE GRAND MANNER. People said, "So you've come here for three days, after which you'll write a book explaining everything that's wrong. Well, we've lived here all our lives and don't understand anything yet."

I never knew whether I was expected to apologize for my arrogance or their ignorance, but I do think an explanation of how a man tries to understand a nation is in order.

I arrived at Singapore airport at dawn. Three newspapermen interviewed me and I had the felicitous good luck to say that I knew nothing about Singapore and hoped to talk with ordinary citizens about their ordinary problems. The reporters seemed delighted that I wanted to learn something.

I then disappeared. Upon arriving in any new country I spend the first three days typing up my notes of the last place visited. This serves many purposes. It allows me to record in actual words exactly how I felt about a land, something I cannot recall six months later. These three days also permit me to immerse myself slowly in the spirit of the new country. I walk a lot to rest my eyes from typing. I eat in native restaurants. I listen to the sounds about me. And I almost never talk those first three days. For I have found that my silence plus the sound of my typewriter working overtime drives the local residents crazy. They become convinced that I am a charlatan who has come to their city, stuck himself away in a hotel room, and is now writing a dastardly exposé without ever having talked to a native. As a result they become my secretaries and arrange for me a plethora of interviews I could never possibly have obtained for myself.

In Singapore I stayed at the rambling and majestic old Raffles Hotel. When the newspaper stories appeared about an American who wanted to meet ordinary people my telephone started ringing furiously and kept it up while I was in the city. Late at night a quiet voice would say, "Am I speaking to the American writer? You've never heard of me but I work in a Chinese store. Could I speak with you?"

"Come on over to the Raffles."

"I wouldn't feel at ease there."

"Where can we meet?"

"There's a very nice restaurant near the K. P. M. building. Tomorrow at noon."

When I reached the restaurant I usually found some very serious chap who wanted to be sure that my country understood the exact stand of his group. I shall never forget those meals. Often the food would bear neither analysis nor description, but the people with whom I shared it were vitally interesting. I met one man who was the center of a world controversy, one who was a leader of the local communist party, a young Chinese whom I suspected of burning streetcars, and assorted idealists whose causes I had never heard of before. Slowly the complex fabric of Malayan life began to disclose itself.

And there was a different kind of phone call. Gordon Jones, the steel-spring Pan American Airways manager, wondered if I could address a businessmen's club, and there I met four excellent men who knew about Malayan economy. Jim Halsema, a wise and witty fellow from the American consulate, phoned to say that the consul, Kenneth Langdon, was giving a reception that evening, and there I met Malcolm MacDonald, British representative in Asia and one of the best-informed men in the world. A subaltern of the commanding general of British troops in Southeast Asia called to say I could see his general, a marvelous rocky crag of a man who told me of his resolute plans to defend Malaya. And handsome Ivor Kraal, of Aw Boon Haw's multimillionaire patent-medicine empire, called to arrange a lunch and we talked of many things.

Most pleasant were the unexpected and inconsequential calls: students and would-be writers and men with burning grievances and one young fellow who wanted a job with *Time* Magazine. I met these men at dinner, where I asked hundreds of questions, checking up on what I had been told that day. It is remarkable how in this way false information is exposed. I have now forgotten the names of these casual visitors, but the glow of those lovely evenings, with the Raffles waiters bringing excellent food, the string orchestra playing in the distance, the hot night all about you, and the urgent talk is with me yet and colors any thoughts I may have about Asia.

There were other important encounters: the chubby freebooting Reuters man who was a provocative compendium of knowledge; the famous newsman whose yarns about Siam kept me enthralled for seven hours; the haunted Englishman who had been knocked senseless in the religious riots and woke up in the river; and the shadowy American who was trading with the Chinese communists.

However, two nights stand out in memorable relief. A friend said, "There's one chap you must meet," and he arranged a dinner with Anthony Brooke, last of the famous white rajahs of Sarawak. Brooke was in some way a pitiable chap, for his luck had run out. He had been evicted from his savage kingdom and now alternately tried as a matter of pride to get back or assured the authorities as a matter of patriotism that he would accept his banishment. I liked Brooke immensely and, improbable as it seems, helped him draft his statement of final abdication. We drank a couple of bottles of wine and arranged for release of the story to newspapers in London and New York. I can see him yet, a kindly, bewildered young man, a living relic of the vanished Pacific days when a white Englishman could actually make himself rajah of a savage domain vaster than England itself.

During my somewhat unusual dinner parties at the Raffles I noticed a heavy-set, distinguished gentleman observing me with what was obvious distaste. Then, as the time for my departure neared, he made bold to knock on my door.

"Michener," he said bluntly, "you've been talking with the wrong people. Don't want you to leave with misleading impressions. Want you to have dinner with me tonight. Black tie." He introduced himself as a colonel from the British Army.

It was an exciting evening. After a fashionable meal we visited a millionaire businessman whose liberal attitudes were refreshing. Then we probed back streets to find a Malayan with a very special story, only to wind up at the famed Tanglin Club, which has for generations been the very acme and symbol of British rule in Asia.

As the orchestra played modern waltzes, as the businessmen and soldiers of Singapore swayed through moonlit dances, and as some of the tastiest food I've ever eaten arrived the colonel said, "Fine crowd, this. Wouldn't like you to make fun of what this crowd accomplishes."

Invariably around the world I have received a hospitality I did not deserve, and almost invariably my host has begged me not to make fun of his country or his ways. What kind of Americans have we been sending abroad?

During my stay in Singapore I listened for fifteen or sixteen hours a day. People of every complexion, of every intellectual or political persuasion talked with me. Never meeting fewer than four strangers a day, I conducted more than sixty interviews. I would have had to be a drooling idiot not to have learned something about Malaya in that time.

I learned mostly how much I didn't know. America should have some of its ablest young men doing for months and years what I did for some days. For unless we know Asia we will never gain the wisdom to make right decisions at the right time. And unless we start making some right decisions, Asia will become by default our implacable enemy. This is avoidable, for every Asian who came to see me in Singapore did so for one very simple reason. He wanted America at least to understand his position. He wanted us to be on his side. We have that to build upon.

THE

NEW

LEADER

Dato Onn bin Ja'afar has attained something that few men in the course of history have ever attained. He is the very first leader of his people. Every other Malay leader who follows Dato Onn will have his work to build upon. Dato Onn had to start from scratch.

"In 1940 I wrote an article deploring the lack of unity among Malays. I warned that without leadership the Malay people could gain neither freedom nor the respect of the world. To my surprise, truly, the Malay people responded by establishing me as their leader.

"The English rulers helped. They tried to force some very unfair treaties upon the leaders of our semi-free states. Instead of being independent states we were to become colonies of the lowest order. And everyone who lived in Malaya—Indians, Chinese, Malays alike—was given one basic citizenship.

"The resistance to this grave injustice centered in me. I was elected President of the United Malay National Organization and we fought for new treaties. We got them. Instead of a colony with no rights we are now a federation of various kinds of states. Instead of one cheap citizenship for all we have a plan whereby anyone who really wants to live in this country and make it his permanent home can become a citizen. But he must renounce ties with any other land.

"We have never been anti-British. No sensible Malay is. We know that if Britain left now, the Chinese would take over at once. Did you know there were more Chinese here now than Malays? Therefore we want the British to stay and guide us until we have progressed to the point where we and not the Chinese can rule the country.

"We object to two things about the British. First, they make no honest attempt to train our people for future government jobs. They still send out totally incompetent young men who immediately assume positions of leadership over Malays of mature age. The British keep saying they will give us Malaya one day. But when?

"Second, the British treat colored people as inferiors. There is always the private club to which no colored man can go. I can honestly say that I do not take these things seriously. For under the Japanese I learned that an Asian is just as good as a European. You cannot understand the effect of the Japanese occupation of Malaya. They were brutal, true, but they inspired us with a new idea of what Asia might become. That's why even I cringe when I have to call an Englishman Tuan Besar, the big boss, while no Malay can ever earn that title.

"I must add right away that it's been better since the war, and I think the British men would give up this silliness in time, but their women see to it that the old ways continue. Even then it's only a few who do the damage, but they're insufferable."

Dato Onn—the Dato is like Sir—is in his middle fifties, speaks flawless English and knows America. "In 1939 I was in charge of Johore Pavilion at the San Francisco Exhibition. This was only natural because my uncle was in charge of the same pavilion at the Chicago World's Fair. My family has been in government service since the year 1200.

"Therefore I consider the future judiciously. Malaya is the only important colony left in Asia. All the rest have kicked out the white man. But I don't think we can stand by ourselves, for we are in the middle of three great pressures: Indian, Indonesian and Chinese. The dice are loaded in favor of China. The prospect is not happy.

"If anything were to happen to Britain, Malaya would be Chinese by nightfall. I try to convince the Chinese that their future lies within a free Malayan state, but I don't think I make much ground.

"For the present the Chinese in Malaya are not communist. The Chinese bandits are, yes, but not the businessmen. Of course, if communist China is victorious in Korea and Indo-China, Malaya is probably doomed. You must remember that even capitalist Chinese always yearn for the bones of their ancestors. And they rest in China, whether it's communist or not.

"What I would really like to see would be the establishment of a great Pan-Malay Union consisting of Malaya, Indonesia, Borneo, and perhaps the Philippines.

"In such a union we could constitute a great nation. Malayan riches would be an important contribution, for even today we are the biggest dollar earner in the British Commonwealth. Everyone wants our tin and rubber, but some day we would like to keep our profits at home. For schools and hospitals.

"So you can see that we stand at a very critical point in history. We remember what the Japanese taught us. We see Indonesians, people with religion and history like ours, enjoying what we do not have. And we watch China starting a violent new movement.

"For the present there is no affinity between Malays and communism. But recently our young people have grown impatient. Several splinter parties have broken off from my leadership and they are definitely left. I would say my group was middle-of-the-road, tending to the right. But I would not say that the new groups are communist, yet. We know that if they lose faith in British promises they will become communist, even though that means throwing their country over to China.

"I do not know of a single Malay boy in the gangs that burn buses at night or destroy taxis. But it is inevitable that frustrated liberal nationalists always end by joining Moscow."

At the conclusion of our talk Dato Onn said bravely, "Sure you can quote me. I want people to know what I think." He was courageous and appealing, possibly the only man in history who was the father of a country that seemed destined never to get born.

Abdul Samad bin Ismail is a wiry, brilliant, extremely nervous Malay newspaper editor. He's a young man, furiously thin and with a penetrating wit.

"So you'd like to interview a Malay leader? You can't. They're all in jail.

"There's one leader you might meet, Dato Onn bin Ja'afar, but he's simply a dear old man signed up by the British to serve as their stooge. No intellectual Malay takes Dato Onn seriously.

"The younger men will have no part of Britain. Obviously there will be a long-range British retreat from Malaya. The only question is timing. Under Dato Onn's leadership the British will never get out. Because Malaya is their biggest dollar earner in the Empire. Our tin and rubber can be sold anywhere, and Britain would be foolish to let us go.

"But the younger men will speed the timetable. Britain has got to go. I am not, however, violently anti-British. I am amused by them. I laugh at their stupid social customs. Their bumbling attempts to create racial tensions between Malays and Chinese. Their stuffy private clubs to which no colored man can go. All that amuses me.

"It is not the British who deserve serious consideration. It is the Chinese. You might expect a liberal nationalist like me to hate the Chinese, but I don't. In order for there to be any trouble between Chinese and Malay there must be the intervention of a third party making trouble.

"To understand Malaya, study our recent riots. They were a great upsurging of Malays against the centuries of British arrogance. No one led the rioters. No one told them what to do. They simply went out and killed all the white people they could find.

"But not a Chinese was touched. Why not? Because there is no deep enmity between the Malay and the Chinese. We can get along together very well, and we will when the British have gone.

"Also be sure to study the bandits. They're all Chinese and they have killed many people. But if a Chinese bandit ever kills a Malay he leaves a printed message on the body explaining just why he had to kill this man. The Malay had been spying or had been seen talking with British soldiers.

"I can say affirmatively that Malay nationalists are not even afraid of the 300,000 Chinese squatters who have crept over the border and who live off our land. They grow the food the Malay needs. In time they may become good citizens.

"As for communism, don't you worry about communism in Malaya. It won't play a very large role in Malaya. Some of the Chinese are communists, yes, but they are of no significance. I choose to believe that the Chinese we have will not follow communism but will instead become a part of a new Malay nation. Their interest is with us and not with China."

Abdul Samad bin Ismail twists his wiry body into a knot and lights each cigarette from the butt of the previous one. He knows a great deal about America. "I read *Life* and *Time* each week. But America has suffered a terrible blow in Southeast Asia when she bombed Korea. No doubt it was justified, but every night Radio Peking and Radio Moscow drum into our ears their version of the barbarism. No, I never hear the Voice of America unless I pick it up on the Manila channel.

"What about Indonesia? You must understand that every Malayan looks at Indonesia with envy and pride. He sees fellow Malayans who succeeded in throwing off the yoke of Holland before we were able to do anything about England. If there is a meeting the visiting Indonesian always acts as chairman. He's quicker, smarter and has shown that he can handle his own affairs.

"Therefore it would be logical for us to join the Indonesian Republic. After all, we have historic, racial, ethnological, cultural, economic and religious ties with Indonesia. One day we will rejoin them as part of a powerful republic.

"You must remember this when you consider Malayan problems. Why did we despise the British so for their handling of the Turk Westerling case? Westerling was a reactionary Dutchman trying to bring disrepute upon the new republic. And the British made a hero of him. They helped him to operate from this base. The local newspapers carried stories about Mrs. Westerling and what she bought in the local shops when she toured them with admiring British friends. We all felt highly gratified when Westerling was shown up for the fool he was.

"It was the same thing in the case of the riots. If the little girl's real mother had been an American woman, and if the courts had handed down the same decision, that she must leave her Muslim husband and go back to her American mother, there would have been no riots.

"But the girl's mother was Dutch. The Dutch Government were paying her legal fees to prove to a bunch of Muslims that Dutch ways were always superior. It was an affront to every Malay, to every Indonesian and to every Muslim. Rioting was inevitable. Especially when the Dutch thought up the idea of showing the little Muslim girl in a Catholic convent kneeling before the Virgin Mary. I think that was what did it.

"Remember that when the riot started the mob asked people if they were Americans. If they were, they got off free. Later on, of course, the rioters beat up every white man alike.

"But I do not think there will ever be any other riots like that. They were not anti-government. The British Government here is adequate. Not what we want, but adequate."

Abdul Samad punctuates important points with violent movements of his long hands. He also laughs at the follies of his time. "I am cursed with a sense of humor. All of this amuses me. The British trying to hold on a little longer. You Americans trying to buy loyalties. We Malays confused by it all. And the Chinese making every penny they can.

"I have a philosophical attitude about it all because I was raised in a very religious household. On every wall in my home there are quotations from the Koran instructing us how to live a good life. It amuses me. The way the Japs amused me during the occupation. When it was over I was put in jail for having collaborated with them. All I did was help them print their newspaper."

I talked with Abdul Samad for many hours and found him ready with some brilliant, sardonic comment on every topic I proposed. I remember his cynical yet illuminating smile. Next morning, when I saw his picture in the paper he was still smiling. He had been arrested as one of the leaders of the communist party in Malaya.

THE

MULTIMILLIONAIRE

On the brass plate at the entrance of the big building you read Lee Biscuit Company, Lee Rubber Company, Lee Pineapple Company, and also the Lee saw-milling, produce, engineering, printing, ice-making and investment companies.

The directing genius of this empire is a slim, bullet-headed, crew-cut, exceptionally able Chinese businessman, Lee Kong Chian. In his early fifties he controls much of the rubber of the world and is a giant in international trade.

"I left China in 1915 and I've never been home since. First I worked in the Singapore government, but with the money I saved I bought a rubber estate during the 1922 slump. By 1925 there was a rubber boom and I was on my way.

"I reinvested profits and soon had one company after another. Now I have established two large subsidiaries in Indonesia, another in Siam, and one in New York City.

"Take Goodyear in America. I sell them about one-fourth of all the rubber they use. Most rubber middlemen never own the rubber they sell. Just gamblers. But every ounce of rubber I sell has been handled by my men. We recondition it. Add something constructive.

"Look at this air photo of one of our big mills. I have many of them. See the hospital? And the school? Fifty acres of landscaped ground.

"We don't worry about the bandits much. For one thing, we build near large cities. For our labor supply. And of course we keep a special police force. You've got to, in Malaya today. Otherwise the bandits run everything."

Lee Kong Chian has a large expressive mouth and nervous hands. He knows the answer to everything you ask and says he has a special regard for America. "It started when I was a poor government clerk. I needed an education, but where could a Chinese get an education in a British colony? So I went to university in America. By mail. Scranton International Correspondence School. In time I am a civil engineer and all the factories I showed you I built from what I learned by mail.

"Today my children go to America. Two sons at Pennsylvania, one at Toronto, a daughter at Smith. I am a very good friend of America."

Lee Kong Chian stresses this because he suspects that you've heard about his father-in-law, an astonishing man who was a Singapore millionaire but who renounced the life of a capitalist to become a red-hot communist. Tan Kah Kee is now in China as a member of the People's Political Consultative Council. He serves as a sort of general representative for Chinese overseas.

"Well, I do sell my rubber to communist China. To Russia, too. I have to. Singapore is a free port. That's what's made us rich. So if Russia sends a boat down here for rubber, I fill the boat.

"How do I decide who gets the rubber? An international price is set. Anyone who can offer that price gets the rubber. If my price is too high neither America nor Russia will buy. If it's too low, I go broke. It's all a matter of business.

"But if the Government were to pass a law saying that sale of rubber to Russia was forbidden, then the Russian ships would go away empty. But in Singapore there is no such law. Here we trade with everybody.

"No Chinese in Singapore are communists. I think that here in Malaya the Chinese and Malays will make one strong country. Always remember that Chinese who leave China always leave as individuals, never as agents of their Government. The Chinese knows he must adjust to local life and make his home there in the new land. He has no ties with home.

"Consider Indonesia. When the great riots began many Chinese were killed, but you don't hear of that any more. Because the Chinese adjusted themselves to the new idea of government and are loyal to the Indonesian Republic. They get along together fine.

"In the same way, during the Singapore riots there were no Chinese killed by the rioters. The Malays knew we were their friends. That's why I think there will never be communism here."

But less than eight blocks from his office, as we talked, a band of fantastically devoted Chinese communists seventeen and eighteen years old upset another bus and burned it. These gangs are determined to disrupt life in Singapore so that communist China will be able to capture the city without much trouble. They burn buses, murder policemen, create public panic. They represent one of the most curious phenomena of our times: individualistic and money-loving Chinese working everywhere in the eastern part of Asia to aid the communist revolution. It passes belief and makes no meaning, but the accumulated hatred of the white man's insults and arrogance makes Chinese expatriates from Singapore to Tahiti one of the most effective fifth columns the world has ever known.

Lee Kong Chian insists that he does not play at this stupid game. "The way to avoid communism is to raise the standard of living, increase social services. Wise men in Southeast Asia should pray for gradualism. They should put their faith in slow change. I myself always try to adopt the British attitude toward change. It's coming, but let's keep it from being too violent.

"In my youth I thought the other way. In 1911 I was a revolutionary fighting for Sun Yat Sen, but when I became a British subject, with a British passport, I took no more interest in revolutions. I feel the same way about the young Chinese here in Singapore who get excited over communism. It's natural, but they'll outgrow it."

That night, of course, not far from one of Lee Kong Chian's rubber factories Chinese communists shot dead four more white planters. When the wife of one of them tried to escape, they chased her into a ditch and shot her, too. So life in Singapore seems to be a battle between rich old men with money and fiery young men with none. In the long run of history the latter usually win. But the multimillionaire concludes, "The city of Singapore will never turn communist." His father-in-law, in

Peking, has said that all of Asia will soon be communist. In fact, it is his job to see that this happens.

I met Hugh Channing in Singapore and he will haunt my conscience forever. He was taller than I, better-looking, better-educated and more gifted in the correct use of language. His skin was whiter and his smile more gracious. In fact, there was only one thing wrong with him. His grandmother had been a native woman.

"Therefore I am nothing. I am not a European. The white people see to that. Nor am I an Asian. Because the white people insist that I never push a rickshaw or clean gutters. I can neither go up nor down. I am the man ordained by God always to be a clerk in some English shop. They don't have to pay me much, for I can't leave. There's no other job I could get. And they don't have to promote me because everyone knows I'm not really to be trusted.

"What am I? I'm a Eurasian. I can never be a European as long as Englishmen despise anyone with even a drop of color. I can never be an Asian as long as my parents bring me up to imitate the white man.

"This was proved in the recent riots. On Saturday night there was dancing at the Tanglin Club. I could never hope to enter such a club. White Englishwomen see to that. They never had a servant at home, but out here they can rule the world.

"On Monday the riots began and a gang of infuriated Malays saw me in my car. With huge bamboo flails they smashed the glass and hauled me into the street. They set fire to the car and destroyed it. They were going to beat me to death but a fearless Sikh rescued me. Eurasians took terrible punishment that night because the Malays looked upon us as traitors.

"This riot was most difficult to understand. We had a fine police force, all Malays, all armed. Four of them watched casually as I was being beaten nearly to death. They stood by with their arms folded. A white priest was almost killed but managed to crawl to a police station where the officers slammed the door in his face. They said that otherwise it might look as if they were taking sides.

"At the investigation the Malay police were astonished that anyone had expected them to interfere with the mob. 'They were all Muslims,' the police protested. 'How could we fire upon our own religion?' A news-paperman explained that in New York if there's a riot, Negro cops will fire on Negro criminals or Irish cops upon fellow Catholics. The Malay police thought this very strange and said the Irish cops must not take their religion very seriously.

"I myself am a Catholic, and this has been a great solace to me. This was the only church that really welcomed Eurasians and I have always felt myself a brother with all Catholics across the world.

"But recently I have begun to wonder if I ought not turn my back upon Christianity, confess my sins and become a complete Malay Muslim. I believe now that my future lies with the Malays."

For many years social scientists have studied the tragic problems of the man who stands astride two societies belonging spiritually to neither but inheriting the prime evils of each. Such men are known as marginal men and in all societies their life has been hell. In Canada, America and India the half-breed has been an object of bitter hatred. Only in chance places like Mexico or Tahiti has he gained a decent home.

"But in British colonies he inherits a special hell. For some curious reason the Englishman has a pathological contempt for the Eurasian. It took my mother two years of daily pleading to get me into a school. I was prohibited from social contact with white children.

"As I became older they treated me with politeness but also with contempt. Then when I reached courtship age the real misery began.

"Of course I couldn't speak to any white girl. But at the same time all the prettiest Eurasian girls were chased by white men. I had two feelings. I was enraged when I thought of myself, but I was also amused when I saw how terrified the white fathers and mothers became when they thought their son might actually marry a Eurasian girl.

"They tried everything. Women wept and men threatened to shoot somebody. I had a sense of revenge when the Eurasian girl went right ahead and married the boy. They were usually driven out of Singapore, but lots of them established good lives elsewhere.

"The case we Eurasians enjoyed most was the recent one when an army officer announced that he was going to marry a Eurasian. His commander huffed and chumped and said he damned well would never marry the girl while he was in uniform. So the officer waited until he got leave and popped out of uniform. The Army countered by ordering him to another post on four hours' notice. He deliberately missed the plane and got married. So they court-martialed him, but a brilliant Eurasian lawyer proved that the Army had no right to send him to another station until they first canceled his leave. This outraged the army lawyer so that he screamed, 'Everyone knows that all Eurasian girls are whores!' Then the court began to sweat, because they knew that if this were published there would be riots, so the commanding officer ordered the lawyer to apologize. But they saw to it that the man who had married the Eurasian girl was ruined.

"Usually, however, the Eurasian harbors no desire for vengeance. He is a playboy. He gives enormous parties and has a good time and never worries about business because he knows he can never get promoted. Sometimes white men come to our parties, but always looking for pretty girls. And the girls don't mind, because if they can catch a white man they may escape to a better life.

"One thing that has happened in Singapore has given us all hope. Today for the first time in history there's one club which any man with a clean shirt and the initiation dues can join. The American Club. We also now have a free library to which anyone, regardless of color, can belong. The United States Information library. These things are important.

"I think that if enough such things happened in Asia there might be some chance of avoiding communism." But things are happening with terrible swiftness in Asia today and even as Hugh Channing spoke, one of the most brilliant, handsome and gifted Eurasian lawyers in Singapore was being arrested. He was a leader of the communist underground. When Hugh Channing saw the headlines he shrugged his shoulders. "What could you expect?" he asked.

THE

SCHOOLTEACHER

I had tried for two weeks to meet this man but constantly I was put off by one group or another. The Europeans said, "Better leave him alone." The Malays asked, "Why would he want to talk with a white man?"

Then, on my last night in Singapore, I tracked through the ominous alleys where everyone crept into shadows as I passed, and finally I met the schoolteacher. I found twenty-two-year-old Mansor Adabi one of the most provocative and yet winning persons I was to meet in Asia.

"I was teaching English to mixed classes in Singapore for a little over $70 American a month. I had this house where my mother boarded students. Things were going well.

"Then on June 1, 1950, a Malay woman I had not known before, Che

Aminah, asked me if I would tutor her daughter in English and I went to a social welfare house where the law had placed her daughter.

"I knew there was something wrong when I saw the girl, for she was a very pretty Dutch girl, a Muslim, who called herself Nar, which is short for Nadra. It was obvious she was not Che Aminah's daughter. I learned that a Dutchwoman was her real mother, but she had given Nadra away a long time ago. I taught Nadra English and when the police would not let me see her I sent her the lessons by mail. She was a brilliant learner and already spoke Malay, Javanese and a little Chinese. She knew no Dutch.

"Then the lower Singapore court announced that Nadra actually did belong to Che Aminah, and not to the strange Dutchwoman who was her real mother. Nadra was allowed to leave the home and on August 1 I married her."

Mansor Adabi points to the wall of his bare living room, and there, tacked to the glaring white plaster is a world-famous wedding picture. It shows him in Muslim garb, very young, good-looking, with rim glasses and very white teeth. It also shows his bride in Malay dress, a sweet square face and winning smile. It is a famous picture because Nadra was thirteen years old that day.

"There are several things I should like to explain about our marriage. First, it was not conducted secretly in order to defeat the British law in case some higher court decided that Nadra belonged to the Dutch-woman. It was very public. More than 100 people attended. I should know because I paid the bills. One thousand dollars. I had saved the money from my salary.

"Second, it was a perfectly legal marriage. Muslim law requires three principles to be observed. A guardian must approve, consent must be obvious and witnesses must observe the ceremony. An important *kathi* performed the wedding, and under Muslim law Nadra was old enough to be married. If you saw her picture and did not know her age you would say she was sixteen or seventeen.

"Third, Nadra herself wanted this marriage. I had known her two months and in that time we had fallen in love. Was any force used? Only the force of mutual attraction.

"Fourth, it is crazy to call Nadra a jungle girl. She is as much a city girl as any girl in Chicago, U.S.A. One of the papers spoke of her dodging tigers in Singapore. Where do such writers think we live? In the middle of a jungle?"

Mansor stops to show several pictures of his wife. She does look to be sixteen. She does appear to be a normal, happy, civilized girl. It is hard to believe that she caused eighteen men to be beaten to death. Another half-hundred men and women will be maimed or crippled for life because of the terrible riots that were launched in her name.

"I had no idea riots would follow. The judge called us into his chambers on Saturday, December 2. Nadra and I were there, Che Aminah and Nadra's mother, Mrs. Hertogh. The judge said simply that the court had decided there had never been a marriage and that Nadra must go to live with her mother.

"Che Aminah fainted. Nadra shouted that she would have nothing to do with her mother and that she loved me. She was embracing me when I told her to be patient. Then she asked me to do everything I could to get her back. They took her away and I have never seen her since. Later they smuggled her out of the country secretly and now she is in Holland."

Mansor Adabi, to perfect his handwriting and English, has on his desk little slips of paper on which he has copied famous English quotations. In ink more recent than the rest is written, "The sweetest joy, the wildest woe is love." In the days following the judge's decision his love became fantastically wild.

"I was in the mosque praying when friends rushed in and cried, 'They are killing white people because of Nadra.' Three Muslim leaders and I got into a taxi and cruised about Singapore shouting, 'We beg you to stop. You are doing an unwise thing.' We succeeded in stopping some of the worst gangs, but in other places the riots went on all night.

"The cause? Muslims were outraged because the courts had said a Muslim marriage meant nothing. They were furious because of pictures in the paper showing Nadra being made to worship a new religion. I think, too, they were angry because the Dutch had engineered all this as a way to get even with the Muslims for being thrown out of Java. It was a Dutchman who tracked Nadra down. All these things made the riot."

Adabi lives as he did before the riots. His mother takes in boarders and he studies in the living room. Its walls look much like those in a college dormitory with pictures of Roy Rogers, Greer Garson and a championship soccer team. While I was there a stranger from Egypt appeared with handwritten excerpts from Middle East newspapers.

"I live in a total blackout of news. No Singapore newspapers report anything about Nadra. The Dutch permit no news of any kind to seep out of Holland. I do not even know where she lives. But Muslims in many parts of the world get what news they can and send it to me through the underground. I understand that when Nadra got to Holland she struck her father and cried, 'I am a Muslim. I want my husband.'

There was a scene when they tried to take her to church. She said, 'My church is the mosque.' "

There were many things Mansor Adabi told me that the British courts refused to accept, but on one point I could not be deceived. This Muslim boy loved the girl he had married. Once, when he showed me a clipping which suggested that Nadra was dim-witted, he broke down, but immediately recovered. His handsome grin returned and he said, "She is a bright, lively girl. She is still my wife. Even for 20 or 30 years she will be my wife. I am fully convinced she feels the same way. We will be united again." I asked him how he thought this would happen. "I don't know. But I believe it because we are in love. In the papers they have written about everything except that we are in love. I think that will bring her back."

THE

MAN

WITHOUT

A COUNTRY

Anthony Brooke is a young Englishman in his early thirties. He has a cleft chin, a rounded face and the gentle half-stumbling accent of a P. G. Wodehouse hero. He is also a delightful dinner companion, witty and wise in many things, as I discovered when we dined together in Singapore on what must have been the most burdensome and regrettable day of his life.

"Damned good of you to come along. I've got to talk with someone. Because I've gone and done it. No recriminations. Never a second chance on this one. This morning I surrendered all claims to be the white Rajah of Sarawak. A ruling family came to an end today. By voluntary action I gave up substantial claims to land larger than England.

"Maybe you've heard of Rajah Brooke of Sarawak. Came out here in 1841 and brought peace to an immense chunk of Borneo. Put the headhunters at ease. They made him their emperor. And he was a real sovereign in every sense of the word.

"For a hundred years my family gave a shining example of how white men could help colored men rule tropical lands. Everyone prospered, but nobody got rich. My grandfather wrote in his will, 'My predecessor never entertained the idea of founding a family of Brookes to be European millionaires.' We left our money in Sarawak and when it was found that anyone could make money off rubber we did not build vast Brooke plantations. We showed our people how to do that job and now they own the rubber. I think I would have been a good rajah in the Brooke tradition."

Young Anthony Brooke, the chap who should have been Rajah, flies the flag of Sarawak from his auto. "I'll have to take that down tomorrow. No more Sarawak flag. Today marks the end of a kingdom.

"How did it all happen? My uncle had been Rajah for twenty-three years when the Japs came. He was an old man, so he fled to Australia. After that he wandered back to England and when the war was over he was too old to come back to the tropics and become a rajah in fact. So he sold Sarawak to the British for one million pounds. What had been a sovereign kingdom was now a petty colony.

"I protested. So did many others. There were questions asked in Parliament and even Winston Churchill, bless him, sided with me. In fact there was so much stink raised that one newspaper showed a cartoon of two Sarawak natives underneath a palm tree asking, 'What's our quotation on the black market today?'

"It became quite messy and Government had to back down. Instead of handing my uncle a million they gave him only one hundred thousand. I was so disgusted that I decided to fly out to Sarawak to investigate on the spot. By terms of the royal wills of Sarawak my uncle had no right to give away the land without consulting me. He ignored this by claiming that he considered me unfit to rule.

"So I started out to Sarawak and discovered the British Government wouldn't hear of my visiting my own land. Said I was an undesirable alien. I fooled them by skipping to America and hopping a chance plane out to Manila. Government had me tailed and when I landed, there was a proper functionary warning me to go back to England.

"Instead I beat my way to Hong Kong where a stuffy colonial chap told me I'd not be permitted to land in Singapore unless I gave assurances not to visit Sarawak or even speak about it. I trapped the silly bounder into putting these restrictions of freedom in writing and cabled them off to London. There was a proper row in Parliament. Freedom of speech and all that.

"So I finally reached Singapore. But then I was stopped. Sarawak lies just over there. But I couldn't get to it. So Sarawak came to me. Loyal subjects filtered across the South China Sea and brought me proof that five of the men who had voted for cession to England—the vote was 19-16—had been bribed. I learned further that most of the natives wanted me to return as their true Rajah.

"Then things took a devilish turn. Regrettable. Government sent in a colonial governor and the natives promptly stabbed him to death. Hot-heads not connected with my group had done it. Deplorable show.

"Of course, after that Government was more determined than ever that I keep out of Sarawak, where things were going badly. Communists grew stronger. Indonesians filtered into the colony and started to claim it. And Chinese merchants began to look to communist China for guidance.

"This put me in a frightful position. On the one hand, I am morally convinced that Britain played me a foul trick. They tried the same thing here in Malaya, but the natives made them back down. No colonial status for Malays. I was the one on whom the trick worked.

"But on the other hand, no sensible and patriotic Englishman can study the paralyzing events in Asia without realizing that only by a gal-lant and concerted effort can anything be salvaged. I served in the Indian Army and I know what obedience is. You close the ranks.

"So this morning I had a final talk with the authorities and told them I was throwing in the sponge. I relinquished all claim to the title Rajah. I don't abandon one jot of my moral position. But I do submit that as between a communist Sarawak and a free British colony I must in honor choose the latter."

The last of the great white rajahs of Sarawak sips his exile's beer and stares across the sea. "It's amusing. In all of Asia the white man is being tossed out. Colored peoples will have none of him. Yet I'm the only white man the colored people want. So the whites throw me out.

"Fortunately my mother is an heiress of the Huntley and Palmer bis-cuit fortunes. I have enough to live on for a while. But it's hell stopping here almost in smelling distance of home.

"And it's most curious that I should be talking to an American, be-cause the most telling blow against me in Parliament came when the Labour blokes pointed out that Britain didn't care much one way or the other about Sarawak, but that America would never tolerate a white rajah in a colored country. One of your constitutional experts recently wrote me that legally you take no objection to color at all. Legally you could have a Negro for President. He said there'd be no objection to a white man ruling a Negro country. It's all bewildering."

When he drove me to my quarters that last night of his term as Rajah he laughed at the flag of Sarawak as it fluttered from the hood of his car. "I don't think I will take it down, after all. Somehow I feel that one of these days I'll be called home to Sarawak. It *is* my home, you know."

Malaya is the most vulnerable country in Asia today. It is split four ways. Its population is divided between Chinese who have recently over-run the peninsula and Malays who invaded it some thousand years ago. The indigenous Sakai have almost disappeared.

Malaya is also split on religion, the Malays being ardent Muslims and the Chinese indifferent Buddhists. As will be seen later, this is an era of resurgent Islam and Malaya's Muslims are excited at the prospect of a spiritual federation with their fellow religionists.

Malaya is also divided on communism, many Chinese and some Malays adhering openly to the movement. While I was in the country, rural Chinese communists murdered an average of three white planters a week while city communists averaged a policeman every other week. The fifth column is stronger in Malaya than in any other country I visited.

Finally Malaya is split on nationalism. Most young Malay liberals hope for an ultimate union with Indonesia. If this materializes the union might help stabilize Southeast Asia. But since Islamic nationalism threatens to run wild, the proposed union might become a cancerous force. There are other Malays who work for a joint Malay-Chinese democracy, although what would preserve such a nation from absorption by Chinese communism no one explains. And some idealists envisage a strictly Malay state under the general spiritual leadership of India, but this seems highly impractical today because of geographic and religious differences. Meanwhile the Chinese say nothing. And in the long run they will determine what happens in Malaya.

By Asiatic standards Malaya is underpopulated with only 5,800,000 inhabitants, 45 per cent Chinese, 38 per cent Malays. The country's disproportionate importance in the world arises from its princely wealth in rubber and tin, export of those two items alone accounting for more dollar income to the British Empire than all other empire exports. Malaya is therefore a land which the Chinese communists would like to have. It is a nation whose independence we ought to encourage.

The Chinese, however, look like the winners. They control Singapore, which is 78 per cent Chinese. They also control primitive mountain areas where their marauders are beginning to prevent rubber production. And they dominate business, since Malays—like most Muslims—have seen no good reason to ape the European in his servitude to commerce.

In time of trouble the Chinese could wreck Malaya. If they ever have to choose between a resurgent communist China and a petty Malay na-

tional state it seems probable they would side with China. They thus
form a potential fifth column of the gravest importance. Only America's
challenge to the communists in Korea prevented China from pushing
down on Malaya. If the push had once started Malaya's tin and rubber
would now be in communist control.

Few Americans realize the enormous advantage China has if she once
starts to run wild in Asia. In almost every nation, every city, every island
from Burma eastward to Tahiti there is a Chinese enclave, many of
whose members remain fanatically loyal to their homeland regardless of
what government happens to be ruling at the moment. Probably not
fewer than 8,000,000 Chinese expatriates live in Southeast Asia (compared to only 2,000,000 Japanese who lived overseas when war started
in 1941). Furthermore, China, like Mussolini's Italy, refuses to relinquish
claim on such nationals, even if they accept citizenship elsewhere. And,
finally, Chinese religion and custom demand that good Chinese return at
last to their homeland for burial. The pull of China is enormous. Precise
figures are difficult to obtain, but a responsible estimate shows 2,500,000
in Thailand; 1,900,000 in Indonesia; 300,000 in Burma; and 120,000
in the Philippines.

More significant than mere numbers is the dominant role played by
the Chinese in Asia's economic life. They control nine out of ten rice
mills in Thailand, eight out of ten in Indo-China and the Philippines.
They serve as bankers, wholesale merchants and shippers. They constitute Asia's most powerful entrepreneur class.

Why then should they fool around with communism? Many of them
don't. In fact, some observers predict that Southeast Asia's Chinese will
be just like Hawaii's or New York's, loyal to their adopted countries.
Certainly they have every economic, social and political reason to avoid
communism.

But two powerful factors lure the alien Chinese toward support of
homeland communism. Agents from Peking have moved into every
Asiatic city, assuring the coolie who earns $3, "When communism takes
over you have nothing to fear. It's the big shot making $30 we're after."
They tell the latter, "Men like you won't even notice the change. It's
the big fellows making $300 we're gunning for." They reassure that
group by confiding that only those making $3,000 will be affected by
communism, and finally they convince the man making $3,000,000 that
only the very rich need worry. Incredible as this seems, it works. Many
Chinese in the near-millionaire bracket support communism!

The second factor is a natural but perverse pride in all Chinese over
the sudden emergence of their homeland as a leading world power. As

a Bangkok merchant told me, "For 100 years everybody makes fun of China. Kick her around. Now China big and rough. People stop making fun of us." And he cheered on the very force that might ultimately destroy him.

The fact that communist China is tied down in Korea has granted Malaya breathing time. Wealthy from her rich stores of tin and rubber, she has an economic margin of safety. Also, many responsible Chinese and Malay citizens are working to create a unified, non-communist state. In the meantime the British are as effective and acceptable as any umpire can ever be. True, they will no doubt attempt to hang on after the hour of departure is at hand, but they will have left behind a most honorable record of men trying to do a job.

When the great change does come, whether by upheaval or peacefully, I am sure that some sensation-mongering journalist will cable from Singapore, "As the world crumbled I stood in the Raffles bar and watched the last Englishman having his gin and bitters, oblivious to the ruin outside."

I think I understand how that Englishman will feel at that moment. My wife and I were in Singapore when a minor riot broke out not far from the Raffles. Some people were killed and for an ugly moment it looked as if the trouble might become general. Then it subsided. We had an appointment on the other side of the riot area. So when the noise had quieted down we dressed, had a gin and bitters, called a pedicab, and set out for our appointment. There was no use moping at home. We had done what we could in the world to prevent race riots and if Singapore blew up in our faces it was too damned bad.

INDONESIA

IF A STRANGER EVER HAD JUST CAUSE TO DISLIKE A COUNTRY, I HAD SUCH cause in Indonesia. When I applied for a visa I was told to come back in two days. In the interval a new landing tax had been assessed, and when I pointed out that I had asked for my visa earlier—indeed, it had already been authorized—I was told I must pay the heavy tax.

In addition Indonesia demands an additional $40 visitor's tax, returnable if you leave the country within 30 days and return to the city from which you originally departed for Indonesia. But I had left from Singapore and was headed for Bangkok. This was irregular and I must forfeit my deposit.

When I finally reached Djakarta all passengers were subjected to an arbitrary delay of two hours in baking quarters, pompous red tape in processing, and a gestapo-like search. Officials in Djakarta seemed determined to be as arrogant and insulting as the consular men in Singapore.

I was about to lose my temper when an Indian sighed and remarked, "Goodness, this is almost as bad as entering New York."

When I staggered through the customs ordeal I was informed that Djakarta was the most overcrowded city in the world and that I had been lucky to get quarters in one of the best hotels. It was a fearful place with one threadbare towel per room. After anyone bathed the sorrowful towel was left to weep in the sunlight, from which the next bather recovered it. The food was dreadful and scarcely enough to live on. The rates were high.

When the Indonesian Government heard of my arrival I was summoned by a press officer and told there would be no need for me to talk with any Indonesians. He was ready to tell me all I needed to know. I said I preferred to talk with people first hand. He said that could not be permitted. I said that was O.K. with me. I would go back to the hotel and sleep and then base my report on what the Dutchman had told me in Singapore. I said some other things and he grudgingly granted me certain permissions.

My life in Djakarta was almost unpleasant. There were constant rumors of riots and threats of retaliations against all Europeans. Local hotheads boasted that one of these days President Sukarno was going on the radio to deliver a real rabble-rousing speech against foreigners "and then we'll see." Curfew came at midnight, but most sensible aliens, especially the Chinese, stayed completely indoors after dark. Europeans with hill homes not far from steaming Djakarta had been unable to visit them for seven months, for brigands on the highway murdered white people.

Once I was returning to my hotel at noon when not far away a motorcyclist approached on the main thoroughfare. A policeman challenged him. Apparently the cyclist did not hear. So the policeman raised a machine gun and blasted the traffic violator. Passers-by hauled the body into a driveway and traffic resumed. I was warned, "If a policeman calls to you in this country, stop! All their guns are on the ready."

Indonesia, having won her freedom, was abusing it. She was mistreating the Dutch just as sorely as the nineteenth-century Dutch had mistreated the Indonesians. Unilaterally she had revoked a treaty with her own state of South Moluccas. And instead of expressing any appreciation for America's crucial help during the days when independence was won, she rejected America and refused even to allow United States ships bound for Korea to put into Indonesian ports.

Djakarta was one of the unloveliest places I have ever visited. Only with bitterness could I recall my happier memories of this city when it was known as Batavia. I was sorely tempted to flee this unhappy land and report that Indonesia was a murderous place.

Instead I found that every shred of sympathy and identification in my body allied me with this new nation. Spiritually I became an Indonesian. I discovered that inwardly I was urging this youthful country on as one urges on some tow-headed boy who has forgotten his lines in a Boy Scout play. I wanted Indonesia to win. If I were a young man in Asia today I would prefer being an Indonesian. The following pages tell why.

A

GRAND

OLD

MAN

AT 36

The single most astonishing thing about Indonesia is the youth of its rulers. Every leading official is under 49. The oldest man in the cabinet is 47. The premier is 38. And the grand old man of the independence movement led the Government when he was 36.

Sutan Sjahrir is a handsome, slightly pot-bellied intellectual whose brilliant mind has provided the philosophical structure of the new nation. Today, at 41, he is the lodestar for most of the best young men in the country, and his spiritual power is enormous.

"I am somewhat different from the other leaders and therefore somewhat under suspicion. I alone did not collaborate with the Japanese. I alone have never called for the complete expulsion of the Dutch. I owe my education and even my mental processes to them, for they picked me out as a promising student and sent me to their university at Leyden.

"But when I came back and they saw that I had developed a mind of my own they promptly threw me into jail. The charge? 'Sutan Sjahrir has conducted himself so that if other Indonesians did the same they might end by contesting Dutch rule.'

"Have you ever heard of Tanah Merah prison in New Guinea? Perhaps the worst in the world, surrounded by jungle and swamps. They sent me there for nine years, along with criminals and murderers of every description.

"Fortunately I was there only a year when out of common decency they moved me to Banda, where I had little to complain of. From Banda I even sent the Government long reports predicting exactly what has since happened. It was in Banda that I formulated my philosophy of social advance.

"It is this. In a new country where 80 per cent of the population were never allowed to read or write one must start first with a few basic things. Education. A workable system of government. Health. The rise of capable leaders. Development of a sense of responsibility. Those are the first requirements and basic to them is a philosophical understanding of men.

"That's why I left the Government. I knew I could do more good on the outside, stressing these fundamentals. If I were enmeshed in actual governing I would be bowed down by too many immediate decisions.

"I would explain our country this way. Under Dutch rule any promising young man found himself in jail. This was not too bad because in jail he found all the other young men who would one day rule Indonesia. Why are there no old men in our Government? None of the old men got into the jails while the big plans were being formulated.

"When the Japanese came Indonesia had an astonishing awakening. The Japs used all the jail-men in setting up a puppet government. This was a very good thing because it taught us how to establish the forms of government which the Dutch had kept secret from us.

"I believe I alone stood out against the Japs. I was sure they would be defeated within three years, but men like Sukarno and Hatta thought they would last for at least ten, maybe forever. Therefore somebody had to co-operate with them.

"So this puppet government was established and for two years the future leaders of Indonesia went through the motions of governing a state. They were given a constitution, which later became the constitution of Indonesia. They had a system of governmental organization, which we kept for our own use. The effect of Japanese occupation must never be underestimated. It showed us we did not need the Dutch.

"When the Japs were defeated we swung their puppet government right into the full arena of Indonesian life, but we expanded it, for it was a structure that could have continued to exist only if the Japanese held all the real power.

"For example, there was no provision for a cabinet or a parliament. Worst of all, there was no responsible premier to execute the laws. So we made Mr. Sukarno a president in the French style, the figure about whom the entire nation rallies. And to my surprise the leaders asked me to become the first premier, in whom the power of the government would actually reside. We made many other necessary changes. I would say that now we are a real democracy.

"The question then arose as to our freedom from Holland. I was sent to the United Nations to plead our case. We were victorious for two reasons. In prison I had learned patience and I worked hard to present my ideas simply, without intellectual or nationalistic arrogance. But even so I would have accomplished little if the Dutch had not sent some of the most stupid, aloof and arrogant men I have ever known. We kept our mouths shut and let the Dutch talk. They argued themselves to death. No one could hear their stupidities without knowing they had no moral right to govern any colony.

"After that I served only as ambassador-at-large, a post I still hold but about which I do nothing. My job is to teach young men what efficient government means, what a good police force is, the relationship between an army and the state. I tell them how free men should live within a free community."

Sutan Sjahrir lives in a modest, slightly broken-down house in a noisy street far from the palatial residences of other government officials. The most memorable furniture in the house is the young men who come there day after day. They make it distinguished.

"We have three parties. The Nationalist led by Hatta is first in power. The Muslim led by Hatsir is first in numbers. The Socialist led by me is first in brains. When I became premier I was embarrassed by communist support but later on the Marshall Plan split them off and I wasn't sorry to see them go. Now they don't carry much weight.

"But I'm afraid that if China captures all of Asia we are doomed. The one thing we pray for in Indonesia is time. If we have time the young men you saw leaving my office will have a chance to provide the country with a good government. It has been said that Indonesia is a nation with lots of generals and many foot soldiers, but no captains. How could this be otherwise when the five-star generals are in their forties? If we have time, I shall provide some of the captains.

"That is why I never mention New Guinea or Malaya. And I think politicians who do simply divert the attention of the people from jobs that need to be done here at home. What Indonesia needs is not more land in New Guinea, but a better land here at home. Right now we need men with low voices and high ideals."

I told Sjahrir that nevertheless I was worried about Indonesia's determination to get control of Western New Guinea. I said that I could foresee the day when possession of Western New Guinea would lead to an attack on Eastern New Guinea and ultimately upon Australia. At that time, I reasoned, America would side with Australia and there would be war.

Sjahrir did not avoid the problem. "I realize the possibility of such dynamics. But I absolutely believe that before such a time comes to pass the entire world will have seen the stupidity of any more conquest. There will be one government, one common interest. That is what I work for. For the day when Australia need have no fear of Indonesia and we need have no fear of China. It is my job to see to it that when such a day comes, Indonesia will be mature enough to find a respectable place in that world government."

Sutan Sjahrir talked for some time, a quiet man with enormous force and enviable good humor. He was interested in all sorts of things and as he spoke I kept thinking of Thomas Jefferson.

HERCULES

WOULD

HAVE

SHIVERED

When you first see Mr. Suwito—like many other Indonesians including President Sukarno he uses only one name—you are astounded that one so frail should have tackled such a monstrous job. He is frail, quick-eyed and dedicated. He is engaged in educating 78,000,000 people, more than 80 per cent of whom cannot read or write.

"Our best agency is radio. We buy thousands of them from America. We hope to place one in each village, but for the present we have to put them only in certain villages, where there has been political trouble or where there is no meeting hall of any kind.

"The head man calls his people together. He can usually read and he tells his villagers what they are going to hear. Then he turns on the radio and the villagers hear a question-and-answer period. We try to guess every single question the troublemakers are asking. Then we try to answer it. But our biggest trouble is trying to find enough technicians to keep our sets working.

"Films are next best. We have mobile units with their own generators, screens, amplifying systems and projectors. We use mostly Indonesian films on such things as health, disease control, what a parliament is, and how to be a good citizen. If we hear of a satisfactory American film we borrow it through the United States Information Service. But we keep our own narrator who puts an Indonesian interpretation onto what the film shows.

"We do that with all films. The narrator stands by the screen and tells jokes and makes the people happy and explains what the people should do when they have finished seeing the film. Sometimes he is very specific, especially on health questions. You'd be surprised at what our people don't know.

"Our film trucks are popular and we shift them about from place to place. People will walk miles to see a film and we think we are accomplishing some good. But I wish we had more films that explain politics.

"Our next trick is probably the most spectacular. In Java we have traditional roadside puppet shows. A traveling troupe puts up a white screen and a flickering lamp to make shadows. A gamelan orchestra plays while women take seats on one side of the screen where they are permitted to see only the shadows while men sit on the other side and see the actual puppets. It's always been like that.

"Then the narrator starts a long account of what the play is going to deal with. This may seem ridiculous because everyone has seen the same play a hundred times, but the narrator is able to bring in local allusions and dirty jokes and lots of good laughs.

"The stories are strange, all imported from Hindu India. And we're strictly Muslim." (I said it was like Americans who listen only to Italian opera and German symphonies. Mr. Suwito said, "I'm glad to know that.") "Anyway, we're Indonesian Muslims but we love Indian Hindu plays.

"The characters are always the same. Kings and nobles and princesses in trouble. And they all look the same. Long-nosed, ratlike faces, flat-chested, immensely long-armed. The only difference between a man and a woman is that the man has a moustache.

"But in the course of time we've added three or four Indonesian servants for the Hindu kings and these are the really popular characters. Their wit and bravery solve the problems. So it's always the Indonesians who save the day.

"Well, we've taken these shadow plays and made little changes. The villain is now a European colonial power. The heroine becomes enslaved Indonesia. The hero is a young Indonesian revolutionary. And the story tells how he overthrows the colonial villain and sets Indonesia free. The people in the villages cheer. And we hope they learn something about freedom."

Like all Indonesian leaders, Mr. Suwito is very young, perhaps no more than twenty-five, yet he helps to spend a huge budget trying to bring political ideas to millions upon millions of people who will never learn to read.

"I used to teach school. You might think therefore that my first desire would be to print a whole lot of books. That would be useless. The best we can hope for is to make our people understand the big ideas of government, what we call the five principles. Belief in God, Nationalism, Humanity, Sovereignty of the People, Social Justice.

"We do print little booklets on these subjects for the head men, trying to explain a few simple ideas. What is a state? Why do we need a president? What is democracy? What is a human right? You see we keep to very fundamental things. If the idea is too complex the head man gives up."

As Mr. Suwito talks you study the map behind his head and you begin to grasp vaguely the enormousness of the job Indonesia is undertaking. From one end of the country to the other is farther than from New York to Berlin. A letter from the capital city to certain jungle villages will take three months. There are no schools, no newspapers, no communications throughout much of the country. Hercules would have shivered at the job of bringing this nation into full political being within the space of two years!

"Yet I learned all I know in Indonesia. I studied English from a book and then went to movies to learn how it was pronounced. I am excited by how much we are accomplishing.

"And the good humor of the people. If we have a big meeting in some village we start with songs and then some dancing and some dialogue between two funny people. Some of our jokes would make you laugh, I am sure. When we have the audience laughing out loud the narrator begins to talk about politics, but he never talks too long. An orchestra plays and we have more jokes. Then the narrator says something more. A meeting in a hill village can be filled with laughing."

Mr. Suwito has no doubt but that in two or three generations his people will be able to read and write. "They'll know what good government is. Until we started nobody had thought Indonesians were capable of learning anything. That was colonialism. Today we know they can learn anything. That's democracy."

I guessed that Mr. Suwito weighed about 110 pounds. Not much for a kid who was making believe he could out-perform Hercules.

IRIAN,

IRIAN!

One of the most powerful married couples in East Asia today are the attractive, intelligent young Diahs, of Djakarta in Indonesia. Muhamad

Diah is a handsome young man in his early thirties, editor of the country's most important newspaper, the daily *Merdeka.*

His wife, Herewati Diah, is the pretty and determined young editor of the equally influential weekly *Merdeka,* the Indonesian counterpart of *Time* Magazine. In addition to editing these journals, the Diahs own a good deal of the stock and also serve as presidents of their respective boards. Definitely, they are young people on the way up.

Their use of the word *Merdeka* as the title of their publications is symbolic and also very good business, for it is the word that typifies all that is best in the very young Republic of Indonesia. In Djakarta the four principal streets are all known as Merdeka. Buildings are Merdeka this and Merdeka that. When President Sukarno rises to speak the crowd roars Merdeka! Merdeka! The word means freedom, and Indonesia gained her freedom the hard way.

Muhamad Diah says, "It would be more correct to say that the crowds used to shout Merdeka. Now, whenever President Sukarno appears in public everyone shouts Irian, Irian! Because our nation has solemnly decided to make the Dutch turn Irian over to us. If they don't, there will be grave trouble.

"Irian is the old and proper name for New Guinea. Why should a great island be known by some alien name slapped upon it by some chance European sea captain? The name is Irian.

"Our claim to Irian is irrefutable. It was once part of the Dutch East Indies. Indonesia is the legal successor to the Dutch East Indies. Therefore Irian should be a part of Indonesia. For the Dutch to hold back Irian is an international crime. We are sworn to correct that crime."

Mrs. Diah, with an M.A. from Columbia and a perfect mastery of English says, "Let's not talk about Irian any more. Our title to it is beyond question." She offers a copy of her magazine *Merdeka* and it deals exclusively with Irian. Indicative of this powerful young woman's wit is the main photograph. An insolent Dutch imperialist lolls back in a native canoe with a palm-frond palanquin over his head while natives paddle him up an Irian river. The picture is entitled "The Tuan Besar."

"An American won't catch the meaning of Tuan Besar," Mrs. Diah laughs. "The Dutchmen made us call them that. It means the great one. Or the all-powerful. We used it with the picture to remind our readers of what we escaped but what Irian still suffers under." She looks down at the pitiful picture and says, "Of course, all the world now knows that colonialism is dead."

I listened with careful attention and not a little fear as these determined young people talked. I knew Irian well, and the problem posed by it is one of transcendent importance to the United States. The Diahs had been honest with me, so I tried to be the same. I said bluntly, "You'll get Irian, then you'll gradually steal Eastern New Guinea from Australia. Then, because you have 980 people to the square mile and Australia has fewer than 3, and because Australia will be only a few miles away from you, lying there rich and empty, you'll have to invade Australia. And that will mean war with America."

Mr. Diah sucked in his breath as if to say, "That's what I thought you came to ask about." Then he said, "Not a single responsible Indonesian has made any claim to Australia's part of Irian. Furthermore, we are not bothered about the stupid way Australians handle their racial problems. If they insist upon insulting all of Asia with their silly White Australia policy, Indonesia will not have to bother with them. They will destroy themselves. And if you should be dragged into a war against all of Asia merely because of Australia you would be very foolish indeed. We are your friends. You must cast your lot with us and work to understand us.

"Therefore you must understand that Indonesia has no aspirations beyond Irian. We don't want Malaya, even though the Malays speak our language, share our religion and were once part of our empire. But Malaya has to gain its own freedom from the British. Then we can talk with them. In the meantime we will be fully occupied with our own problems.

"The same is true of British Borneo. It is filled with our people and is carved out of our land. But we have no aspirations against it. We will have our hands full getting our own house in order.

"You ask about Portuguese Timor. Now here is a completely Indonesian island cut in half, with imperial Europeans controlling our people. But we are not fighting Portugal, are we? All we want is Irian."

I said, "For the present all you want is Irian. But the people after you, they'll want Malaya and Timor and Borneo."

Mrs. Diah said, "No one should speak for the future. But if you read our journals you'll see that Irian is ready to co-operate peacefully with anyone, even the Dutch."

It is difficult to convey the bitterness which brilliant young Indonesians like the Diahs feel against the Dutch. Mr. Diah says, "They controlled Java for more than three centuries and they left 92 per cent illiteracy. They sent a few of our brightest young people to their universities in Holland, but if the students showed an inclination to patriotism, into jail they went for life. They robbed and ruined and plundered our islands. And they gave us nothing in return.

"You may find it difficult to believe that they did not even give us a language. The Japanese did that. When they arrived only a few Indonesians could write their own language. But the Japs made us stop using Dutch and in that way we were forced to learn the language you see today.

"Gradually we are erasing the ridiculous Dutch spellings. It isn't Soekarno or Soekaboemi any more. It's what it always should have been. Sukabumi. It's also Djawa, not Java. We have other original devices, too. In Indonesian we have many duplicated syllables and even whole groups of syllables. The word *surat* is a letter, but *suratsurat* is letters. We print it *surat2*. The word *satu2nja* means that you say the *satu* twice."

Mrs. Diah interrupts. "You must not think that we loved the Japanese. They taught us much, but they were also very cruel. They collected shiploads of young girls for university training in Japan, then dumped them in places like Rabaul and Singapore for the soldiers' special uses. The fact is that we want no masters, not Japanese or Russian or Chinese or Dutch. We want freedom. We fought for it and we want it."

But as we drove home through the incredibly ugly commercial section of Djakarta Mrs. Diah waved her hand contemptuously at the massive, inappropriate Dutch architecture. It was heavy and brutal and uninspired and she said, "We haven't had time to tear such buildings down." Then she laughed at her own melodrama and said forcefully, "Please don't write that we hate the Dutch. We don't. Many wonderfully good Dutchmen are working for our Government right now. But when they were our lords they did such horrible things to Djawa. We must erase all those things."

When I reached my hotel I saw that the day's issue of Mr. Diah's *Merdeka* announced that President Sukarno was going to deliver a flaming oration on the crime of Irian, and an English lady said, "Oh dear, I hope he doesn't. That might be the spark that would set off the next batch of riots. The ones all Europeans fear. We'd all be murdered and thrown into the canals, the way the Chinese were."

But Sukarno spoke and there were no riots, but all through the city you could see those bannered slogans, "Irian, Irian!"

THE

CRYING

DUTCHMAN

There is an ancient legend of the Dutchman who sinned and who was condemned to a life of endless wandering across stormy seas. Today there is another kind of condemned Dutchman and you find him in strange ports throughout the East.

"After we were kicked out of Java"—he calls it Yava—"my wife and I went back to Holland for a try. We couldn't live there. After you've lived in the big-spirited East you can't coop yourself up in Holland. It's too religious, too parochial, just too damned unpleasant.

"We couldn't eat the food. And the family insisted upon dining at six. We used to eat anywhere between nine and midnight in Yava. And we couldn't get excited about local politics. Our friends watched how our minds wandered and they knew we were thinking of Yava. In time every-one in Holland got to dislike us as much as we disliked them.

"What we missed was the East. If you live out here for more than a year you're lost. You miss the wonderful hot weather, the rich food, the dark hot nights, and the blue sky. Your mind is forever changed. And you cannot leave."

The Dutchman looked down at his glass. He was working in an English office for pittance a week. "I used to own a vast plantation in Yava. I would wake in the morning and feel like a real man. I would see mists rising and feel the sun pulling sweat from my arms. That was a good life.

"We built railroads to ship the rubber. Factories to work it. We accomplished such things on Yava as the world will be proud of for generations to come. We made that land one of the richest on earth. It supported a thousand people to the mile and there were no murders or plagues."

The Dutchman sat twirling his glass, staring at the meaningless patterns its wet bottom made on the marble table. He had massive hands. "I still don't understand exactly what happened. We governed Yava well. But the Japanese conquered us. That was no disgrace. They conquered your Philippines, too. But in Yava they established a puppet government out of all the scoundrels who had been causing us trouble for years. Listen to what I say. Every leading Indonesian politician today served the Japanese like a slave during the war. No exceptions. They proved themselves to be liars and cheats and frauds. Read this official whitewash of the present premier: 'During the Japanese occupation Natsir's basic and abiding interest in educational affairs led him to take up the task of Head of the Educational Affairs Department for three years.' A fancy way of spelling traitor.

"All right. Let's admit he had to do this to keep his neck, although not one Dutchman did such a thing. What passes understanding is what America then did. When Yava was freed America and England would

128 INDONESIA

not give Holland ships to transport our troops to put down the Japanese puppets. Instead you encouraged them to become established.

"Next Australian communists refused to permit any Dutch ships to sail for Yava with aid for the legal government. In the black years to come when Indonesia threatens Australia, when Indonesia and Asia threaten California and Seattle, remember that you Americans and the Australian communists dug your own graves. This was all your wish."

The Dutchman puts his glass aside and you see that beads of sweat have broken out upon his forehead. "I went back to Yava like a licked dog and tried to work my land, but no respecting man could stomach the tricks they pulled on me. And what I saw made me sicker still. The machinery we so patiently built is broken and rusting. The great electric plants we engineered are being ruined. Damned fools have destroyed all that we built.

"The Army is totally corrupt and rents its guns at night to brigands. Your newspapermen have been killed on main thoroughfares. The rural officials are completely debauched so that everyone tries to squeeze his way into the safety of the cities, where the officials are even more crooked. Soon there will be epidemics and death and starvation. There will be real chaos.

"Well, I stuck it out for two years. I swallowed their insults, obeyed their filthy stealing laws and paid the enormous bribes. But when I saw this glorious land slowly going to rot I had to leave.

"The present Government may last another three years. Then will come great religious riots during which most white men will be murdered. A fascist religious state will follow. Then the Chinese will take over in the cities and the whole forsaken land will go communist. In Yava there will be destruction and mass death.

"It's there now. Each night there are murders. People are afraid to leave the cities even in daylight. The Government controls perhaps one-third of the land. The rest is bandit country where a white man is apt to be shot on sight. This is what the Japanese puppets have accomplished."

The Dutchman is absolutely relentless in his recital of Java's predicted history. Although much of what he says is true, he will never admit that men like him deserve any share of the blame. The muscles on his neck stand out.

"They are good-for-nothing stupid people. The dogs aren't capable of an education. The few who were we sent to college, in Holland. I could shout with rage when I read in English papers Doctor this and Doctor that. Where did they get such titles? From Dutch universities, their expenses paid by Dutch money, and they brought their education back to undermine our rule.

"When communism was fashionable, they were communists. When Japanese fascism was popular, that's what they were. Then American dollars bought them to be staunch democrats. Next they'll be devout Muslims killing everyone who isn't. And pretty soon they'll be communists again. A fine thing you damned meddlers have done. You've destroyed Yava."

And then you see that the despairing Dutchman is crying.

OBSERVATIONS

If Korea is a test of America as a nation, Indonesia is a test of Americans as individuals. Do we really believe in democracy? Do we really believe in self-determination and government by the people?

Few Americans visit Indonesia today without instinctively wishing that the Dutch were back in control. Say, the way things were in 1935. There were no serious uprisings. American ships were not scorned in Javanese ports. No American newspapermen were murdered on the highway. And the investor's dollar was safe and returned up to 12 per cent annually. Those were the good old days. The Indonesian knew his place and there was none of this jabbering about freedom.

Comparing 1935 with today's near anarchy one begins to rationalize that perhaps even the Indonesian himself was better off under Dutch rule. True, there was political injustice then, but if the Dutch had been given time, sooner or later reforms would have been launched. There were many economic wrongs in 1935, but you could trust time to show the Dutch that these should be eliminated. Many indefensible aspects of colonialism persisted in 1935, but any day now the Dutch were going to initiate Christian equality.

Rubbish! If American slavery had not been terminated once and for all in 1865, there would be good-souled men today in Atlanta and New York who would be saying, "There are some injustices, yes, but any day now slaves are going to get a square deal."

The evil fact about colonialism in Asia is that the laudable reforms were always just about to take place. They rarely did. There was only one alternative: Indonesian revolt and Indian revolt and Indo-Chinese revolt and general Asiatic revolt.

We helped create Asia as it is today. We must accept that creation and co-operate with its people as they work toward something better. Indonesia is a good place to start. We must understand this mighty nation. We must work patiently with it on Indonesian terms. And we must dedicate ourselves to the accomplishment—after present temporary annoyances have passed—of lasting friendship between the Republic of Indonesia and the Republic of the United States. This course will have difficulties. But we know that the old days are gone. We have a chance to co-operate in working out something better. To do so we must understand a few basic facts.

Indonesia today is an oligarchy. Its government is in the hands of a few men who perpetuate themselves in office. There have been no general elections. The present Government is merely an extension of the puppet government established by the Japanese as an insult to the Dutch. As in every oligarchy there is an almost irresistible centripetal force tending to crystallize the present Government into a fascistic monolithic state.

In these respects Indonesia typifies most of Asia. Oligarchs rule the continent. There have been no general elections in China, India, Pakistan, Burma or Indo-China. After the turmoil of war the ablest men available were self-appointed to govern these nations. This does not mean that the oligarchs are venal. Most of them rule well. But power breeds a love of power and we should anticipate throughout Asia an inevitable tendency of the present oligarchical powers to become fascist states.

Why does Asia prefer oligarchs? Why have there been no general elections? For one simple reason. Up to 90 per cent of the people are illiterate, and people who cannot read cannot rule. Since they are illiterate they cannot understand words like democracy, elect, judiciary, or parliament. And modern democratic life depends upon such terms. Since an illiterate cannot know his nation's history it is impossible to judge whether a given politician conforms to the nation's historic ideals. It is almost impossible to have a responsible government where there are no schools. I used to be a schoolteacher but I never even dimly sensed the importance of my job until I went to Asia. The single most significant difference between America and Asia is our public-school system. In years to come, when Asia has acquired one, there will be about the same difference between an Asian and an American as there now is between an Italian in Rome and an American in Dallas.

The world is lucky that for the present the oligarchs honestly prefer representative government. Because they led the fight for independence they have inherited office. This was natural, for these men are true patriots comparable to George Washington or Thomas Jefferson, who also inherited office. They do not want to establish dictatorships. I am convinced that men like Sjahrir, Sukarno, Nehru, and Nu of Burma would, like George Washington, gladly surrender power right now if they could look forward to the kind of self-governing nation Washington could contemplate in 1797. Excepting the dictators of communist China who subordinate the interests of their people to the pattern of a communist revolution, the present oligarchs of Asia are men whom America can support with honor.

At the same time we must remember that inevitably the course of history in Asia will be away from the oligarchs and toward the people. When the benevolent oligarch Chiang Kai-shek failed to keep up with his people they turned against him. Should the oligarch Nehru fail to keep abreast of his people, they will desert him. Ultimately in Asia we must side with the masses of the people. For they always win.

Our policy in Asia therefore faces a most difficult task. We must support the oligarchs—and really support them with our faith, money, and if necessary planes—just as long as they provide Asia with responsible government. But we must always remember that America will never possess enough money or planes to keep one Asiatic oligarch in power after the people of his country no longer want him.

Here is a problem in faith and timing. We must base our faith on the people of Asia. Sooner or later we must be ready to shift our support from the benevolent oligarchs to the responsible people.

The faint hearted among us will always look back. Today many Americans huddling within the confines of Djakarta are afraid of Sukarno and long for the safe old days of Dutch imperialism. Tomorrow those same Americans, confronted by the Indonesian people themselves, will yearn for the safe old days of Sukarno. At that moment, if America rejects the legitimate people of Indonesia some other nation like Russia will embrace them. If this occurs generally in Asia the Europe-Asia coalition will have become a fact and our encirclement will be at hand.

That is why I am for Indonesia today. I am for the young men trying to build a nation. I am for the schoolteachers trying to create literacy. I am for the men who harangue on the radio trying to build an electorate. I am even for the bewildered people who think that if they can only wrest Irian from Holland somehow everything will magically be better. I am for Indonesia because the quicker it becomes an integrated nation the better chance America has to build a permanent friendship with the people of that part of Asia.

In the meantime Americans must be patient. I wrote an essay on Indonesia in which I foresaw expropriation of American holdings in Indonesia. My editor, seeking to check such a statement, sent the manuscript to Indonesian officials in the United States. They were outraged! "This man doesn't know what he is talking about. Here is a malicious

man. Indonesia will never expropriate American property. We are even
passing special laws to protect American capital." I felt like a fool. Somewhere I had been misled. But three days later a new premier took office
in Djakarta, backed by a more radical bloc, and his first fiats were that
foreign capital must go.

We are going to see many strange things in Indonesia in the next few
years. I would gamble that nationalist leaders—forced by political necessity—will demand expropriation and expulsion of foreign interests. That
is the temper of the times. But when the political fiction of expropriation
has been carried out, Indonesia will still need our help.

At this time it will be tempting for outraged Americans to shout that
ungrateful Indonesia has betrayed us. There will be demands for retalia-
tion. But the same thing happened in Mexico and everything worked
out rather well. We remained firm friends with Mexico. We must remain
so with Indonesia.

There remains one crucial point to consider. Ultimately Asia and the
United States will face one another along an extended and potentially
explosive frontier. Alaska and Japan will be the northern anchors of that
face-to-face frontier with Formosa and the Philippines forming the central pillars. Australia will be the southern anchor.

To comprehend the strategical importance of Australia, Americans
should think of it as a fifty-first state, right after Alaska and Hawaii.
Australia exists today solely by virtue of the American Navy and Air
Force, a fact generally acknowledged in Australia with no disparage-
ment to Europe-occupied Great Britain and certainly no lessening of ties
to the British crown.

But crucial Australia, about the same size as the United States, has
only the population of New York City. Australia has 2.8 people to the
square mile. Indonesia has an enormous population which in Java
reaches the unheard of density of nearly 1,000 to the square mile. And
Indonesia is only 300 miles from Australia.

Sooner or later Indonesia will get Irian. Then the pressures on Australian New Guinea will become great, for Australia has not the people
to colonize New Guinea properly. And New Guinea is only 90 miles
from Australia.

Finally, in the early years of this century French and Dutch colonial
cupidity arranged a deal whereby thousands of Javanese were trans-
ported to New Caledonia for labor in the nickel mines. Offspring of
those Indonesian citizens are beginning to crowd New Caledonia, some
900 miles east of Australia. With their remarkable fecundity they will
probably duplicate in New Caledonia the Indians' absorption of Fiji,

where in a relatively few years the offspring of imported laborers out-numbered the native population.

Great empty Australia is thus threatened on three sides by Indonesians. For the present there is nothing to worry about, for Indonesia has neither an air force nor a navy. Two or three generations may pass somnolently. But ultimately Indonesian and American interests must clash in Australia.

That is why I am for Indonesia today. I want the present oligarchs to build a strong nation. I hope to see the day when a general election is held in Indonesia. I want a true republic down there. For if we are fast friends with such a nation we have a chance of working out our Southeast Asia problems. But if Indonesia runs wild and if we are unable to retain contact with her, then only disaster can result.

THAILAND

I HAD DECIDED NOT TO GO TO THAILAND, FOR OTHER MAJOR NATIONS seemed more important than this small self-governing land. But as I was preparing my itinerary a famous newspaperman rushed up and cried, "My God! I just heard you were planning to skip Siam!"

I replied that I had other more important work to do and his face became mock-ashen. He grabbed me as the Ancient Mariner must have intercepted the wedding guests and said, "If you miss Siam you miss Asia. Siam is the sanctuary in a troubled world. Siam is the air-conditioned room in hell. The padded cell in the insane asylum. Siam is all things to all men and its girls are the most beautiful in the Orient.

"Take the revolutions. In Siam they're very simple. The Army kicks the Navy out and then the Navy kicks the Army out. The revolution is always finished by breakfast so that everyone can spend a full day in his new office. Practically nobody gets killed except army or navy men and they fill their ranks by forced enlistments.

"I remember one particularly swift series of revolutions. I wired New York, 'Army's in again.' They wired back that I was to stop being a wise guy and submit full details. So I drafted a masterful cable but by the time I was through there'd been another revolution so I added at the end, 'Flash. Now it's Navy's ball again.'"

I interrupted the torrent of words and said I hadn't come to Asia to make fun of quaint customs. The famous newspaperman dropped my arm and said, "Look, chum! Who's making fun of whom? I love that crazy land. I love any country which in an atomic age can be perfectly screwball. In Bangkok they have one of the world's most beautiful post offices. Very modern. Eight different drop slots for letters. City Mail. Air Mail. Up Country Mail. Up Country Air Mail. Europe. Asia. North America. Africa. Then at five o'clock a little old man with a cart comes along and empties each box into one big pile."

I protested again that I wasn't in search of wacky yarns, but he said, "Damn it all, I'm not reciting these as ridiculous items. They prove that there's one nation left on earth that doesn't take itself too seriously. A Siamese friend of mine had been to Oxford and decided there ought to be better Anglo-Siamese relations, so he translated *Macbeth* into Siamese and put on a whing-ding performance. But no Siamese audience would tolerate a play without dancing, so when Lord and Lady Macbeth welcomed the king they were going to murder, there was a big dance, after which Mrs. Macbeth sang *Danny Boy*. I said to my friend that he had made some pretty substantial changes in the play, but he said he thought William Shakespeare was big enough to take it."

I said I wasn't interested in such stories and that anyway I understood the name of the country was Thailand. "Don't you believe it!" he cried. "There were two shipping companies. The Siamese Forwarding Company and the Siamese Shipping Company. When the nation changed its name to Thailand, the latter company became the Thailand Shipping Company overnight. But the first company kept on with its old name. You see the second company was owned by English money and they wanted to please the Government. Whereas the first company was owned by the Government and they said it would be ridiculous to change the name of a business firm just because the country had a new name.

"In 1941 when New Zealand declared war on Siam, which turned out to be a Japanese ally, the local government sent the declaration back to New Zealand and said they couldn't accept it. The name of the country was misspelled. So when it came time for a peace treaty they found none was necessary because Siam had never been at war with New Zealand.

"There was a problem with personal names, too. Siamese spelling had been worked out by two missionaries who had been to college. They decided that Siam should have the world's one scientific spelling system.

So the name Bipul isn't pronounced Bipple, it's Peebun. The B is P, the i is ee, the p is b, and the l is n. That's what the two geniuses decided was the world's best system.

"So I started to call Bipul Peebun in my dispatches and the office raised hell. Said names were to be spelled the way the Siamese spelled them. Some time later I received word that the Voice of America was going to send a special broadcast to Siam. I told all my Siamese friends and they listened, but the Voice of America didn't check on the pronunciations I'd sent in, and names like Peebun came out Bipple. Next morning my Siamese friends said, 'It was a lovely broadcast. Came in very strong. What country were they talking about?'

"Politics is very simple, too. There was this politico Pjumpbh. He double-crossed the British something fearful. But later on he reformed and I saw a confidential report in which the British Government kept referring to the New Pjumpbh. But at the bottom of the page some cynic had written in red ink, 'It is important to keep the distinction between the New Pjumpbh and the Old Pjumpbh. It was the Old Pjumpbh who so dastardly betrayed the British. The New Pjumpbh hasn't betrayed the British . . . yet.'

"But don't let my talk of politics obscure the fact that Siamese girls are the most beautiful in Asia. There's also the thieves' market where you go each morning to buy back what they stole from you the night before. They give you two quotations on a pair of stolen pants. Two dollars plain or three dollars with what was in the pockets.

"The Siamese census was something special, too. The United Nations asked every country in the world to conduct a census in some year ending in o. Well, the Siamese calendar ended in o in 1947, so they had a census. To do the job right they bought a whale of a lot of first-class IBM machines, the kind that handle the complete United States figures in about five weeks.

"Half a year went by, a whole year, a year and a half and still no census report. They sent a special investigator down to the IBM room to find out what was wrong. There, at the end of the line, they had one Chinese girl with an abacus. She was checking the machines' figures and was fourteen months behind schedule.

"But don't let this talk of business make you forget that the girls in Siam are adorable. You've got to be careful, though, when you take a bath. When you pull the plug out of the tub snakes and frogs come at you. But the snakes aren't poisonous, so it's really not too unpleasant.

"The story which explains Siam best was my interview with a high court official after the late King's death. This dignitary was trained in

Europe and had a fine command of logic. I said, 'The King was found dead. What happened? Was he murdered?'

"The official frowned and said, 'Murder, what an ugly word! Who in Siam would dare to murder the King? Who would want to do such a devilish thing? The King was a fine gentleman and a true friend of the people. Murder is one theory that can easily be dismissed in this case.'

"So I asked, 'What about suicide? They say the King was depressed because of the revolutions. Was his death suicide?'

"The official threw his hands over his face and cried, 'Suicide? That's the one thing it wasn't. Why should a man in the King's robust health and high spirits commit suicide? The very thought is repugnant. You would do Siam a great favor to put such thoughts out of your mind. Besides, no one could have inflicted such wounds upon himself. It's out of the question, it wasn't suicide.'

"Practically everything else had been eliminated so I asked, 'Then it was really death from natural causes? An illness, maybe?'

"The court official sighed and said sorrowfully, 'No, it wasn't illness either. To be sure, the court physician had announced that it was death from natural causes. Stomach trouble, the physician said. Upset stomach.' But this theory didn't take into account one stubborn fact. The King had a bullet wound right through his head, and after four hours of insisting that it was stomach trouble, the court physician had to admit that the bullet wound right through the head had something to do with it.

"I waited for the court official to tell me what had happened, but he folded his hands as if to say, 'Well, that's that.' So I banged the table and asked how the King had died. The official said, 'I've told you.'

"'Wait a minute!' I cried. 'If it wasn't murder or suicide or natural death, what was it?' The court official bowed and said, 'One of those strange things in nature, a complete and perfect mystery.'

"But don't let this talk of murder make you forget that the girls of Siam are delectable. There was this elevator in the main public building. The sign read, 'This elevator will be fixed later.' I was away two years but when I got back the sign still read, 'This elevator will be fixed later.' I've been all over the world and Siam is the best place I ever visited."

Seven hours later the famous newspaperman said, "I'm sorry I kept you up so late. But I'd hate to see a friend of mine get so close to Siam and then miss it. I would rather be stationed there than any other country I know of. Please take my word and go to Siam."

No friend ever gave a traveler better advice. When I stepped from the plane I heard people actually laughing, the only time I heard this in all of Asia. I could roam the streets at night without fear.

Siam is the joyous land. Bangkok is the Paris of Asia. Never in my life have I left a land with more regret. In many ways Siam is a foretaste of what all Asia may some day become. Its business procedures break the hearts of American businessmen, I'm told, and absolutely no one keeps an appointment. But the nation has prospered under its own haphazard guidance for some 2,000 years. It is a gentle and wonderful place.

THE

BUDDHIST

MONK

I met Par Anake Angkanarlong one hot midnight in Bangkok. The Buddhist temple near where I was trying to sleep was conducting a whale of a carnival, so I slipped into some old clothes and went out to join the fun. I had been there only a few minutes when this little man in thick glasses and saffron robes accosted me and said, "You speak English? Never mind."

He took my arm and led me to a row of 135 gold Buddhas, each about two feet high, depicting Buddha in all the traditional poses remembered by his followers. The great religious leader who lived half a thousand years before Christ was shown blessing the poor, entering Nirvana, seeking protection from a mighty snake, and in more than a hundred other poses.

"What day you born?" Par Anake demanded abruptly. He led me to a Buddha standing with outstretched hand. "This your Buddha. Two ticals, please." He handed me a slip of paper written in Sanskrit. "This your fortune. You can't read? Never mind." And he tore up the paper.

Then he led me to the temple and said, "Shoes off! Follow me! Never mind." He took me to the high priest who rubbed charcoal on my face and gold leaf on my tongue. Then he blessed me and Par Anake said, "Twenty ticals, please. Never mind."

We had a fine time that night, the little monk and I. He led me to the tree where thousands of bits of paper were tied to branches. For three ticals I grabbed the one he suggested and won a bottle of indelible purple ink. He looked at it in disgust and said, "No damn good. Never mind." And he gave it back to the monk who tended the tree.

He took me to the dance where lively couples did the ramwong, a processional dance in which partners never touch. A Chinese hot-dog man offered us a mess of that wonderfully jumbled and delightful food cooked on the spot, but Par Anake refused. "Monk eats only twice a day.

Five in morning. Twelve at noon. But I can have soda water. Never mind."

Par Anake had only a little English and I had no Siamese, but we knocked about Bangkok together for several days. For some months I had been arguing about politics and wars and economics, and it was a great relief to see this little man in saffron robes come swaying down the street with a bright hello.

"We go my room. You see how monk lives." He led me down a very dark and dirty alley to a row of dormitories in back of the temple. Some of the rooms were pretty bad but he led me at last to a fine, clean platform at the top of which he lived. It was spacious and had fifteen gold Buddhas. "I worked hard to get this room. Very nice." He hired a servant who kept it clean.

He slept on a mat 1/16th of an inch thick placed on polished boards. At the head of this bed he had a vase of rush tapers which he lighted from time to time to the accompaniment of brief prayers.

Par Anake was popular with the younger monks, many of whom clustered about him to borrow books or to argue. While they talked I peered down from the platform and saw on one of the porches a remarkably pretty girl of twenty sitting with a monk playing gin rummy.

"Very bad!" Par Anake said. "Monks not touch girls. Not talk lovely-lovely to girls. Not play cards." He sent a young monk, not yet ten years old, to tell the girl to go away. But the gin-rummy game continued.

Next door to the monastery there was a Chinese theatre and the younger monks had ripped down some of the corrugated-iron wall so they could watch the plays. Par Anake did not approve of this, but from his platform I watched the performances. They were noisy and a lot of fun. Sometimes as many as forty monks would be crowded about this broken wall.

Par Anake said, "I thirty-five years old. I a monk now for one year. I stay two more years. No money, no clothing. Anything I need my younger brother give to me. Suppose I break my tooth, he pay dentist."

He took me to see his brother, a collar-ad young fellow with a beautiful wife and two children. Par Anake said, "My fine brother do all things for me. Give me much money." I noticed that the younger brother's wife took a rather dim view of Par Anake and we soon left.

I rose early one morning and watched the monks go out to beg their daily rice. It was a moving and colorful sight. From all over Bangkok appeared the saffron robes, the rice bowls, and the good women of the city who appeared with huge buckets of rice from their kitchens. The monks ate copiously and did not say thank you, it having been directed by Buddha himself that religious people feed the monks each morning.

At midday the monks went out again, this time for more substantial food. Par Anake said, "I allowed to smoke cigarettes. Good thing. Most Siamese men be monks for three months some time in their lives. Shave their heads. Put on robes. Beg for food. Very good for all men to know this."

I told him I had heard that criminals habitually flee to monkhood when the police are hot after them. Par Anake said, "Some bad monks. Never mind. We all pray to one god. You good Catholic maybe? Ave Maria Gloria Plenis. O.K. Or maybe you say Father, Son, Holy Ghost. O.K. Never mind. I pray to Buddha. All means same thing. Never mind."

I tried in vain to discover why Par Anake had become a monk at 34. He explained sorrowfully, "My father died. I very sad. Heavy heart. I become a monk." I was impressed and asked when his father had died. "Twenty-two years ago. But my aunt die, too. I very sad. Heavy heart." She had passed on twelve years ago. "Other things, too," he added. "I tired of working at custom house."

I grew to like and respect Par Anake's gentle religion. It had done much for Asia in providing a substantial, matter-of-fact moral code without morbid qualities. Every statue of Buddha must show the saint smiling with benign compassion.

Then one day to my surprise Par Anake said, "All right, we go see my family." He led me along the interminable winding footpaths that probe into the interior of Bangkok city and we came at last to his home. I was astonished to find that he had a wife, two children, a living room with an immense colored photograph of June Allyson, and a Buddhist shrine with five gold Buddhas. He was annoyed to find that his wife had won a naked kewpie doll at a fair and that she had placed it among the Buddhas. He made her take it away.

When she brought us drinks he made her put them on the floor from which his servant lifted them to his hands. "I not touch anything my wife hold in her hand. I not live here while I am a monk. I never talk lovely-lovely to my wife. One year I not talk lovely-lovely. Two more years. My brother he pay all bills but my wife she work too when she can."

His children were delighted to see him and he banged his son up and down on his knee, but his daughter he would not touch. On his way back to the temple he said, "Buddhism very gentle religion. Everybody kind. Buddhism make the heart pure." Then he frowned. "But if commu-

nists capture Siam they destroy Buddhism. Laugh at our religion. That
very bad thing, I think."

AND

JUST

A LITTLE

MAGIC

The most painful interview I had was with a wonderful old Siamese
man who looked like a benevolent Buddha. Nai Yok Nuyphakoi was a
famous doctor, renowned for his ability to cure any nervous trouble. The
brilliant tropical sunlight was causing me eye-strain headaches, and I
sought him out.

He lived at the end of a filthy alley whose paving stones sprayed
geysers of mud as they rocked back and forth under my feet. The houses
along the narrow passageway were old and shabby and unpainted, and I
could hardly believe that a great specialist lived in one of them.

When Nai Yok's door opened a laughing face peered out and I was
told to kick off my shoes. His office floor was soft and polished like a
work of art and he said that I should lie down upon it.

He was delighted to have an American patient and talked to me
steadily for four hours. I didn't understand a word he said but by ges-
tures, pictures and the help of a taxi driver who knew a little English we
had a rare time together.

Nai Yok's theory of medicine was simple. The body is composed of
blood vessels which need stimulation and nerve canals which need torture. He would kneel over me as I lay on the floor, grab my leg with his
powerful hands, apply enormous pressure and suddenly relax with a
delighted cry, asking me if I didn't feel better already.

A treatment took two hours, during which all major blood vessels were
choked off for varying intervals. Each nerve was also explored from its
thinnest beginning to where it hurt the most. He did this with his iron-
like thumbs, which were unbelievably powerful. Once he simply grabbed
my leg well above the knee and compressed it with his thumbs until all
blood ceased to flow, and he maintained this pressure for four minutes.

I had intended to take only one treatment of such torture, but when I
went back to ask him further questions about his study of medicine he
said that since I was already there I might as well take another session on
the house.

Nai Yok—the Nai is an honorary title—said that he had studied with the wise men of Thailand and that for a time he had been a monk in the temple where spectacular cures have taken place. He told me of several cures that ought properly to be termed miracles, the kind that through history have occurred in the temples of all religions.

He said he had a very high regard for European medicine, especially surgery, and tried never to treat a patient who needed European medicine.

He himself was allowed by law to administer drugs, and he had a large supply in his office, but they were mostly exotic things like barks, fish essences and the omnipotent horn of the white rhinoceros.

The cab driver said that Nai Yok had absolutely cured his leg when the European doctors could do nothing with it, and he called in several neighbors whom Nai Yok had hammered back into shape. I suspected that the old man had tortured the legs so much they had walked away in self-protection.

Nai Yok said he was not a specialist on the head but that he could cure almost any headache, and he was willing to work on mine. He did so by practically pulling my neck apart and snapping it back into position. He also applied heavy pressures on the eyeballs and on the ear bones. Pretty soon I didn't have a headache any more.

He then asked me if I felt equal to his famous foot treatment and I said go ahead. So he moved me to a spot near a window, whose sill he grabbed with both hands while he walked up and down my body. When he found a good place to stop he started to apply subtle and overpowering pressures with his toes. At one point he placed his big toe on the inside blood vessels of my leg and pressed down until I thought I must break in half. The foot treatment ended by his jumping lightly off and grinning at me as if to say, "Feels good, eh?"

It did feel good. It felt wonderful. He told me that he was especially skilled in constipation and invited me back any time I happened to be in Bangkok. He said I was a good patient. Never hollered once.

So we had tea and sat cross-legged on the floor and he said some unexpected things.

"America has the atom bomb. Why don't you use it? If China is not stopped soon they will surely overrun us. What can Thailand do against China? Many thousands of Chinese live in Bangkok already and would create great trouble if war started."

The cab driver said, "We don't complain against the Chinese who are here now. Most of them are good people. But the communists who control China now will never let our Chinese alone. The doctor is right.

If you have the atomic bomb, why don't you use it? Now, when there is some chance of doing good with it."

The doctor spoke excitedly. "All America does is threaten. You say you are going to get mad pretty soon. Pretty soon nobody will worry about your threats any more. They will laugh when America says she will do this or that."

The cab driver said, "This is important to us in Thailand. What can we do against the Chinese? We can't use magic, the way Nai Yok does."

I asked what the cab driver meant by this and he said that he meant Nai Yok accomplished wonderful cures with magic but that Thailand couldn't depend on any magic against Chinese armies.

"What magic does he use?" I asked.

"In Thailand doctors know many things Europeans don't know," the cab driver said seriously. "See my leg." He showed me a badly misshapen leg on which no one could say how the nerves and muscles functioned. "The European doctors said the leg was rotting and would have to be cut off. But Nai Yok saved it with his magic."

"What magic?" I asked.

The cab driver and the doctor argued heatedly for some seconds and I became aware that Nai Yok did not wish the driver to tell me about the magic, but finally the latter said, "He did it with holy water and white lotus blossoms."

"What!" I cried. The doctor nodded aggressively. That's what did the trick, holy water and white lotus blossoms. I met three other patients who had been cured of leg atrophy by white lotus blossoms.

"Wait a minute!" I said. "How does the white blossom cure a withered leg?"

The cab driver said, "Nai Yok puts the water and the flower on the leg. Then he rubs the leg every day for a long time. The magic works."

In sign language I asked the old man if this was true. He laughed and said yes. Put the lotus blossom on the leg and then rub very hard for a long time. But he added that the cab driver was right. There was no magic like that that could save Thailand if the Chinese wanted to come in.

I shall always remember Nai Yok, not because of the torture he inflicted on me, but because he was absolutely the only man in Asia I met other than politicians who was seriously worried about the threat of communism. He knew that magic alone was not going to stop them. You put the lotus leaf of hope upon the wound, but you also rubbed like the devil.

In the old days in Asia, American travelers were often repelled by the experience of having rickshaw boys haul them about Shanghai or Hong Kong. They were sickened by the heaving muscles, the gasping lungs and the straining blood vessels.

Today it is not the rickshaw boy who deserves sympathy but the American visitor. For the rickshaw boys are fast disappearing and in their places have come an aggressive new capitalist class, the samlor boys.

The samlor is a fine innovation. The rear wheel of a bicycle is replaced by two wheels on whose axle is slung a cushioned seat for two. The outfit is geared very low, so that even a little pedaling sets the contraption spinning through the streets.

Samlors differ from country to country. In Formosa the boy rides behind the passengers and pushes. In Indonesia the samlors are handsomely decorated in garish colors. In Burma they are swung beside the driver and look like Irish jaunting carriages, one passenger riding forward and one backward. But in Siam the samlor has reached perfection.

Pon Paknakin is twenty-one years old, the kind of brash youngster people like wherever he is found. He smiles constantly, is extraordinarily clean, and has become a professional in guessing where Americans want to go in Bangkok.

"Sure, I know! Burmese Embassy!" He seats you carefully, flashes that big grin, and leaps upon his saddle. In two swift pumps of his powerful legs he has the samlor rolling through the narrow streets.

One of his steady patrons said that Pon didn't know the meaning of fear, traffic lights, brakes or an honest fare. I came to know him well and concluded that he must have learned to steer a samlor after piloting jet planes.

The traffic of Bangkok is terrifying. Buses, trolley cars, private trucks and samlors compete for every inch of space. Of them all, the samlor is by far the most daring and rapid. Pon, in his immaculate Samlor 13, likes to dash for an opening, ring his bell furiously, glare at truck drivers, grin over his shoulder at his passengers, if they haven't fainted.

"Never had an accident," he boasts. "Never will. Because this my own samlor. I pay $300 for it. From Chinese merchant. Then I paint it and polish it and clean it every day. Finest job in Siam. I change white seat covers every three days. You notice I never wear same shirt more than one day. Change my pants every two days. Very important I look neat.

"I work seven days a week. Eight in morning till one or two in the next morning, if I have a customer who pays well. During day I catch some sleep when no business. Sleep in samlor then, but at night have my own bed. Many boys sleep in samlor all night, but mosquitoes bite them and they get fever very bad.

"I make good money. I have to. Need money for laundry and paint for my samlor and new clothes. I don't save money yet. I young. I like lots of girls. I spend much money on good clothes. Six dollars for suit. Three dollars for shoes.

"Some day maybe I get married. Then I got to save money."

One of the other samlor boys standing in the crowd says, "He'll save then. I'm married. I have two children. Pretty soon I'll be forty years old. Too old to samlor any more. What can I do then? When a samlor boy reaches thirty-five he begins to worry."

Pon interrupts. "What will I be at forty? A storekeeper. Save my money and buy a store. Keep it very clean for Americans. I not worry. Three years ago I have nothing at all. I rent a samlor from rich Chinese and pretty soon I own this one. I work all night and day to pay for it. I'll get store same way.

"Eighteen years old is the earliest you can be samlor boy. Police give you badge for $7.50 a year and inspect your brakes and lights. I have special battery for my lights. Charge it once a day for five cents.

"I never been to school but I samlor boy only few days when I know that to make real money got to speak English. So I find American and say I samlor him everywhere if he give me lessons one month. Then I go to American movies each night for long time and study how to say things. I like Errol Flynn best and Tyrone Power next.

"English very important. Two weeks ago fat man came to hotel, very big shot. I tell him I take care of him fine. One week I carry him wherever he want to go. He give me one hundred dollars."

It costs slightly more to ride on Pon Paknakin's samlor than it does to ride in a New York taxi. He never quotes a price but grins in a professional boyish embarrassment and says, "For me whatever you think is right." But if you offer him less than a dollar an hour there will be trouble.

Most of the samlor boys have studied Siamese boxing and Bangkok police records are filled with cases in which tough sailors from foreign ports rode the samlors and then tried to bully the skinny boys. The samlor jockeys whistle and a gang rushes to the scene. Sometimes the sailors have been kicked to death before the police get there.

"I never fight," Pon says solemnly. "Might break my samlor. Ruin my clothes. What I do fight for is to get American passenger. He best pay there is. Europeans next. I won't take Siamese in my Samlor. Too stingy. Chinese? If I see Chinese coming my way I run. Never take Chinese."

One of the other samlor boys winks and says, "Pon he very rich." A moment later I discover why. An airline bus draws up to the hotel with a new covey of tourists. In a flash Pon, impeccably clean and grinning like a clean-cut kid from next door, darts swiftly among the passengers. Ignoring the Englishmen and Dutchmen and Indians, he gloms onto every American in the crowd, saying very confidentially, "In the morning, sir. Remember. Samlor Number 13. Very lucky samlor, Number 13. The clean one over there. Number 13."

When the passengers have filed into the hotel he comes back and resumes our talk. "I get to them very fast. I got to. Because I got a lot of money tied up in this samlor."

OBSERVATIONS

There were four of us in Bangkok, the Indian newspaperman, the Burmese merchant, the Indonesian official and I. We were talking of freedom.

Indian: I was saying this morning that Thailand has a noticeably different air. You can sense it the moment you land from India or Burma or Indonesia.

Burmese: Indeed, that's right. In no way can Siam compare with Burma, so far as wealth goes. Nor do I think the people are so good as ours. But they have a quality we have not yet acquired.

Indonesian: It's easy to define. It's freedom. Thailand has been a free nation for many generations. It makes a difference.

I: What you say is true. The big difference between Thailand and your countries, fine as they are, is that in Thailand people laugh.

Indian: I've noticed that. Thais smile at you when they meet you.

Indonesian: In my country we do not smile yet because we were so recently slaves. It will take us a long time to feel decent and confident the way the free Thais do.

Burmese: We are the same way. We were slaves so long we developed a national inferiority complex. Therefore when our American friend here smiles at us, we scowl back. We are not yet sure of ourselves.

I: That word "slaves" sounds silly to me. Neither the Dutch nor the British made anyone out here slaves.

Indian: A man is either free or he is a slave. There is no compromise. Thailand was free. We were not. Therefore we had generations of thinking like slaves.

I: I can't accept that, really. But if Russia invades your lands, you'll really know what slavery is.

Indian: We will have to take that risk. And no one here believes that Russia could be worse than England and Holland and France.

I: I do. I think Russia would be far worse.

Indonesian: I don't.

Indian: The brutal fact is that not a single European country ever built in any Asiatic country as many schools as they built jails.

Burmese: I agree. Europe controlled us for three centuries and left us all illiterate.

I: Didn't China do the same with her people?

Indian: It seems to me they have rather powerful and capable leaders today. Chinese leaders.

I: And you don't fear China, either?

Burmese: We don't fear fellow Asians.

Indonesian: We were speaking of Siam. Let us admit that it is not a first-rate country. It will never be as great as Indonesia will be some day. But it is a free country. What a magnificent difference!

Burmese: And everything that's wrong with Siam can be blamed to the Siamese themselves. They don't have to be mad at anybody.

I: I'm glad and astonished to hear you say these things. I sensed them when I got off the plane at the airport. The luggage man actually smiled at me. I have always felt that freedom was a real thing, like rice or water. That it could be measured, like cloth. But never before did I realize that it could substantially change an entire population.

Indian: I do wish you would explain that to your American friends. You must be patient with us while we taste our freedom.

Burmese: Yes, you must humor us in our beginnings. For example, all during this talk you've called me a Burmese. We don't like that word. I'm a Burman.

I: This gets confusing. In China a man hates to be called a Chinaman. He's Chinese. But you won't be a Burmese. You're a Burman.

Burman: That happens to be the way we want it. It's ridiculous, maybe. But we want it that way.

Indian: Such as never calling human beings Asiatics. They're Asians.

Indonesian: Such as never referring to the East Indies any longer. It's Indonesia.

Indian: You won't appreciate these things, but I'm an old man and I've watched Englishmen and Americans come to my land for generations. Why did you consider yourselves so superior? Not because of greater intelligence or spiritual power.

Burman: I'll tell you why. You knew you were free. You walked with an aura about you, and you did not have to prove your worth to anyone. You had been nourished on freedom.

Indonesian: This inherent self-respect is so terribly important in building a nation. Look at Indonesia. The youngest nation on earth. We have no tradition of freedom, so less than a hundred thousand men terrorize Indonesia. Why? Because they happen to have some machine guns left behind by the Japs. So they use them. If you asked our brigands what they were fighting for, they wouldn't know what they wanted. They just want to fire their guns. Because to them that's freedom.

Burman: In Burma the same way. If you asked our rebels what they wanted they could not say. They think that as free men they have a right to shoot their guns against the Government.

Indian: We were talking some time ago about why India has not yet had an election. It's simple. Nearly 90 per cent of our people are illiterate. Would you believe me if I said that in my town not one-third of the people know what a parliament is? Therefore we appoint our members. We have not the knowledge of freedom's ways that comes with long acquaintance.

We stopped this discussion and went out to attend the Siamese boxing matches. To an American they were astonishing, for the boxers used fists, elbows, knees and feet. It was like a general roughhouse between a windmill, a cement mixer, an electric fan and an egg beater. The crowd especially liked it when one boxer kicked his opponent in the face as the latter was falling backward.

The main bout was between the champion billed as "Famous and advanced fighter possessing the lion-hearted character to trespass and never retreated by ruthless action to roll the opponent down by K.O." and a wild man from the provinces described as "Topmost advanced fighter being composed of kick and elbow attacking ferociously in self-defense with hot action that instigated the fans."

The point is that Siamese boxing is ridiculous by Western standards. No American or English boxing club would tolerate it for a moment.

Indian: This is what I meant by freedom. This is outrageous boxing but the Siamese like it. Can you imagine what would have happened if Siam had been occupied by the English? Some colonel would have seen a match like this and that night he'd have reported to his club, "Awful affair, you know. Kicking and gouging and all that sort of thing." Next day he'd have organized the Royal and Ancient Siamese Boxing Club. And thereafter all Siamese boys would fight the English way or not fight at all. And rich colonels would loll back and cry, "Well struck, old fellow. Well struck."

Burman: And these white colonels would enter the club by one gate and the Siamese would crawl in through a lesser one For colored people.

Indian: And the Englishmen would have a wonderful time, having brought civilization to the savages. And the Siamese would hate it, and soon there would be no more spontaneous fun in boxing.

Indonesian: The Americans would have been as bad. If they took over Siam they'd cry, "It's gook boxing, that's what it is. Why don't they stand up and fight like men?" And they'd organize a tournament and give big prizes and make the boxers stop praying to their gods in the middle of the ring. Then heaven help the poor Siamese who fought in the old style. He'd be disqualified and your magazines would carry witty stories about the poor idiot who actually preferred his way of doing things.

Indian: What we are saying, my friend, is that we Asians want freedom. The freedom to do things our way. No matter how good or wise or rich the white man happens to be, we don't want any more instruction from him. We've had his benevolent help for three hundred years and it has got us nowhere. Absolutely nowhere.

I: But yet you are willing to take new lessons from Russia?

Burman: No, we do not want that either. We want to be left alone.

There was a wild flurry of fists and feet and the "topmost advanced fighter with the ferocious character" went down like a teak log. The crowd cheered wildly as they hauled away the body and I thought that a Siamese boxing match was a strange place to learn the exact meaning of freedom.

INDO-CHINA

AMERICANS FACE A DIFFICULT INTELLECTUAL PROBLEM IN ASIA TODAY. It is a matter of words. Specifically, there actually are such people as agrarian reformers. We must not forget this, merely because the phrase has fallen into ill repute.

There is little doubt that a group of pro-communist sympathizers sold America a bill of goods that the Chinese revolutionists were simple agrarian reformers who would never associate with Russia and who could thus never cause us any harm. Actually, there was from the beginning a hard core of Moscow-trained revolutionists who were determined upon world revolution.

But there were also, originally, many peasants who were indeed agrarian reformers. All over Asia today there are agrarian reformers. Indeed, I would state categorically that unless some kind of agrarian reform takes place in India within ten years the nation will have to go communist. The same applies in Iran, Pakistan, Burma, Indo-China, parts of Indonesia, parts of the Philippines and the southern part of Korea.

No matter how tarnished the phrase agrarian reformers, it is the one scientific phrase to identify what is necessary. There must be a new system of land ownership, a new system of taxation, a new system of agriculture, a new system of exchange and new governmental agencies to support and supervise these innovations. In the section on India I shall exhibit some simple facts proving these contentions. In the meantime we must not, as a nation, blind ourselves to the inevitability of these reforms. If we do not sponsor them, Russia will. What is worse, if we brand every young man who calls for agrarian reform a communist—and most of them aren't that at the beginning—they will have no option but to become so.

We are not now fooling with words, even though we were once badly bitten by the phrase agrarian reformers. We are considering the evolution of an entire continent. In doing so we'd better line up with the legitimate agrarian reformers early in the game and keep them on our side. Specifically, we should abandon any idea that we could possibly prevent land reforms in Asia. There isn't a chance.

That leads properly to the question of Indo-China. I doubt seriously if Ho Chi Minh could ever have been led away from communism, but most of his followers could have been led away from Ho Chi Minh had there been legitimate systems of reform to which they could have rallied. Now it seems too late.

As for Bao Dai, he is best considered a temporary, unfortunate and perhaps inescapable stopgap. When the Western nations studied Indo-China they were, understandably and forgivably, thinking more of China than they were of Indo-China. A wrong decision appears to have been made. Its only justification is that world conditions as a whole had to be considered at that time. I doubt if the French and Americans together can spare the equipment necessary to enforce that unfortunate decision.

What we can hope for is that the French, awakened by the military genius of de Lattre de Tassigny, will find some political genius to equal him. Together two such men, fortified by French, British and American good will, might work out some reasonable solution. But unless that solution takes into account agrarian reforms it will be useless. Indo-China will then be in revolt for a generation to come. And the final result can only be the overthrow of the French.

Let us therefore not be tyrannized by words. Or better still, let us coin new words to remedy old wrongs. Democracy, freedom, justice are some that come to mind.

THE

SCOURGE

OF EMPIRE

It seems ridiculous to speak of Ho Quoyn as a scourge of empire, but that's what he is. A small wispy man from Indo-China, he is only five feet two and weighs less than a hundred pounds. His cadaverous face and frail beard first attracted my attention in 1944, on the New Hebrides, just south of Guadalcanal. I've known him intermittently for eight years.

At our first meeting he told me, "I was born in a peasant village in Indo-China. My parents were unspeakably poor. They rented a rice paddy and a filthy home where they raised eleven children. But more than half their rice crop went to the French.

"In order to escape starvation, my wife and I signed indenture papers to come here to the New Hebrides and work copra plantations. The papers were strict and made us slaves for five years.

"I was here when you Americans captured the island in 1941, but I wasn't interested in war, because my indenture was over and I was eager to go home. But the French said, 'Sorry. There is a great war. You can't go home. Your indentures are extended automatically for another five years.' I said, 'But I don't want to be a slave for five more years.' They said, 'Sorry. It's war.'

"What happened? Our food got worse. My wife had more babies. Have you ever seen the houses they give us?" He led me to one of the infamous pens where, in a dismal hovel smaller than an average American bedroom, he had lived for five years with his wife and five children in one room with no window.

"You can stand such a place for five years, when you know you'll be going home with money in your pocket. But not for six or eight or ten years."

When I next saw Ho Quoyn he was very happy. He had been made schoolteacher. Dressed in a black alpaca jacket and armed with an immense stave of pandanus wood, he taught his thoroughly cowed students the French alphabet. At the slightest mistake he would wallop them over the head with his club. "It's better than working copra," he grinned. In two years he managed to teach them to read simple yarns about Paris and Normandy. And each year he tried to get back home to Indo-China.

"But always the French plantation owners say, 'Don't bother us about getting home. Speak to the Government.' And the Government says, 'Sorry. War.' And our indentures are extended for another term. Some day there will be trouble."

So on July 4, 1945, a large number of Ho Quoyn's people assembled at the plantation where he worked, and in desperate fright the French owner shot into the mob. Two Tonkinese were killed. Many were wounded.

A kind of civil war followed, there at the edge of the great jungle. American troops, being white, naturally sided with the French and helped put down the rebellion, and an armed truce was arranged.

Now Ho Quoyn's teaching stopped. The rice ration was cut. Life became very rough, very wicked. I last saw the little man in September, 1945, and he had become something of a leader among his countrymen, for he had stolen a radio and could listen to broadcasts from Asia telling about the uprising in Indo-China, where his countrymen were at last facing up to the French.

Between 1945 and 1949 I quite forgot Ho Quoyn. I assumed he was back in Indo-China, probably fighting against the French; but in early 1950 I returned to the New Hebrides and found to my astonishment that he was still there.

"The devilish French!" he stormed. "During the war we couldn't go home because the Japanese held our land. In peace we couldn't go because there were no ships. Now we can't go because of the communists. When can we go?"

The news he got over his radio was confusing. "What are these communists? Ho Chi Minh is not a communist. He said on the radio he is only a nationalist. I wish I could get home."

He now had a store of his own, immaculately clean. His six children lived in a quonset hut, very well lighted. "I must admit the French have made things better for us, here in the New Hebrides. The bad laws have been lifted. I even have my own taxi. The French say I stole the weapons carrier from the Americans, but I had a possession slip. How I got it is not your business.

"You want my opinion? I think France cannot hold Indo-China. It is fourteen years since I was home, but I can remember a good deal. We had no land, no food, nothing. Everything was for the rich French. Of a hundred men in Indo-China, ninety-nine must be working with Ho Chi Minh.

"Communism? I didn't know that word when I was in Indo-China. Of course, I was only twenty-four when I left and I wasn't interested in politics. Only girls and gambling."

I did not see Ho Quoyn again for some time, and then we talked only briefly. He was no longer a young fellow interested in girls, nor a frenzied schoolteacher clubbing his charges, nor a revolutionist listening to a secret radio. He was a determined, mature man.

"I want to get home. I have saved American dollars and French francs. You say I ought to be contented here. Would you be? Would you want your children to grow up away from home?

"If the French can't find us a boat, let me try. I understand charters. We'll get our own boat. But we'll never get home until Ho Chi Minh drives the French out of Indo-China. You know why? Because every Frenchman knows that each man they send home from here is a soldier who will fight against them the minute we reach Indo-China.

"There has been some talk that we might get home if we signed a pledge not to fight when we got there. I would never sign. Let me tell you that I remember Indo-China as it was under the French. No land. No food. No hope. If I can fight to get those things, I'll fight. I'll make my boys fight, too.

"Communism? You keep asking about communism. I told you before I don't know what communism really is. But when I see the years go by and never a ship home, I think I am beginning to learn. And if it takes communists to drive the French out of Indo-China, all right. I'll be one. There seems to be no other way."

THE

COMMANDER'S

LETTER

I have never met Chhuon Mochulpieh, but I owe him a debt of gratitude, for he permitted me to experience one of the most majestic nights I shall ever know.

We were visiting Angkor Wat, that enormous and inscrutable mystery of the Cambodian jungles. Our party had been flown in from various quarters: Saigon where the French were being murdered nightly, Bangkok where life was superb and sleepy and Singapore where the riots were still a fresh memory.

But at Angkor Wat these troubles were forgotten, for here we saw the mighty ruins of a nation that once had an army of 5,000,000 men, cities of more than a million population, a civilization that exceeded China's, and a grandeur that must have been stupefying. At its height, Angkor Wat was the spiritual center of a mighty world.

Then mysteriously the grandeur vanished. An entire civilization of more than 30,000,000 people disintegrated. The cities were destroyed. The temples crumbled under the weight of giant trees that grew upon them, and even man's memory of this vital culture was erased.

For a thousand years the vast temples, major architectural and sculptural masterpieces, were forgotten. We do not even know the name by which this civilization was called. Then, in the early 1900's archaeologists chopped away the invading trees and set old statues straight. The result is a historical ruin of such magnitude as to bewilder the mind. In these days when other civilizations are being weighed in the delicate balances of history, it is reassuring to see Angkor Wat, this symbol of a totally destroyed culture. Your mind sees things in a better perspective and you are less scared about the little things that have been happening to us.

But on the night when I thanked Chhuon Mochulpieh for his graciousness, there was a full moon and the French director of Angkor Wat said that he had arranged a special celebration for us. He added cryptically that we might never again have an opportunity to see what we would see that night.

We arrived at the towering ruins two hours before midnight, when the moon hung directly over the jungles that hid the temples. Then, as we turned a last corner, we saw a sight so unexpected that one could hear gasps of delight, for along the great causeway leading to the distant main gates of Angkor Wat flickered hundreds of reed flares, smoking in the moonlight. On the face of the entrance gate itself, more massive and majestic than many entire cathedrals in Europe, other torch bearers had climbed. And far beyond, on the topmost tower of the temple itself, one solitary beacon quivered in the night.

Then, as we started to walk down the magnificent causeway, we discovered that our torches were being held by very young boys, seven and eight and nine years old. Sometimes the torches were taller than their heads, and they stood there, silent and bronzed, their slanted eyes staring solemnly into space.

Next they broke ranks behind us, and the causeway became a medley of darting lights as we entered a spacious square in front of the great arched gate and there in the moonlight women of the village danced the ancient Cambodian rituals that had been performed in the temples nearly two thousand years ago. Above the dancers rose the towering pillars of Angkor Wat and the sculptured heads of Angkor's gods.

When the dance ended we were invited to pass through the gates and along another enormous causeway up to the temple itself. There it stood in the moonlight, a pale, gray-silvery ghost of a mighty civilization. Three of us, aided by intrepid boys with faltering torches, climbed to the very top of the temple, from which we could see the vast courtyards, the majestic corridors, the battlements and the sickening drops of Angkor Wat.

Beyond us lay the jungle, that green and twisting serpent that had once torn down this temple and would do so again sometime. Along its edge we could see the enormous man-made lake to which barges and rich ships from all Asia had come. And we could imagine the extensive city that once must have rested where the jungle now stood. But even its name was lost, and I thought of Chhuon Mochulpieh.

Why did I owe such a memorable experience to a man whom I had never met? Well, it's easy to explain. He was the commander of the local communist outlaws. For some months he had been killing Frenchmen and making the land around Angkor Wat untenable. His leader, Ho Chi Minh, was for the present far to the north, but in the meantime Chhuon Mochulpieh's irregulars did what they could.

In fact, they did so much that trips to Angkor Wat were stopped, so Chhuon sent a letter to the Government saying, "In order to put an end to the one-sided rumor according to which there is danger for the tourists to visit the Angkor buildings, tokens of the prodigious past of the Cambodian nation, I beg to confirm you hereby that all tourists may peacefully move about the ruins whatever may happen. Because of their interest in the Cambodian art and civilization they will be looked after by my Independent Cambodian Command."

The letter was posted on all government buildings and is instructive on several counts. First, the communists praised local traditions as if communists alone treasured such things. Second, national pride of the Cambodians was appealed to, it being the hope of the communists that the Cambodians will rebel against the French. Third, the bringing of tourists to Angkor is good for local business and the communists always pose as friends of the small businessman.

But as I left Angkor Wat that night I saw on the lintel of the great doorway the stains of fresh blood. And the priceless uprights of the door were clearly pock-marked by machine-gun bullets. I asked the guide what had happened.

"Communists," he whispered. "They killed seven French partisans and fled here, knowing we wouldn't fire upon them in the temple. But some Legionnaires had friends among the seven who were murdered and they stormed the temple. They killed the communists right here." Then he added confidentially, "That's what will happen to all the reds who come this way."

But when he left, another man sidled up to us in the darkness and said, "That isn't blood. It's betel juice. But if the Frenchmen stay in this country much longer it will be blood."

Then I understood what the guide had meant when he warned us that this might be the last moonlight ceremony for a long time. Chhuon Mochulpieh and his communists were getting restive. At any time he might withdraw his permission for strangers to come to his Angkor Wat. It seemed that in the timeless jungles the civilizations were changing guard once again. At least one of the civilizations involved was going to be damaged in the process, as centuries ago an entire cultural world was totally erased. Remembering the destruction of Angkor Wat, one had to pray that it would be his civilization that triumphed.

**B
U
R
M
A**

To UNDERSTAND WAR YOU MUST GO TO BURMA. FOR NEARLY A THOUSAND years Burman warriors have been going forth to sack Southeast Asia or fleeing homeward to await the shock of invasion. At times the narrative of Burmese-Siamese wars becomes as disgracefully confused as the record of war in Europe. The Burmans have been extraordinarily brave, conspicuously nationalistic and willing to wage war against any enemy or among themselves if no aliens were available.

About the size of Texas, Burma is composed of several autonomous states and this separatism enabled the British to wage war against the country. Burma defended its freedom until 1886, when civil wars so corrupted it that the last strongholds fell. During World War II Burmans naturally sided with Japan against the British and then rebelled against the Japanese.

After the war Burma gained dominion status and promptly dropped out of the British Commonwealth, establishing the Union of Burma, a federation of various states, some of which already seek independence. Since the total population of the Union is only 18,000,000 the resulting nations would be trivial.

But the addiction to warfare is so ingrained in Burmese culture that no fewer than seven separate armies launched operations in various parts of the Union. Some of the armies were communist, but each with radically different programs. Several were simply the personal armies of powerful generals whose war aims have never clearly been stated.

Back and forth across the hilly face of Burma these armies have raged. The destruction of food and capital goods has been heartbreaking. What was once a rice-surplus area is now a rice-deficit area. What was once the leading teak-producing land on earth now barely lumbers enough for local use. What was a land of great mineral production is now a land with barricaded mines. In fact, Burma at peace could have the richest and best-rounded economy in Asia, not even excepting miraculous Malaya. But ripped apart by a thousand years of war, both external and internal, this most gifted land is an unproductive shambles.

It is difficult to portray the tragedy of Burma. In many ways it is more pathetic than Korea, for there the damage has been done by two great and irreconcilable external forces. In Burma the Burmans themselves have sacked the land.

The tragedy is deepened further by the fact that in Korea the contending forces at least represent incompatible interpretations of life. When I was in Burma I read six manifestoes issued recently by contending generals and I could not comprehend one of them. The armies were fighting for nothing. They had inherited arms from the Japanese or British; therefore they fought. I showed the manifestoes to a Burman and asked his help. He said, "Three of the armies want to establish separate states. The official communists want to establish one big state. Three others want to take over the state we already have. The Government is trying to protect itself."

What are the chances for peace? I have no idea. I do know that the Burmans are the most attractive people, physically and intellectually, in Southeast Asia. They had originally the highest percentage of literacy, now terrifyingly low because no schools can operate in many villages. They have a strong unifying religion, Buddhism. And they have a rich wonderland in which to work. Unless their addiction to war is a poison that can never be expelled, I should think Burma's future might be very bright.

But in Burma today the difference between civilization and chaos is war. To comprehend war's terrible cost in decaying civilization—no trains, no teak, no schools, no social progress, no money in the bank, no ships at the dock—go to Burma.

THE

PATRIOT

I had finished my work in Burma and had gone to the airport when a long black government car sped into the enclosure and a worried man of sixty hurried out to speak with me.

I had talked with this man several times in Rangoon, and while he had said nothing that I considered startling he had made much sense. I thought of him with respect and affection, for he was a dedicated and intelligent public servant.

But now he was distraught. He said, "Last night I reviewed what I had told you, and I talked it over with my wife. We agreed that I had been imprudent. May I implore you to tear up your notes? And promise me you will not use my photograph."

"You said nothing disloyal to Burma," I protested.

"You don't understand." His hands moved nervously and he began to perspire. "You might not think it dangerous, what I said, but if it appears in American papers it will surely be spotted by our embassy official in Washington, who will report it back to Rangoon. Then I might get shot."

I promised him that I would use neither his name nor his photograph, for as we talked there at the airport I had to acknowledge that, harmless as were the things he had said, they still might cause him to be shot. In this respect he represented 80 per cent of the intelligent men I had met in Asia. They knew the various disasters that threatened to overtake their countries and they knew that this time they simply had to guess right. They had to guess which side was going to win, because if they backed the loser they would get shot.

This likable Burmese official said, "I have a wife and three children, all girls. I cannot afford to have the communists angry at me. For we don't know who is going to win in Burma. Or in Asia, for that matter. And I have already been through too much hardship.

"What do you think? Will America start a war in Asia? If she does, then Burma is doomed to another terrible disruption. The communists will invade us from the outside and terrorize us from within. America will be too occupied elsewhere to give us help, and China will occupy us within a few weeks.

"You asked me why we don't face this problem now. Why don't we do something? All right, I ask you: What can we do? We are a little country. More than any land in the world we have been devastated by war. We will not listen to any policy that might lead us into another war.

"You Americans cannot understand this. Look at Rangoon! A tired, dirty, frightened city. Before every main building a barricade of barbed wire to give us a little time if another revolution starts.

"Our main roads are barricaded, too. In the northern hills it's unsafe to walk about. And on all sides rebels threaten our national security."

In the hot sunlight this man spoke like a person who cherished the land in which he was born. He spoke like the hero in one of Robert Sherwood's plays, his back to the wall, his mind agonized by the insuperable problems he must face.

"Burma is one of the loveliest countries on earth. It is one of the richest, too. Our teak is the world's best. We have mines that produce essential metals. We produce an abundant surplus of rice. Famine does not strike our land. And you yourself said the Burmans are delightful.

"Then why is so favored a land so impoverished now? Because when the Japanese invaded us they set in motion forces that no one has been able to stop. Eight different rebel armies have attacked the Government at one time or another. For what? For nothing. Some of the leaders say they want freedom. Others say they want a petty state to be a sovereign nation. Some fight for a communist state. Others fight because they have the guns.

"Here in Burma you can see the true terrors of war. A magnificent country devastated. Civil life at a standstill. You must remember this when we say we want no more war. Especially not if we have to choose sides between America which is very far away, and China which is on our border."

I asked this nervous man, "Then you do not fear communism?"

"Yes! The Government does, too. Perhaps even a majority of the Burmese people do, too. But as between communism and another war, they'll take communism."

"But don't you realize that communism will be worse than the Japs?"

"There you are wrong. I was in Jap hands. This scar came from them because I was known as a democratic liberal. When I refused to work with them they slapped me in the face and took everything I had. Believe me, my family knew what true poverty was. We could not stand that again."

"Communism will inevitably be worse. Communists don't slap liberal democrats in the face. They shoot them."

"That I know," the government man said. "That's why I hurried out here to make you stop that story about me. Because if the communists arrive I don't want to be shot."

"Do you think they will arrive?"

I have no idea what this man really thought, but he said, "No, I do not think they will come this far. For one thing, Burma has no large Chinese colony to cause trouble. For another, Rangoon has no large slums to breed a communist movement. For a third, we are Buddhist and that means spiritual opposition to communism. Most important, we side with

India in international affairs, and Pandit Nehru says India will not be overrun by the Chinese."

"You believe that?"

"Yes, I do. In this respect we must believe Nehru. Burma will go along with India in foreign affairs. We live or die with India and can have no separate life of our own."

"You agree with Nehru when he says there is no danger from Red China?"

"Yes."

"Then why do so many people in Burma fear communism—as you yourself have been saying?"

There was a long pause and the government man said, "We have got to weigh various possibilities. Remember that the rebels were in Rangoon itself not long ago. We drove them out that time. Who knows? Who can foresee what will happen by this time next year?"

This sensible man—he spoke English fluently and said that the British had been the salvation of Burma, starting her on the path to freedom—could have been speaking for 500,000,000 Asians: "We prefer democracy. We cherish national freedom. But the American Navy and the British Army are a long way off. We had better not make the communists too angry. Because who knows? Maybe this time they'll be the winners."

HOUSEWIFE

IN ASIA

North of Rangoon, in the Shan Hills of Burma, an astonishing gray-haired American woman in her fifties is giving a demonstration of what democratic co-operation means. To see her at work is to gain new heart for the big jobs we have ahead in Asia. People like her are America's answer to Russia.

Mrs. Otto K. Hunerwadel, of Gainesville, Florida, accompanied her farmer husband out to Burma on his spur-of-the-moment agricultural job sponsored by the Fulbright Scholarship people. He was assigned to the local government to help them on problems of local government.

Mrs. Hunerwadel was happy to be able to come to Burma. Her two children were finishing their education in America and she had no work to keep her at home. Furthermore, she says, "I was past fifty and had never traveled. People said I was crazy to go to a place like Burma, but this was the kind of place I wanted to see. Different.

"Otto was sent way up into the hills to work, 400 miles from Rangoon.

At first the people paid no attention to us. Partly because we were white. Partly because they knew we couldn't know anything about their problems. And partly because we were both so old.

"In Burma you retire at fifty and are kicked out if you stay to fifty-five. I peeked at a message one of the officials sent to Rangoon: 'Please get a jeep for this fine old couple. They are getting restive.' The Burmans were quite astonished when they saw how much work Otto could do.

"Before you knew it, he had hundreds of the local people interested. He showed them how to grow better crops, how to use them when they were grown, and even how to make brooms.

"Yes, his broom factory was a brilliant success. He introduced a tough broom grass, found a kind of tree that would provide suitable handles, and rigged a machine to do the binding. Otto's very resourceful."

Mrs. Hunerwadel looks like the beaming country housewife in a Thanksgiving Day ad. She talks rapidly and with infectious enthusiasm. Her eyes dance with humor and she has great respect for the Burmans.

"I can honestly say I've never been happier than I am here. It's like a new life. But mostly it's because I've been so busy myself. I got started in an interesting way.

"I had been in Burma for some time, doing nothing, and it hurt. At home I was always busy. When Otto was county farm agent in the States I traveled with him and got to know a lot about farm life. So one day I had the idea that it was senseless for me to be in Burma doing nothing. I started a class. In canning.

"Yes, I finally got sixty-four students, all men, of course, since Burmese women aren't allowed out much, and I showed them how to use the rich foods that God had given them.

"Burma is very fortunate where food is concerned. Everything you can think of in greatest abundance, but it ripens one month, a little is eaten, the rest goes to rot, and then the people are hungry. I showed my students how to can everything from corn to exotic Burmese dishes like fish curry, pork stew and ripe mangoes. They kept asking, 'How long will this food keep? One week?'

"So at the end of four months Otto and I served a big village dinner. And each dish that night was food that had been canned at least three months before. From soup to nuts, literally.

"The feast was a sensation. After that everybody wanted to know how to can. Food that for centuries had been allowed to rot was gathered and we canned everything imaginable.

"Now I don't mean that we were putting up single jars of food. I mean real commercial canning with tins and labels and all that. The result was that I had dozens of hard-headed businessmen with real money in the class. They were quick to see that here was something they might make some money on.

"But I hadn't the necessary machinery to do the job right. So I went back to America and marched up and down the country begging equipment from big firms. I couldn't pay them what the machinery was worth, but I could convince them that America ought to be doing work like this in Burma. Sears Roebuck gave me a fine new range. Du Pont gave me seed fumigators. Other firms kicked in and pretty soon I had what I needed.

"But I didn't have the money to pay the freight out to Burma. I could have wept when the solution came. The Burma Government said that they were so impressed by what I had accomplished that they would pay the freight. What they sent wasn't quite enough, however, so Otto paid the rest out of his salary.

"Now we went to work in earnest. Otto, while I was back in the States, had invented a new kind of mattress in which the Burmans could use their cotton and kapok. Beds became easier to sleep in. He also taught them principles of rural sanitation.

"But it was the canning project that held people's attention. So Otto gave up what he was doing and helped me. We proved to the Burma Government that large-scale canning was economically sound by one simple trick. We canned some mangoes, and they were delicious. That same day the government gazette advertised for $40,000 worth of canned fruits for the Army. They were importing expensive pears and peaches from Europe while they left the fruit that their men really liked rotting on the ground. A government official estimated that a real cannery might save the country up to $50,000 monthly."

As Mrs. Hunerwadel relates one hilarious experience after another—she practically became a Burman—her tall, bright-eyed husband laughs. He had become famous in the hill country for his ability to tramp over the fields, work on the farms and do everything the younger farm hands did.

"That's what made it so impressive when Otto lectured the local governor. The man had lost a leg in the insurrection and was despondent. 'Why didn't they shoot me altogether?' he moaned. Otto argued with him that the mere loss of a leg needn't end a man's usefulness. The governor cried, 'It's all right for you to preach. You have your legs.' So Otto pulled up his trousers and showed the man his own wooden leg. He had worked in Burma for two years and not a soul knew about that leg."

There is a great deal more to Mrs. Hunerwadel's story. Of how she worked with the missionaries. Of how she had to leave during the rebellion, trekking over jungle trails, of how she was one of the first to come back in. In fact, you can't be with this remarkable, happy woman without being proud that it was your country who sent her to Burma.

THREE

RUPEES,

SAHIB

Sikantor hailed me late one afternoon along the water front at Rangoon. He was a tall, ultra-mournful-looking sampan man with a scraggly moustache and piercing eyes which flashed brilliantly when he saw me.

"Sahib! Sahib!" he shouted. "You are looking for me. I am looking for you."

"All I want is a quick trip over to the other side and back."

"Sahib, better than anyone on the river I can do that for you."

"How much?"

"Sahib wants to see Rangoon from the other bank. Very well. I shall take you to such a spot as you can see the entire city."

"How much?"

"Five rupees, Sahib. Wait! Don't leave. Sahib, I very poor man. I got wife, many children. So I got to have money. For you, Sahib. Three rupees."

Sikantor knew this was too much—a rupee is twenty cents—but he nevertheless put on his most mournful face and pleaded with me to give him the job. Since there was just a chance that he did need the money, I climbed into his sampan.

He stood behind me and rowed by running up and down along a raised platform, pushing the oars in rapid strokes. They were lashed to the boat by heavy strands of wet rope, so that at every stroke the ropes groaned and squealed as if they were crying, "Rangoon, no, no. Rangoon, no, no."

The city lies on one of countless channels of the great Irrawaddy River, one of Asia's most powerful. The Rangoon River, as this branch is called, is big and brutal and brown and dirty. Squat steamers from Asiatic ports call here. Ugly dhows and blunt barges line the shore, while along a far stretch of the river the wharves of Rangoon line the mud flats. Rangoon has one of the ugliest river fronts in Asia and now from the opposite shore I could see the ugly outlines.

Then I noticed that the whining oars had halted and above me I heard the soft voice of disaster. "Sahib, this view very ugly. But up there . . ."

"I've seen what I wanted. Take me back."

There was no response on the oars and Sikantor came to sit with me while the sampan drifted downstream.

"Sahib," he reasoned, "I do not like for you to see only this much of my city. Up there is a fine view. Towers. Mosques. Turrets."

"How much?"

"Five rupees altogether."

"Take me back."

"But already you've spent four rupees."

"You said three."

"That's true, I did. But while we've been talking the boat has drifted downstream. An extra rupee for the long pull back."

"You allowed us to drift. Three rupees."

"But you were doing the talking. Look, Sahib. Four rupees already. For one more only you see the lovely view. Good."

He returned to his oars and worked like a maniac, finally pulling up at a spot from which I could see the great golden spires of the Buddha temple and the exquisitely lovely monument to Burmese freedom.

"See, Sahib!" Sikantor glowed. "I always speak the truth. Now down the river . . ."

"Take me back. Five rupees."

There was a long pause and I looked back over my shoulder. Sikantor looked more mournful than ever. "Sahib, for you to miss the view down the river . . . No!" He stood like an immovable rock and slowly held up eight fingers.

"Eight rupees!" I yelled. "You take me back!"

"Sahib, I cannot make my arms move. For only three more rupees, what you will see."

"What will I see?"

"A vision. A true vision."

So he led me down through a maze of dhows and mud flats and barges. He cursed at the other sampans and finally nosed his into the mouth of a canal that wound its way back into the dark interior of Burma. The scene was indeed engrossing.

"You like, Sahib?"

"Yes. What is it?"

"For ten rupees we will go down the canal and see."

By this time I felt like a man in a dentist's chair. His face has been pumped full of novocaine and the dentist says, "There's one more little cavity back here. Shall I?" Numbly I told Sikantor to go on down the canal.

So he took me along an incredibly filthy waterway that somehow or other had a positively Dantesque beauty. Little houses hung along its edge. Men and women struggled with life wherever tillable land could be squeezed in. Barges of all description lined the shores and tiny boats sped back and forth across the dirty water. Here was Asia itself, living in its dirty barges, fighting, screaming, laughing, living its life out along one of the great waterways. Then, dramatically, the sampan stopped.

"Magnificent, eh, Sahib?"

"What's that around the bend? That big crowd of people?"

"That would be twelve rupees, Sahib."

So we probed farther down the canal and came to a huge collection of rice mills. Unthreshed brown grain lay spilled in filth. Smoke stacks rose high into the air, and men finishing their day's work lay along the canal banks and shouted to others lying on the other side.

It was now dusk and the canal seemed a forbidding and even frightening place to be. Silent men appeared at the sterns of the barges, staring at our sampan as their wives cooked the evening meal forward. There had been much trouble in Burma and white people were advised not to move carelessly about after dark, and this canal seemed to be about as careless travel as one could find, so I advised Sikantor to return to Rangoon before night actually fell.

He was adamant. "Sahib! To come so far. And not to inspect the mill itself."

"Let's get home."

"The rice mill, Sahib. You'll never forget it. Fifteen rupees."

"I don't want to see a rice mill. Home and twelve rupees."

"For you, then, fourteen rupees to see the rice mill." And so, whether I wished it or not I was led ashore in the gloomy dusk and shown the rice mill, cavernous, dusty and foreboding.

We climbed back into the sampan and, as night collapsed about us, we crawled back along the foul canal. The smells of cooking were heavy. The soft calling back and forth of unseen voices echoed behind us. And then we shot out of the dark canal back onto the bosom of the great open river.

A breath of clean salt air struck us and across the river the varied wonderful lights of Rangoon shone in the darkness. The temples were gaudily ablaze and the tower shimmered in the darkness. It was a magnificent sight, breath-taking and superb. Here were the rivers of Asia, magnificent and enormous and crowded with life. Here were the stars of

Asia, spectacular in the night sky. And there was Sikantor behind me, laughing, for he had planned it this way.

He said nothing as we sped across the awe-inspiring river, for he was content with what he had accomplished. But as I climbed ashore he grinned and said, "Sahib, forgive me, I had to keep you at the rice mill. To wait for the stars. Was that not worth the fifteenth rupee?"

Without argument I gave him the money, but as he accepted it with his right hand, he thrust out his left. His face became tragically sad and he bleated in a soft whimper, "Baksheesh for the rower?"

This was too much. I pushed him aside and walked back to my hotel, where I found that a hot-shot commission of big-time American businessmen had arrived to advise the Burmese Government on ways by which Burma could make more money. I had the curious feeling that the wrong men had been sent to the wrong country.

OBSERVATIONS

In two respects Burma represents much of Asia. It looks to India for leadership in international affairs. And it is completely indifferent to the world-wide struggle between democracy and communism.

Most Americans underestimate India's leadership in Asia. Indonesians, Malayans, and Burmans in particular consider India Asia's unifying force. When Nehru speaks of Asia's spiritual values, he strikes a vibrant chord in these nations. When he sponsors a third way between communism and capitalism, he expresses their hopes. While I was in Burma one of the leading newspapers stated that Burma could have no foreign policy that did not coincide with India's, that in effect Nehru was Burma's foreign minister.

Like the average American I was shocked to find that most of Asia is quite bored by the American-Russian struggle. They deem it merely a contest between capitalism and communism and cannot project themselves into the fight. They have known Western capitalism unfavorably. They understand that communism is no relief. Their hope is to escape each of the systems.

I met few Asians who were pro-communist. Patriots especially recognized that their homelands would lose much if Chinese communism swept Asia. But they were not paralyzed by the prospect, admitting that perhaps in the long run a home-grown communism might be both inescapable and constructive.

On the other hand, they also admitted that given time and growth, a capitalism like America's might be even more advantageous. But to get excited about either system was useless. A slang phrase was current at the time which expressed the average point of view: "Korea? We couldn't care less."

I think it probable that for many years this indifference will continue. But if we find a chance to demonstrate the pragmatic values in our way of life we may win Asians to our side. I stress pragmatic values because if we merely mouth our slogans expecting Asians to read into them the heritage of freedom and decent living that we read into them, we will accomplish nothing. An Indian told me, "If an American and a Russian were to stand at the edge of a river and shout their opposing slogans to Asians on the other bank, the Russian slogans of 'Land, food, jobs' would gain converts and the American cry of 'Freedom, democracy, industry' would not. But if you Americans could cross the river and exhibit your substantial proofs, I think you would win every time."

Along with those pragmatic facts will have to go spiritual content. It has become the fashion in America to laugh at Asia's reputed spirituality. This custom developed because at a crisis in our national history Nehru said the Asians did not necessarily accept American motives at face value. Asia applauded.

I think Nehru was wrong. I think that our courage in Korea saved Nehru's neck. But simply because Nehru offended us is no reason to reject his insistence that there is a spiritual content to Asiatic life that must always be taken into account.

Religion is more important in most of Asia than it is in America. Philosophy is much more important. Spiritual speculation is, too. Almost no lasting heroes of Asiatic life were generals. Saintly men won immortality.

The nature of our contacts with Asia has prevented intercourse of a high philosophical nature. It would be ridiculous to expect aggressive pioneering businessmen to be addicted to cosmological speculation. And a missionary by definition goes abroad to effect religious conversion from what is defined as a lower religion to what he believes is a higher. Asia has not been particularly impressed with the spirituality of such visitors.

But now America is a grown nation forced to exercise a considerable world leadership. If we continue to send Asia only pragmatic businessmen and hortatory missionaries, we will lose contact with those very Asians whose friendship we need.

Inescapably I am once more driven to conclude that our job in Asia is going to be difficult. If we merely shout slogans, we will lose to Russia. If we merely parade industrial efficiency, we shall fail to inspire the spiritual leaders of the continent. What we must do is exhibit a well-rounded society. Fortunately, most aspects of our society warrant such exposure and those that do not ought to be changed.

I was therefore delighted with what I saw of the job we are doing in war-torn Burma. American businessmen were sharing new processes with Burmese businessmen. Fulbright Fellows were exploring fields of scholarship with Burmese students. People like the Hunerwadels were explaining to everyday Burmans how American society works. A superb United States Information Service library demonstrated some of the things America has accomplished intellectually. And an efficient military mission was giving aid and comfort to the established Government.

Any American could be proud of the exhibition we were giving of a nation strong in material things, rich in humanity and gifted in the arts. If we can continue patiently to present such portraits of our nation we have a good chance in Asia.

INDIA

IT IS INSTRUCTIVE FOR AN AMERICAN TO APPROACH INDIA FROM THE EAST. For in the nations east of India he learns the focal importance of this crowded land. He finds that the leadership of Pandit Nehru is both spectacular and applauded.

Burma, Thailand to a degree, Malaya and Indonesia—whose very name, Islands of India, bespeaks an ancient association—look to India as the spokesman of their rights. Perhaps one day the Philippines may join this orbit, and though Ceylon is presently outside, due to a millennium of distrust, it is likely that Ceylon will gradually reach a rapprochement.

The sources of India's influence are historic. To most of Southern Asia, India brought civilization and culture. The literature and drama of nations like Thailand and Indonesia were borrowed from India. Religion particularly was disseminated from India, reaching even China and Japan. There is historical basis to the claim that India has been the spiritual reservoir of Asia, and there is some likelihood that this condition will continue. It has become fashionable in America, recently, to laugh at this claim, but we would be exceedingly foolish to underestimate spiritual forces in an area like Asia, where fatalism and poverty combine to make intense spiritual experience almost a necessity.

Equally important is the basic intelligence of India's people. It is high. Today inadequate education inhibits this capacity and Westerners are thus deluded into believing it does not exist. But when Indian students have had a chance to apply themselves to science, medicine, astronomy, philosophy, poetry and practical agriculture their accomplishments have been notable. There seems no good reason why India should not in time make the same thundering strides forward that Japan did after 1880.

I am not overlooking the perilous present. In the interviews that follow, the overwhelming problems that plague India become apparent and make any prospect of stability seem quite remote. And it would be remote if India sat back and bemoaned her bad luck—a partition that wrecked her economy, a land that cannot feed her people, and the largest collection of critical decisions to be made in all Asia—but India is not doing that. A national effort is being made to get India on a sound basis. Vast reforms are under way. Hydro-electric plants and factories are being built. And an enormous population supports the government that has launched these measures.

India is of inestimable importance in the world. It is the second largest nation. It is the key to the Indian Ocean. It is the best remaining link between the Western world and the mainland of Asia. Every American who can possibly do so should visit this great sub-continent. In the thirteen interviews that follow I have barely brushed the infinity that is India, but I have indicated some of the major problems. If tomorrow I were directed to spend the rest of my life overseas doing what I could to help America, I would not need a moment to choose. I would go to India, for sound American-Indian relations could be the foundation to our entire policy in Asia.

THE

GREAT

DEBATE

Today India is conducting a debate of critical importance upon the merits of a bill which if it becomes law will revolutionize Indian life. It is called the Hindu Code Bill and brings into formal codification a mass of what was formerly fragmented law and unwritten custom. The code will govern the religious, social and economic life of nearly 350,000,000 people, probably the largest single religious-political community in the world.

The code deals with marriage, adoption, guardianship and family life. In those categories there is little that is new or contentious. But three other proposals are so revolutionary as to have evoked a hurricane of protests among orthodox Hindu believers.

First, polygamy is forbidden. Frequently Hindu men prefer two or three wives at the same time. There is overwhelming evidence that these wives live together harmoniously and seem not to mind too much. One of my acquaintances has two wives who appear in public always dressed the same way, as adoring sisters do in America. Polygamy has never featured seriously as a national problem, but where injustices to women have occurred, they have been so flagrant as to warrant legal prohibition of the practice. Orthodox Hindus object to government interference with individual rights.

Second, divorce is legalized. This is a major shock to the orthodox, who consider marriage so inviolable that in the old days widows were encouraged to throw themselves upon their husbands' funeral pyres and burn to death. Even today, a child-bride of nine who has the bad luck to become a widow before she has even so much as kissed her husband must remain a widow for life. Remarriage is unthought of among the orthodox. Therefore, publicly encouraged and legally sanctioned divorce is held to be an outrage.

But even with the above "scandalous" provisions the code would probably pass if it were not for the third provision which really rocks Indian tradition to the roots. It is proposed that daughters shall be eligible to inherit money and land from their fathers. At present this is forbidden by law in most of India, and the new proposals have shocked everyone. If adopted they mean that Indian girls will be able to support themselves and will no longer be under the domination of their men. Therefore many sentimental Indian men cry in public, "We don't want our glorious Indian women ruined by European ideas. We must preserve the old traditions."

The fight over the Hindu Code Bill is further aggravated by the personality of the remarkable man who has fathered the bill. Dr. B. R. Ambedkar, the Minister of Law in Nehru's Cabinet, is one of the intellectual giants of India. He is also the focus of violent hatreds and rapt adulation. I found him by all odds the most provocative man I met in Asia.

Big, slightly stoop-shouldered, black haired, this fifty-year-old lawyer has a huge mouth that droops at the corners when he is brooding, but which widens into a big grin when he is pleased. Friends and foes alike —India divides about 30-70 on that score—acknowledge Dr. Ambedkar's incorruptible love for India.

"Our legal system has sometimes been called the envy of the world," Ambedkar growls as he lectures you over his desk in Parliament. "I have dedicated my life to it. Our penal system could hardly be improved upon. But where we lag has been in social legislation. And now we've taken that up. In one giant bill we will revolutionize life."

As you listen you are impressed with the determination of this giant man. You recall that he was one of the prime figures in giving India a splendid constitution. "But the Hindu Code Bill will be 100 times more benefit to India than the Constitution," he says emphatically. "We are building a new society here, and we are doing it with justice and law."

As he speaks, you understand why his enemies call him "arrogant, intellectually cruel, unsympathetic and destructive of ancient ways of life." In Parliament, there is no one who is so ruthless a foe of the sloppy argument or the inapplicable analogy. He simply withers the opposition with phrases like: "Thus we can see that there is not a shred of reason in what he has proposed." On one occasion, when friends were suggesting a surrender of minor points to gain major ones, he shouted, "I will have this code apply to all of India or to none of it. There will be no compromise."

He laughs when you ask him why he is so tough in debate. "I have to be. If I wavered, then all would be lost. I have no explanation of why I am in Parliament. I have fought the leaders of India for a generation. Many of them hate me, and I despise some of them. But they called me and said, 'We want you to enter the Cabinet. We need a mind like yours.' So I accepted. But my value would disappear if I surrendered on any point, however small. Because I don't care whether I'm in Parliament or not. I have no personal ambition. I don't want money and I don't care whether I'm re-elected. What do I want? A decent, fine India. I will do anything to help attain that."

But Dr. Ambedkar's association with the Hindu Code Bill is even more astonishing than his fiery temperament indicates. His writing of the bill which will revolutionize Hindu religious life is one of the greatest tributes to modern India. For Ambedkar is a man who has been a bitter critic of the Hindu religion. To many orthodox believers even his name is unspeakable.

It happened this way. Dr. Ambedkar was born an untouchable. He knew intimately the cruelest kind of social ostracism. As a boy, he got an education by building a separate hut alongside the regular school so that he would not contaminate little Hindu boys who might otherwise brush against him. His life was a mortification salvaged by the miraculous intervention of the Maharajah of Baroda, who sent him to Columbia University for a law degree.

When he returned to India, Dr. Ambedkar joined the fight to free his untouchable group. He rose to a position of eminence, where his voice carried weight, and he helped to build the new India.

He holds no brief against Hinduism as such, but he does wage incessant war against the Brahmins who have insisted upon continuance of what he calls "evil patterns." He has been relentless in his exposure of fake Brahmin writings which impose rigid systems upon once-fluid India. He says, "What annoys one is the intolerance of the Brahmin scholar towards any attempt to expose this Brahmanic literature. When any non-Brahmin makes an attempt to tell the truth, the Brahmin scholars engage in a conspiracy of silence, take no notice of him, condemn him outright on some flimsy grounds or dub his work useless. I've been the victim of such mean tricks."

From his long battle against the tyranny of untouchability, he came inevitably to a consideration of the same kind of tyranny directed against women.

The rare old fighter calls the Hindu code "my bill" and proudly states that it is merely one more shot in his unending war "against injustice, tyranny, and oppression wherever it is to be found in Indian life." Therefore he will make no concessions on his epochal code, and it is on the interpretation of social justice for women as Dr. Ambedkar sees it that the great debate rages.

THE

CASE

AGAINST

THE

NEW

WOMAN

Deputy Speaker of Parliament Ananthasayenam Ayyangar is against the Hindu Code Bill. This fifty-year-old Bombay lawyer doesn't hedge. He's against the bill. He says it will ruin India.

In fact, Mr. Ayyangar is so irrevocably opposed to the code that he needed no questions from me to keep the discussion going. He anticipated all of my arguments and gave an excellent example of a powerful and logical mind in action.

"To understand the Hindu Code Bill," he said, emphasizing his points as if he were addressing a jury, "you must remember two things. India is terribly poor. And in order to combat that poverty we long ago invented the joint family. These two ideas are basic to Indian life, and the joint family is the unit for all life.

"Such a family consists of a man, his wife, his sons, his sons' wives and their children, and if need be, the man's own parents when they are too old to work. The joint family is India, and anything that threatens it is evil and must be opposed.

"The joint family lives on its little plot of land, growing its rice, sharing its poverty. It is more than a family. It is the social legislation of India. We have no federal unemployment compensation, for the family insures that. We have no old-age pensions, because the family takes care of that. We have few orphanages, for the family keeps all children. Every proposed Indian law can be judged by one question alone: Is it good for the family? If not, then it must be bad for India.

"Now as to girls. Girl children are part of the family until they marry. Then they become part of their husband's family and they are cut off from their original family as completely as if they had died. They do not look to their mother for guidance, but to their husband's mother. They do not ask their father for clothes, they ask their husband. The girl is of his family now and forever, and it becomes the responsibility of his family to provide for her, to care for her children, to feed her in her old age.

"That is why there are no unmarried women in India. A father and his sons, worried about a girl's future, work very hard to get her married early and settled securely. They will pay much money to accomplish this. If necessary, they will travel great distances to find her a husband. And they will give her money for a dowry. But when she is married, then the girl is no longer their responsibility. She has joined a new family.

"Now as to the land. No European can understand how an Indian thinks about his land. The parcel is so small that most Europeans wouldn't call it land at all. Rarely is it more than an acre. But it belongs to the family. Only the family can sell it, never an individual. If it makes money, that money belongs to the family. On the day a son is born he owns, in Hindu law, an equal share in that land and it may never be disposed of without his consent. The father, who heads the family, may not make a will giving the land away, for the son owns it as much as he. But the daughter owns no portion of it.

"And if a man has five sons then he must take them into consideration. By law he must give each son an equal share in the family wealth. But if he has five daughters then he alone owns the land and the daughters must look to their husbands for land.

"Now you can see what a horrible thing the Hindu Code Bill is. It says that in addition to the ancient rights of the sons in family property, the father must consider his daughter. Thus the wealth of India will be broken down into smaller and smaller pieces. And soon this great land will be totally ruined.

"Now consider the land. If you have seen an Indian rice paddy you know that individual fields are already so small they can barely be farmed. We are starving for lack of rice. But the code says that these tiny fields must be fragmented further. It's national suicide.

"So if a man had no objections to the code other than this attack on the joint family, the code should be defeated. Actually there are other, more serious objections."

Mr. Ayyangar now draws his legs up under him and leans forward from his chair. At first it looks as if he might teeter off, but he raises his right forefinger dramatically and launches into a legal annihilation of the bill.

"First the women who are shouting for this code want it mainly for one reason. So they can get hold of a little hard money and leave the villages. They want to live in big cities like Western girls. They don't want to marry early and become a part of Indian life. They want to get away from family supervision. We are asked to ruin India for such selfishness.

"Second, the divorce clause in the code will have a disastrous effect on Indian life. Oh, the woman will get her divorce all right, but then what? No Hindu man will marry her. There is in our religion an absolute repugnance against association with another man's wife. An orthodox Hindu won't even shake hands with a married woman. What will these divorced women do? If they have no money they will be able only to drift into the big cities.

"Third, if a young wife enters her husband's family bringing along some money of her own it won't be long before she'll want to establish a home of her own. To get away from her mother-in-law. But where will she find a house? There aren't enough to go around now, when we have joint families. Or where will she find the land on which to build her home? It's all being used now. More houses, more new homes are an impossibility.

"Fourth, if you weaken the joint family you speed the day when Communism will succeed in India. If you build up a landless wandering population, India is lost.

"Fifth, there is another point you may not understand. Please don't take offense. The Hindu Code is called modern because it will bring India in line with Western customs. Why should we be brought in line? What is there about Western social life that is so impressive? Are all the girls in New York married? Are all the men in California happy? Are old people looked after in your country? Tell me, which is better to give a girl: a typewriter or a home?

"Sixth, the Hindu Code is going to make an impermanent India, whereas under our old customs India has become the most ancient continuing society in the world. India has withstood a hundred assaults. The Aryans invaded us and we absorbed them. The Muslims came, and our joint family withstood the shock. The English came and we outlasted them. Our marvelous family system has never been weakened from without. But now we are asked to destroy it from within.

"We Indians don't want Western divorce, Western girls roaming around unmarried and unhappy, their children in Western orphanages. Above all, we don't want our aged thrown into the street when they reach sixty. If you have a joint family, one extra mouth is no great burden. But if you have to pay for that old person's room and board it becomes something to be avoided. Do you think America's way with old people is better than India's?

"Finally, the Hindu Code Bill is an attack upon an ancient and gentle religion. Hinduism is the oldest successful religion on earth. Like the joint family that goes with it, Hinduism has withstood attacks for five thousand years. It is the very structure of our society. If a proposed code threatens that structure, then it ought to be fought and fought and fought. That's what I am going to do."

IN

DEFENSE

OF THE

NEW

WOMAN

It is not difficult to find proponents of the Hindu Code Bill. Almost every educated Indian woman favors it. In Parliament there are twelve women members who have fought for such legislation consistently. The most dramatic is a handsome woman in her forties, Mrs. Renuka Ray, one of the leading people in modern India.

In America you would take Mrs. Ray to be the president of an important woman's club or perhaps the manager of a New York store. She has a fine sense of humor, extensive knowledge and a patient understanding of why her program offends orthodox Hindu men.

"They quote old religious books and beat their breasts and cry, 'Indian womanhood is sacred.' They protest that if these sacred women are given any rights at all the great mystical life of India will be destroyed. They get very excited about protecting Indian womanhood. But when the shouting ends it all comes down to this: they don't want to surrender economic rights.

"I started this fight when I was in college, back in 1927. I've heard every lame old argument. They don't hold water.

"The orthodox old men say, 'Hindu custom forbids women to be the equal of men.' But for every passage they can quote, I know three which prove that in ancient days men and women were equal.

"The men shout, 'This is an offense to religion!' But I can prove that in the old days women served as Hindu priestesses.

"The men cry, 'It's sacrilege to change old customs.' Well, there was an old custom some years ago in the Malabar region of India. All land and wealth were vested in women. Men could own nothing. Believe me, the men of India changed that law fast enough. We heard no outcry from them about disrespect to old customs.

"They are particularly fond of saying that if the Hindu Code Bill passes, rice lands will be fractionated into even smaller parcels. That is correct. But the evil is that even now land parcels are too small. (In one region 15 per cent of farms are less than a quarter of an acre each.) What India must do is not hold women down because the land system is wrong, but change the land system so that women and men alike can be free. If the land system is changed then there would be shares to give daughters. What the orthodox want is to continue a ruinous land policy which benefits them and keep that as an excuse for maintaining an equally ruinous policy toward human beings. We must ask which is more important: old land customs that lead to starvation or human beings working freely under new systems which provide enough to eat.

"The men also say that giving a share of family wealth to girls would destroy India's moral life. But in Bengal fathers from time immemorial have been free to include daughters in final settlements if they wished. Bengal has remained moral.

"The men say our Bill will lead to easy divorce. But the provisions are just about what they are in enlightened European countries. Most people stay married there.

"The men are bitter over the fact that the code sanctions intercaste marriages. But these have become common in recent years and are almost a mark of distinction.

"And the orthodox opponents of the Bill have one very strong point. They say that India has always been governed by religious custom and that we want to substitute civil law. But the fact is that what Brahmins like to weep about as religious custom is really nothing but their own caste prejudices as they were foisted upon our English conquerors in the eighteenth century.

"When the English arrived they sought advice as to how they should rule India regarding civil and religious affairs. Whom did they ask for advice? Brahmin priests, some of the most bigoted men on earth, and these Brahmins saw a chance to establish all their petty preferences. Consequently the British pressed down upon the people of India harsh and ridiculous and cruel laws, believing that these were the historical customs of the land.

"The worst to suffer were the women. I used to be on committees that implored the last viceroys to reinstate the ancient laws that gave us freedom, but the viceroys always said, 'We musn't interfere with local custom.' And I would say, 'But that's how the trouble started. You did interfere with local custom. Back in 1750.' And they would reply, 'But that was a long time ago.'

"The Hindu Code Bill does nothing but restore to women the rights they held in ancient times but which were taken from them by the priests and the British."

I have given Mrs. Ray's reasoning in rapid order, losing completely her wit and hilarious comment. She laughs a lot as she talks of her long fight and is in no sense a grim-faced embattled shrew. Pressing you to take more of her delicious food, she laughs as she puts on a long face and says, "Think of it! Twenty-five orthodox old men are keeping this Bill from coming to a vote. They know very well that in the informal caucus of the Congress Party it passed 118-22 and that if we can ever force a vote it will become law.

"But Nehru is terribly occupied with many problems and he cannot allocate a full month of uninterrupted sessions to this Bill, during which we could kill the filibuster. So the orthodox old men make long speeches and almost weep about the glories of Indian womanhood, while they see to it that Indian women remain medieval chattels."

Mrs. Ray saves her three most important points till last. She says, "I really want you to understand this Bill, because in some ways it represents the very best in Indian life. It also represents one of our greatest problems.

"I get very angry, therefore, when I hear the fearful misrepresentation that is circulated about this Bill. Ignorant women are told that if the Bill passes their husbands can divorce them that afternoon and they will no longer have any kind of family. You find few Indians who have read the Bill who are against it, but most of them have not read it.

"Second, I am ashamed to admit that most Indian women seem to oppose the Bill. I think from what I've just said you know why. They have been told that if the Bill passes they will all be like the homeless women you see in Calcutta. But I'm sure uneducated women in America fought against vaccination. And village women in England were sure suffrage would hurt them.

"There is, however, a third point that is most hopeful. India has not split down the middle on the Bill, with all women for it, all men against it. The finest people in India are for this Bill. Some of its most powerful defenders are men."

I myself judged that, since powerful old men are against the Bill plus almost all uneducated women, it would not become a law. Not this year. But it is inconceivable that women like Mrs. Ray and men like Dr. Ambedkar will stop fighting for a modern India. Next year—perhaps.

MARRIAGE

FOR

LOVE

Aruna Banerjee is in her mid-twenties, a lovely and brilliant young Hindu wife who is attending college in Calcutta while her husband works in a village some sixty miles to the east.

She is remarkable in many ways. Her tomboy laughter is both infectious and incessant, providing a gay sparkle to all around her. She is also well informed about Indian life. But she is interesting to a Westerner primarily because she represents a complete fracture between past and present. For she selected her own husband. And she married him not because her parents advocated him but because she loved him.

"My mother was horrified when she heard I was thinking about doing such a thing, so when I actually got married I didn't tell her. Later I sent her a letter explaining what I had done, and she almost died to think that a daughter of hers had turned out to be a bad girl. Now she accepts it and is rather proud of me."

To appreciate what a monstrous crime Aruna committed in her mother's eyes, you must know something about her village. On a dusty plain where all the land is cut up into small rice fields, Aruna's village rises among a cluster of trees. Its houses are built of mud. Its roofs are rice thatch. Its floors are pounded earth.

At meals no spoons or forks are used. Every one reaches into the common pot and licks his fingers appreciatively. There are no lamps, no beds, no sheets, no books, no radios. And the life of the average woman in Aruna's village is almost exactly what it was three thousand years ago.

"The girls are married at eight or nine to husbands who are in their twenties. This isn't as bad as it sounds, for the young brides stay with their own parents until puberty. Then the babies come pretty fast."

At this point Aruna summons Hridea, a good-looking young fellow of the village. He has a moustache of which he is proud and a wife of ten. He stands shyly in the doorway and explains that he had never seen the girl before he married her. In fact, the first time he ever saw her was when she lifted her veil after the wedding. He says proudly that she was a pretty girl. He now sees her once or twice a week, if her parents permit.

Aruna continues. "When the marriage is finally consummated, the bride goes to live with the groom's parents. Then her mother-in-law is all-powerful. The young wife may never speak to her husband during the daytime as long as his mother runs the house. She may talk with him only at night. She may never be seen with him in public. That explains those strange carts you see passing our house."

In the blistering sunlight oxcarts go by, each with a large wicker basket lashed upside down onto the creaking boards. Inside the basket, cut off from all air but open to the blinding dust, hides the wife, wrapped head to foot in cloth. At the great public market not a woman can be seen. They lie huddled in the baskets while their husbands haggle for hours over the family purchases.

"There is one curious law," Aruna explains, "which states that a married woman must absolutely never speak her husband's name to anyone else. That's so that if she should ultimately fall into disgrace no one need ever know it was such-and-such a man's wife.

"My mother has been a long time accepting my new way of life. I wear no veil. I appear in public. But the thing she has never forgiven me for is that once at her home, when she had friends in, I spoke my husband's name. There was a silence of death, and every woman there felt sorry for my mother that she had reared a shameless girl. I had said my husband's name.

"After this the women of the village started the rumor that I had had my baby before I was married. Of course this wasn't true, but it helped them to understand me. They knew that something terrible must have happened to a girl who would speak her husband's name in public.

"Now if you and your wife call upon my husband and me, you never see me. And my husband never sees your wife. We women must keep together in a dark back room. And if I wish to visit your wife, I cannot do so alone. Some older woman must accompany me, and I should properly return and report to my husband within the hour.

"One of the worst scandals in our village has been Hridea, whom you met. The other day his wife wanted to leave her mother's home and go to the home of her aunt. Hridea took her through the village, and it was a public outrage. That a man should walk in public with his wife while she still lived with her parents! People are still talking about the scandal and the old women pass from house to house whispering that Hridea has no regard for his wife's good name."

It is possible to live in Aruna's village for several days and never see a woman. Shadowy figures, covered with veils in hundred-degree heat, are sometimes glimpsed darting behind walls. Occasionally a very old woman, too crippled to disappear, huddles beneath her veil and glares her defiance.

Aruna says, "The position of widows is specially difficult. We found a fine woman who could have helped us in our work, but we could not bring her to this village. For no widow may eat from a common mess. She must cook her own food. She may not eat meat or eggs or cheese or anything good. She must shave her head and wear no colors of any kind, no jewelry. She may speak to no man, nor may she ever marry.

"If Hridea were to be killed today, his widow, a girl of ten, would have to live the rest of her life that way. There is some talk of a new law to help widows, but whenever such a law is actually proposed all the conservatives shout that the old customs of Hindu life must be preserved. So more harm is done than good."

That very week, in a responsible magazine, appeared a statement by a famous writer to the effect that it was better in the old days when widows burned themselves to death upon their husbands' funeral pyres. He said that the glory of Indian womanhood had originated in such willing suicide and accounted for the fact that Indian women were the finest in the world. He went on to say that recently he had taken his own womenfolk to a movie in which disgustingly immoral scenes were shown. "Girls winked at men and one girl showed her leg up to her knee." He said that he had sent his women home to protect them from such contamination but that he had stayed on to see just how bad the movie was.

New laws have been proposed improving the lot of women, but when they are discussed in the Legislative Assembly fiery orators rise and shout that such freedom merely means that instead of being the monarch of India, as she now is, the liberated woman will have become a political tool. As in other legislative bodies, strong men weep over the glory of womanhood.

There are thousands of Indians like Aruna Banerjee who have fought individual battles for freedom. Some of them hold Cabinet positions in the Government. Others are in Parliament. Many are learned specialists in business, law, medicine and education. Increasing numbers of them do as Aruna did. They find a man they love and marry him.

But it is correct to say that nearly 160,000,000 Indian women live more or less according to the old rules. Most of them are illiterate. Many of them marry before they are twelve. Girls like Aruna Banerjee shudder at the thought, but a large percentage of Indian men and women seem to prefer it that way.

BREAKING

THE

CASTE

SYSTEM

When you meet Jibon Banerjee, a rollicking chap in his late twenties, it is difficult to realize that you are meeting a hero. It is even more difficult when you are told that his heroism consisted of marrying a beautiful girl like his wife, Aruna. For if a young man ever got himself a lovely, hard-working, happy companion, Jibon did.

But it took a good deal of courage on his part, for he is an upper-class Brahmin and Aruna is a lower-caste Kshatriya and until a few years ago for Jibon to have married beneath his caste would have been the same as committing social suicide.

Even today he has caused his family and friends considerable pain. "I met Aruna in Calcutta, away from village life, and we fell in love. We argued about caste for a long time and decided that our parents would never understand. So we married secretly and told them about it by mail.

"My mother was furious and outraged. She's completely orthodox and still makes trouble. When she visits us she can't eat anything Aruna has cooked. To do so would be a horrible sin in her eyes. So she cooks her own food in special pots and eats it where Aruna can't see her."

Aruna laughs and says, "My own parents objected, too. They said a Kshatriya girl must have no self-respect to marry outside her caste. Even though Jibon was a Brahmin.

"The women of the village were especially outraged. They said that if a girl could marry anyone she wished, soon there would be no sense to Hindu life. They have never accepted my marriage."

No American can appreciate the meaning of caste, and comparisons are useless. The word itself is not Indian but Portuguese and of recent arrival, but the system is as ancient as India. Originally the word for caste meant color, which reflects the early determination of the Hindus to keep the white-skinned superior classes free from contact with the dark-skinned inferior groups. An ancient instruction said, "All that is white is good. All that is black is bad."

Caste determined everything. You were born into the caste of your father and you could never leave it. Your caste settled all problems for you: what you ate, where, how; what jobs you did; whom you married; how you lived and what they did with your body after you died.

When new occupations developed, new castes were ordained, for the system is meticulous, with special categories for those who deal in salt or fish or mend shoes or conduct wars.

It is impossible to guess where in the social scale a particular job falls. Barbers are extremely low, but shoemakers are even lower. Artists and musicians who blow wind instruments are near the bottom of the list, but even high-caste Brahmins can play stringed lutes.

At the top of the scale comes the Brahmin. They control education, religion, government and philosophy. The veneration in which they were held even through the first half of the twentieth century is difficult to believe, especially since they were originally only in the second category of caste. Over the years they gained control of culture and actually rewrote the history of India to prove that they had always been the highest caste.

At the bottom of the scale come the untouchables, a pathetic group called by Gandhi, their inestimable friend, the Harijans, or children of God. Traditionally they were treated by Hindus as inhuman slaves. Along with the criminal caste whose members were taught to commit crime and the abysmally low aboriginal tribes, these subhuman castes total 85,000,000 people even today and their continuance has been characterized by Indian leaders as "an abomination, a diabolical contrivance to suppress and enslave humanity."

Today, fortunately, the worst features of the caste system are disintegrating. In the eyes of most Indians the finest thing Gandhi, himself a Brahmin, did was to lead the fight against the intolerable injustices of the system. Nehru, another Brahmin, has carried on. In fact, neither his daughter nor his sister married Brahmins. In all large cities, as education slowly percolates down through the 280,000,000 illiterates, the older customs are dissolving. Today men shift fairly free from one job to another.

But that is not true of Jibon Banerjee's village. There caste determines precisely what work a man will do. He is either a farmer or a fisherman, or, if he is of particularly low caste, he may do the menial village jobs. The more fortunate residents do weaving for a living and are of a slightly higher caste. A few villagers are of high caste and enjoy a veneration that seems pathetic to the outsider.

Jibon says, "I would like to see a casteless India. But it may never come. You'd be surprised how the old customs live on."

Aruna says, "Our parents have been interesting to watch. They fought against our marriage and predicted everything bad. Now I think they like us. But they would not permit their other children to marry outside of caste."

There are many who defend the caste system as a bulwark of the state. "A man knows where he belongs and he harbors no ideas about revolution." It is a fact that communism has made little headway among the peasants of India, for they do not understand its appeal to rise and throw off one's chains.

On the other hand, the caste system, with its encouragement of a permanent illiteracy, has meant that India is governed by an astonishingly small proportion of its total population. In an America of 150,000,000 probably 100,000,000 could conceivably help govern the country if needed. They could understand political problems and might acquire the skills to deal with those problems.

In an India with a population of 350,000,000 probably fewer than 1,000,000 citizens could understand or help run the Government. Actually, the effective number must be far smaller, somewhere nearer 300,-000.

Therefore any conspiracy to win India to communism need only gain control of a small number of influential leaders, and the vast nation is in communist hands. Conversely, to keep India in the ranks of the democracies it is necessary to retain the loyalty and dedication of a relatively few leaders.

But whichever side first taps the capacities of the villager will win the ultimate victory. In that inevitable struggle the Hindu religion will operate on the side of the democratic system. But the caste system and forced illiteracy will not, for it is generally believed today that the lower castes could be swung over to communism without their ever knowing what had happened. It is only if they understand and appreciate freedom that they will actively prefer it.

THE

HUNGRY

OLD

MAN

One hot afternoon I was walking along a village road in India. It led through a grove of trees and a group of children recognized me as an Englishman and took me proudly to the one man in their community who could speak my language.

He was a handsome, gaunt old man of seventy-three, tall and stately. He cried in a loud high voice, "S. C. Mojindar, sir. Retired British civil servant. Living on a pension and having a fine time."

He insisted upon joining me as my guide to a local point of interest, and as he strode along the intricate country paths I was unprepared for what he called back to me over his shoulder. "I'm almost totally blind, but I've walked these roads since I was a boy. I hear perfectly."

Like many Indian villagers, as opposed to the city people, he laughed freely and enjoyed half a dozen little jokes. "The British taught me to speak their language. They gave me a job. Now they give me a pension of $19 a month. So I help to kick them out of India.

"Fine, decent people, the British. When we built bridges in those days they were good bridges. Not like the ones we build today."

Mojindar is very thin. He jokes, "Nobody in India gets enough to eat these days. Even if you have the money you half starve. A man needs three pounds of rice a day. We're lucky if we get two. That's why I'm so thin. Not enough to eat.

"Cloth is even worse. Those naked children you see. You think their mothers want them to go naked? Not at all. No cloth. Do you suppose a man like me enjoys wearing such clothes as I wear? Not at all. We are a hungry and a naked people.

"We were all right when we had the rice fields of Burma and Muslim Bengal, but now we've lost them and our own fields don't produce enough to feed us. Rice is terribly scarce. Government brings in a little American wheat, but we don't like it much. Too hard for our delicate stomachs to digest. But we have to eat it anyway. Maybe our children will learn to digest it.

"The big trouble is that we've had floods again this year. Last time we had floods that destroyed the early rice was in 1943. That year the monsoons didn't come and a drought followed. You know what happened."

I did know. Since coming to the old man's region I had heard many times about the terrible year of 1943. In one state alone 1,866,000 people starved to death. Actually, the total deaths from allied diseases must have been nearer 4,000,000. For India as a whole the tragedy was unbearable. In Mojindar's village two people out of every five died.

The old man recalls, "I tramped over the countryside begging for the water that rice had been boiled in. I added grass and that kept me alive. In the morning I would walk through a village and see six men lying dead in the road. On my way back at night there would be two dozen.

"We ate anything we could find. Anything. It is terrible to know that in an entire region there is absolutely nothing to eat. Not even rats or mice.

"I often saw men who were true skeletons. They would lie down and you'd swear they would never be able to get up. But somehow in the morning we'd be up looking for food. I was a skeleton like that."

The famine of 1943 was the worst in memory in Bengal, for the war prevented ships from bringing in emergency grains. The big city of Calcutta was black with death.

"Many villagers from here wandered into Calcutta, but their journey was useless. Soldiers kept them at the edge of the city and they died in big camps. But we quickly forget such years when the rice grows. But this year is starting like 1943. The floods have destroyed the crops again. If we should have a drought, too, we'd have to go wandering again."

Mojindar lives in a communal group of some twenty families who have built a kind of medieval mud-wall village in which they share their goods to a limited extent.

"We are all paupers in this village. Only six middle-class families. The rest of us are coolies with six children minimum. What we ought to have is better agriculture."

Here the wise old man had identified India's problem and her peril. Yearly her farm land is becoming less productive, but he was aware of only one of the reasons.

"The trouble is the splitting up of rice paddies. Look at these fields. No bigger than a cart each way. A farmer will have six paddies, all in different locations. Why? Because when fathers die the land is split up among the sons. Soon there will be more land in the ridges separating fields than there is in the fields themselves."

The second reason for the death of the soil is a reason as old as India itself. The land teems with cattle. India has one of the greatest cattle herds in the world, but the manure never goes back to the land. Women jealously clutch it from the fields, mould it by hand into cakes, and bake it on the thatched roofs of their houses. Then they use it for firewood. Thus millions of tons of prime fertilizer are lost each year.

"So as we get less rice, the Government takes more of it," Mojindar explains. "Teams come to collect it for the cities. Soon there will be riots." Again he was right. The day after I talked with him three government men who were expropriating rice from a village near Mojindar's were killed by an angry mob.

As we talked the old man kept turning his face toward the sky. "It's getting hotter. Pretty soon it will be monsoon season. Then we'll see."

He is worried lest the monsoon fail again this year. If that happens it will be famine again. Mojindar's state alone has 90,000 villages which exist mainly on rice, and in such villages a famine can be too terrible to describe.

It's as simple as this. Unless the rains come by June, 3,000,000 people will starve to death.

THE

REFUGEE

The division of India into two separate nations, Muslim Pakistan and Hindu India, is indefensible on any but religious grounds. Economically it is a tragedy and has caused the uprooting and exchange from one country to the other of perhaps 15,000,000 people, or twice the population of the entire continent of Australia.

Nowhere is this tragedy more apparent than in the leading state of Bengal, which originally contained the enormous population of 61,000,-000. It was then the economic center of India, located between the mountain states to the west and the rice states, including Burma, to the east. Its capital, Calcutta, was one of the world's major cities, commanding the trade of a vast area.

Now Bengal is chopped in half and once-mighty Calcutta, swollen to fantastic size by refugees, hangs like an afterthought on the edge of India while its rice fields and economic hinterland belongs to Pakistan. It seems to be a city with no future but with somewhere around 6,000,-000 people. To complete the tragedy, in Hindu Bengal there continues to be a Muslim minority of more than 5,000,000 while in Muslim Bengal there is a Hindu minority of 11,000,000.

Common sense would dictate the reuniting of Bengal, but its two religions are almost immortal enemies and any kind of peaceful co-existence is impossible, so long as national leaders call for holy wars of extermination. Hindus eat pork but revere cattle as sacred, whereas Muslims enjoy beef but will burn down their houses if a fragment of pork is thrown upon them. It is understandable why riots and communal massacres have been common in recent years.

As a result of these mass murders, and because people fear a new outbreak at any time, millions of people have fled back and forth across the India-Pakistan border. They are known as refugees and they constitute a grievous social problem. But there is one light-hearted refugee who views the whole business with a delicate detachment which is wonderful to see. In people like him there is some hope for the future.

Sudha Ghosh is one of those rare human beings, an authentic wit. Everything he says makes you laugh. Since Bengali has no sound like the English *s*, he pronounces all his English words with a *sh* and grins when he produces some hilarious effect.

He also has a tolerant and forgiving attitude toward politicians, toward great national powers like America and Russia, toward conflicting religions and toward the hard facts of economic existence. He reminded me of Voltaire.

Sudha Ghosh is a wiry little Hindu, about thirty years old, and a native of that part of Pakistan where the riots were specially bad. "Completely ridiculous," he says. "A bunch of stupid Hindus running around screaming 'Jai Hind' and a lot of equally stupid Muslims shouting 'Pakistan Zindabar.' Each phrase is very patriotic and means 'Long live my peaceful country and extermination to the dirty scoundrels across the line.'

"I was a Hindu amongst Muslims at the time. Their papers reported that every Muslim had been massacred in Calcutta. Later I saw the Calcutta papers and they said that all us Hindus had been assassinated in Pakistan.

"Well, our little village felt out of things, all this going on and not a single murder. So one night when a Muslim was giving his wife her regular beating, her cries became unusually loud and we Hindus thought the murders had really started. So we started to run for safety. When the Muslims saw us running they decided we had killed somebody, so they started running after us, shouting 'Allah hu Akbar.'

"So our little village had its riot. But it didn't turn out to be much, for some wise Muslim leaders came to where we Hindus were hiding and told the crowd to go home. These leaders were very brave, for in another village the crowd got mad when that happened and killed the leaders.

"The riots were caused by four things. Politicians on both sides wanted trouble to make their own positions more secure. Killing nearly a million people accomplished that. Accumulated hatreds were available to be worked upon. Lies were spread about the religions. And a lot of people thought that if they killed off their enemies, they would inherit their lands.

"Mostly the riots were an expression of city life. In the country we knew our neighbors too well to believe the gossip. Yet I do think there is still danger of further riots in the cities.

"For myself I have no bias at all. The Muslims I knew in Pakistan were fine people. If I could find a good job there, I'd go back tomorrow.

"The main reason why I can't take all this too seriously is because of what happened to me. When I lived in Muslim Bengal, all my neighbors were Hindus. Then I fled to the safety of Hindu Bengal, and all my neighbors are Muslims."

He was aware, however, of the heartbreaking experiences of other refugees. Near Calcutta many of them had squatted on whatever land they could find and there they lived a primitive and often starving existence. In the Punjab region farther west, where the mass evacuations were greatest, the hardships were epic.

But soon Sudha had to laugh again. "It's so totally ridiculous! They move millions of people out of lands that always have a surplus of rice and dump them into areas that always border on starvation. Only religious leaders could dream up a thing like that.

"And then there's the case of the abducted women. Every week great patriots in Pakistan and India cry bitterly, 'Where are our abducted women? When will we get back our abducted women?' Let me tell you about the abducted women of my village.

"When a killing took place all the women got very scared. They hid in barrels and under the rice straw and wherever they could disappear to. When the trouble was over, all the men looked for their women. Then when it came time to report the number of women abducted they turned in the complete list. After a while the women decided the men were through killing, so they came home again. But the list remained as it was. Now troublemakers on each side scream, 'We want back our women.' I think most of the missing women are in Calcutta. They don't want to come back. They're smart."

Sudha has great faith in the Indian villager. "I don't think there will be other riots here," Sudha says. "Certainly not religious riots. We are all hungry first and Hindus second. If we had any real sense we'd join Bengal back into one state and make it part of India again. But that's too much to hope for."

The easiest man to interview I ever met was Shri Dev Kanta Borooah, member of the Indian Parliament for Assam, one of the more backward states. A plump, energetic extrovert in his forties, he had the quickest mind I met in Asia. In fact he had so much to say that I rarely had to ask a question. And although he had never been in America, he illustrated most of his points by reference to our history.

He was fun to know because he was a real optimist. "India's going to be one of the great nations," he assured me. "We resemble America when she started her great adventure. We have everything in our favor and if we can only be spared the time to solve our problems, we'll be a famous success.

"I've been in politics for twenty years. First went to jail in 1930. Been in prison four times so I understand politics pretty well.

"Haven't the slightest grudge against the British. They did the best they could. Nobody in India hates the British. That's very important to understand. They threw me in jail, true, but they had to. I never forget the jails but I also never forget the twenty universities they established in my land. Nor the legal system they gave us. Nor the ideal of good government.

"Their time was up, that's all. Like your own revolution. There wasn't much wrong with the British, but their time was up, so we had to throw them out. But look how graciously they left India. To tell you the truth Englishmen are more loved and respected right now than they ever were. I don't like to say this, but they're much more popular than the Americans.

"Let me give you an example. On a certain day I think of, all Indians were united in the threat that if England didn't get out we'd assassinate them all, Viceroy Mountbatten first of all. The next day Lord Mountbatten turned the Government over to us. At five-thirty that day we had what we wanted, the right to nominate of our own free will our first locally chosen Governor-General. Whom did we nominate? Lord Mountbatten, of course.

"Sometimes Americans ask how we can be a republic and still remain in the British Commonwealth paying respect to the King. I don't know how to explain that except that Britain made a graceful exit and we feel indebted to her for avoiding bloodshed. She really behaved magnificently.

"That's why we're not aggressive toward other countries. Look at Portugal. They own a big section of India at Goa. We could take it any day we wanted to send our troops in. But it isn't worth a fight. We mustn't waste our efforts on little annoyances like Goa when we have our own problems to worry about.

"Same applies to French Pondicherry. We could occupy the French holdings any morning we had a mind to. But more important is that we mend our own problems.

"We feel the same about the Indians in Fiji. There aren't over 100,-000 of them and we have 350,000,000 to worry about at home. Solving the little problem of Fiji won't help us escape our own larger problems.

"What are they? I would name seven. First, we must create an adequate food supply. Everything is secondary to that. Second, we must manufacture more things for our people to use. Third, we need *lakhs* of schools—a *lakh* is 100,000—for our illiteracy is disgraceful. Fourth, we must improve the standard of living. We know that millions of our people live below the poverty level. Fifth, we must lower the price scale. We're on the brink of real inflation and it must be stopped. Sixth, we must continue to break down the caste system. I myself married outside of caste. So did Nehru's daughter. It will take generations to destroy caste, but we must try. And seventh, we must improve the national health. Our life expectancy is 26. Think of that.

"So you'll agree that if we attend to our own problems we'll have enough to do."

Congressman Borooah was so rational and restrained that I felt brave enough to ask the unmentionable topic: "But why does India refuse to negotiate with Pakistan on the Kashmir problem?"

It was like backing into a buzz saw! "Pakistan has no claim to Kashmir! Indians will never give up Kashmir. It's ours and we'll hold it."

After some minutes I managed to ask, "But I thought that when Hyderabad, which is largely Hindu, was dragged legally but unwillingly into Pakistan by edict of its Muslim ruler, India protested and even started armed intervention. You moved so fast and took over Hyderabad so completely that Pakistan never had a chance to defend her claim."

There was another explosion during which Mr. Borooah explained the Hyderabad problem almost exactly as I had done, so I asked, "Isn't it a fact that Kashmir is heavily Muslim but its Hindu ruler keeps trying to drag it into India?"

"Kashmir's different!" Mr. Borooah cried. I have heard fifteen Indians explain why Kashmir is different, why a plebiscite is not the way to settle the question, and why the good offices of mediating nations cannot

be trusted. I even heard Prime Minister Nehru discuss the problem for
forty minutes, but it always came back to what Mr. Borooah had cried,
"Kashmir is different. No foreigner can possibly understand Kashmir."

Yet I liked Mr. Borooah immensely. It was good to see a patriot eager
to defend his country against all comers. "China invade India? She'll get
a terrific black eye if she tries it. Russia force communism upon us? We'll
throw Russia and her communism both out. We are not a nation for
communism. Pakistan? She'd better not dare to make a move in Kashmir.
We've been very patient with Pakistan.

"America? Your attempt to bully us in the United Nations is disgraceful. Your attacks upon Nehru are insulting. He speaks for all of India.
We refuse to be drawn into a war between Asia and the West. Whatever
he can do to avoid that war he does with our approval.

"But the average Indian, I assure you, likes America. The trouble is
that we've become suspicious when you back Chiang Kai-shek, when
you refuse to recognize China and when you treat your Negroes the way
you do. How can we think of you as our long-range friends?

"As I said before, today it is Britain that understands and champions
Asia. Let me express it this way. If I were on a ship that was sinking and
I had to jump into a lifeboat, I'd jump into the one that was commanded
by an Englishman. I'd reach shore more slowly, perhaps, but we'd be
sure to make it.

"But India has passed the point where she'll have to jump into any
lifeboat. We are really accomplishing the dreams of Gandhi. Never underestimate that saintly man. He kindled in us all that was best. He tried
to remove all that was worst. I would feel safer if he were living today.
But we try to keep his spirit alive in India. That's why we'll solve our
problems."

THE

CYNIC

During their long battle against British rule Indians became adept in
harassing governments, pouring scorn upon any positive action and with-
ering the opposition with diabolical wit. Today the free Indian Government has inherited these professional crepe-hangers, and it is a strange
sensation to have one of them pin you down at a party and start to
explain in acid detail everything that is wrong with India.

"Look at the Parliament-wullahs," my cynical young friend lamented.
"All of them over sixty. In 1921 my father started his fight for Indian
freedom. Later on he joined the Congress Party. What do we find today?

The same people who led us in 1921 lead us today. India, the land of the tired old man. India, the land of lost visions and youthful ideals.

"We face a terrible danger in India. The Congress Party is going to crystallize into a monolithic one-party government. Even now it has no opposition, and the conservative old men lop off the heads of any young men who try to assume leadership. India will go the way of Russia. They had a brilliant revolution, but the leaders became jealous and narrow bureaucrats. Inevitably India must become a fascist state. I think it will happen three years after the death of Nehru. That's why every good Indian prays each night, 'Keep Nehru alive for ten more years.' By then we might have a two-party system.

"Without that there is no hope for the Congress Party. It's terribly corrupt. People joke, 'What's the difference between a thief and a Parliament-wullah? A thief steals and goes to jail. A Parliament-wullah goes to jail and then steals.'

"It's disgraceful. India has no rice to eat and no cloth to wear, but the Congress Party condones black markets and racketeering. Rich people with rupees can buy anything they want, while the working people with annas starve and go naked.

"All we get from Government is talk about the mystical soul of India. Look how it operates with women. On the one hand the mystical soul says that the Indian woman is the monarch of her home, but we keep this monarch a stupid, broken-backed peasant who moulds cow dung all day. We close our eyes to how India is changing but have you read the matrimonial advertisements in our papers? Here's one. 'Wanted. Lovely young virgin nineteen seeks mature husband. Must be mill owner or highly placed in Government. Caste no bar. State income when writing.' And she gives her full address."

The young man showed me a column of such proposals. By their frank phraseology they denied the pietistic claims of orthodox Hindus that Indian women would never break away from the old patterns. Even widows were now free to marry again, an absolutely vital affront to Hindu orthodoxy: "Handsome and dashing army officer income Rs. 1200 will marry widow under thirty. Caste or children no bar. Must have house in own name."

"The mystical soul of India leads us to many stupidities. My nephew came home with the new Hindi textbook on botany. 'What is the purpose for which flowers were put on earth? So that with them we may pay reverence to the gods.' An article on hydraulic pumps states that the gods of deep water push the water up from the bottom of the lake. A bill is seriously proposed that all European-style doctors be banished from India and that everyone go back to Ayurvedic medicine men. Another is being circulated to prohibit the killing of any living thing. That includes cows, pigs, fish and chickens. While we starve they discuss such an idea.

"I used to be a devout Hindu and still respect the sacred cows, though why they should fatten on our grain while we go hungry is difficult to understand. But to find something totally impossible, look at the suggestion that any Indian who wears factory-loomed clothes be expelled from the Congress Party. This in a land that is going naked from lack of cloth.

"Our nationalism has reached the ridiculous state. We have twenty-four major languages and none is common to any great part of India. The two best were English and Hindustani. But English is to be dropped for obvious reasons, and Hindustani is outlawed because it contains Urdu words, and Urdu was chosen by Pakistan for their national language. What we settled on was Hindi, which is like Hindustani except that it drops Urdu words and replaces them with ancient Sanskrit. So we have a national language without a literature and the average educated Indian can understand the B.B.C. radio programs from London better than he can his own Hindi broadcast from Delhi.

"And you can have no idea of how badly we need a language that people can share. We are almost totally illiterate. An American journalist visited one of our villages and asked a peasant, 'What do you think about America's intervention in Korea?' The peasant blinked and asked, 'What's Korea?' So the journalist chose a simpler question: 'What do you think of America's offer of wheat?' 'What's America?' asked the peasant. The American saw that he was completely off the track, so he asked, 'Is life better since the English left?' And the peasant asked in surprise, 'Were they here?'

"I must admit that such people are too stupid to vote intelligently. Although I despise Congress Party, I know they have no choice but to stay in power and keep on postponing the elections. It will be years before we can seriously discuss political problems with our people, and in that time something will probably explode."

The oblique mention of revolution led the cynic to that one topic upon which he was not supercilious. Subhas Chandra Bose. This remarkable Indian leader had died in a way to enshrine himself as an immortal. He seems to have boarded a plane and set out across the ocean to get help for India. The plane disappeared mysteriously and has never been heard from. Millions of Indians know in their hearts that Subhas Chandra is biding his time and will shortly appear from the skies to lead them to a new national greatness.

"When Subhas Chandra comes back," my cynic said with great excitement, "the Congress-wullahs will be through. Subhas Chandra understood India. He even defied Gandhi. He defied Nehru. He joined the Japanese Army to lead an expedition against the British. He was a great leader."

Now the cynic's eyes grow bright. Above his desk is a colored litho of Bose, a big-faced, handsome, placid man with enormous forehead. But what my cynic did not know was that I knew where these millions of Indians believe Subhas Chandra to be. They think he is hiding in Moscow, being instructed in the principles of revolution. They know he will return. Eagerly they await him, not because he is now a communist but because they are fed up with the Congress Party. They remember Subhas Chandra as the dynamic adventurer who was going to overthrow the rich, launch a new India and become their leader. As my cynic said devoutly, "I am certain that some day the plane of Subhas Chandra will return."

THE

GRACE

OF

ASIA

I am always amazed when Americans ask, "How did you manage to get along in Asia? Can you speak Asiatic?" Or, "Were you able to eat that funny food? Did it make you sick?" Or, "I suppose you know they're all crooks out there. They'll steal the gold fillings out of your teeth."

To all such questioners I can express only one wish: that they could spend some time with Sohan Lal, of Delhi, India. He is a little fellow forty-four years old, a brilliant, darting, handsome hummingbird of a man. He stands five feet one, moves with compulsive energy and talks with brilliance, spicing his observations with inviting wit.

Like most educated Asians he speaks excellent English for he was specially tutored in the language for many years. It is, in fact, his native tongue. But he apologizes. "I am not really so good in English because my education was interrupted. I should have gone on to Oxford but my father died prematurely. I had to stay home and start assuming control of some of the family interests."

Who's Who states that by the time Lal was thirty-six he was chairman of six companies (including electricity, wool, trade, banking); director of three (in manufacturing and farm products); guiding hand in a private high school, a public college and a religious movement; chairman of his chamber of commerce, member of his city corporation and state legislator in Punjab.

The word Punjab is important. For when partition came Sohan Lal lost his wealth, his titles and his positions. He was a Hindu in Muslim Lahore, one of the great cities of Asia. His voice chokes when he speaks of Lahore.

"Finest city in India. One of the oldest. A superb center of civilization for more than two thousand years. The gateway to India. Now it's gone.

"I had to flee. I left everything behind. Printing presses. Woolen mills. All my life. But above all I had to leave Lahore."

How does he live now? He has set up a printing press in Delhi and some woolen mills in Bombay. His Delhi Press has been in the news recently, for from it Lal has issued a series of pamphlets written by himself which suggest to the Government of India means whereby it could govern better. His first pronouncement dealt with the refugee problem. His second contained suggestions for a better foreign policy. And his third dealt with economics.

"I feel a citizen has an obligation to share with the Government any ideas he might have. I take government seriously. I'm like a lot of Indians in that respect. I flee my homeland without a shirt but pretty soon I'm telling my new Government how it ought to behave."

Lal himself behaves with extraordinary grace. I met him one night at the sedate and vaulted Gymkhana Club. To the strains of a military band he danced waltzes and polkas energetically with slim dark ladies in shimmering saris.

I shall never forget the Gymkhana Club. Once no Indian would have been allowed within its formal portals. A few subservient rajahs or chinless princes might have squeezed in but the white men would have resented them. Now with the white men gone, Indians control the club. Across its stately floor dance turbaned and bearded Sikhs, officers in bright uniform, handsome men in full dress and Sohan Lal in his bejewelled achkan.

Lal never looks better than when he wears this traditional suit: ankle-hugging white chudithar pyjamas and black-silk tight-collared achkan. "It's a wonderful costume," he explains enthusiastically. "Very cool in hot weather. The cloth is so thin." You notice that instead of buttons or links he wears large rubies studded with diamonds. The effect is dazzling.

The dance continues and sprightly Mr. Lal insists that each lady dance with him at least once. And now you watch not this handsome little man but the graceful women of India as they go by in their diaphanous saris. It is an unforgettable delight to see a dimly lit room filled with beautiful women in flowing saris. For this must be one of the finest gowns ever devised, especially for waltzing.

At intermission Lal fans himself energetically—he never does anything halfway—and jumps up and down with pleasure when food is announced. He personally escorts three women to the table, fixes their silverware, talks with everyone and whispers, "I have three sons and two daughters. They'd love this dance."

To see Sohan Lal at his best, however, you must visit him at home. It is a modest apartment in one of Delhi's hotels near the Kashmiri Gate. "I'm re-establishing myself," Lal says brightly, jumping up to meet you. "In Lahore we had a fine home, I can tell you. Here it is work and starting a new life that is important."

His guests include members of the Turkish, Canadian, Burmese and French delegations to India. Lal says, "I like to have people from all over the world in my house. Listen to them talk!"

Then as if motivated by sheer joy he claps his hands and cries, "Now we give the Americans our specialty. They must guess what these are!" He brings a silver tray containing a biting sauce and a towering mound of little brown balls. With a swoosh he dips one into the sauce and pops it into your mouth. "What is it?" he demands. There is no clue except that the taste is delightful.

"Chicken shami kebabs," Lal cries. "Chopped chicken and special spices and flour made from a pulse which we call channa. Very tasty, yes?"

You try two more and he becomes impatient. "More, more! I always have eight or nine."

Then from the other side of the room someone asks about America and Lal stops clowning. "I've been there several times," he explains. "From New York to California and back. It's a fairyland. Even the magic lamp of Aladdin could not reproduce the wonders of America. The marvelous limits of human enterprise in material things have been reached there. To those of you who have not been to America I cannot do justice in general terms. But when I am in America I always think of India. Because Americans are very healthy. They enjoy many comforts. India and America must make strong efforts to remain friends, for we can learn from one another."

Then his irrepressible buoyancy takes over and he cries, "But what I liked best in America was that wonderful Waldorf-Astoria. Oh, what a heavenly place! You push a button and order anything you want. You push another button and the newspaper arrives. I was in the Waldorf-Astoria many times and never ate one meal except in bed. I thought,

'This is what people mean when they talk about living like an Indian rajah!' No rajah lives half as well."

There are other Indians who do not share Sohan Lal's enthusiasm for America. I recall a brilliant dinner party Lal gave when he introduced me to a group of his Lahore expatriates. He pointed at them laughing and joking. "You'd never think they were refugees! Ah, we Indians forget misery in a hurry."

One of his guests was a famous Indian editor. I had better call him Bahadur. He was extremely handsome and spectacularly brilliant in conversation. I had barely got into my chair when he let fly about the Korean war. How did any American justify such behavior? I started to explain but he was absolutely too much for me. He shotgunned me with facts, figures, fragments of American history and the latest scandal from Texas. It was an overwhelming performance and Lal whispered, "You think his manner of arguing too aggressive?"

"No, I can take it. I'm interested in what such a man thinks."

"Perhaps this will explain him," Lal said. "He's been invited to visit Moscow. A special trip arranged for by the Russian Government."

Americans ought to know that men like Bahadur are common in Asia. Brilliantly educated, gifted in debate and politically alert, they feel no identification whatever with America. Having fought England all their lives they consider us merely an extension of their old enemy.

I read Bahadur's paper carefully and could find no apparent pro-Russian bias. True, it printed scare headlines about Negroes receiving injustice in America. True, it took a crack at us whenever our communiqués from Korea tallied up the newest number of Asiatic dead, but it was neither pro-Russian nor anti-American. It merely illustrated that classic Burmese phrase: "America or Russia? I couldn't care less!" But in the case of this brilliant leader, Russia is taking careful pains to get him to commit himself. When he returns from Russia he may have made up his mind.

Bahadur had to leave Sohan Lal's party early and a beautiful young woman at my side said, "He talks very well. But his ideas aren't always clear." Hers were particularly clear. She said, "All of us tonight are old Lahore people. We have all lost our old way of life. But now we have a nation we can call our own. That's worth whatever price we had to pay.

"When I was a girl my family had a summer home in Simla. It was lovely and cool in the hills but suddenly that home became an insult. For the English chose Simla as their summer capital. And we Indians were forbidden even to walk on certain streets."

The beautiful refugee makes no effort to hide her unforgiving bitterness. She turns to watch a well-behaved party of Englishmen rise and start to dance. "Look at them!" she whispers impishly. "Surely they are the most clumsy people on earth." Then she confides, "Don't you worry about what the editor said. If Americans will only avoid the mistakes of the English you will find India your lasting friend. Any time I see a white man in Delhi dance well or show courtesy or appear to be interested in India I know he's an American."

Another of Lal's guests has other ideas. He takes me to Parliament where I witness the finest, most dignified and intellectual governing body I have ever seen in action. It's been my good luck to watch most of the world's great parliamentary bodies—Congress, parliaments in Australia, Great Britain, France—but I have never seen one that surpasses the Indian for attention to business, brilliance of debate, responsibility to the nation, and average caliber of the membership.

The reason for its excellence is at the same time a castigation of its insecure foundations. For the Indian Parliament is appointive, as perforce it must be, for India is a vast oligarchy which for the present must appoint its senior officials. If the American Congress were made up of the 531 men and women best equipped to govern our land, it would be a pretty dazzling spectacle. But no appointive body is ever superior in ultimate political good. At best it is a stopgap until the people learn enough to elect their own officials. When this happens it is inevitable that some pots and crocks will get elected along with sagacious men. It is curious, therefore, that the Indian Parliament will be a better body when it includes a lesser breed of man thrown into office by the will of the people.

Lal's friend whispers, "You have observed, I'm sure, that our Parliament is based on English procedure. India owes England an enormous debt. Our law is English. Our language. Our universities. Our medicine. Many Indians hate England for the wrongs she did us. But we must all acknowledge the good, too."

I spent about a week in Parliament listening to the birth cries of a new nation. It was an inspiring experience to hear Ambedkar cry that everyone wanted the Indian princes put in their places, but that there was in the world something larger than mere revenge. The spirit of law. And even if it was tempting to pass recriminatory legislation against the arrogant princes, it was better not to do so.

But it was terribly disturbing to hear Pandit Nehru address this Parliament. He spoke for forty minutes on the Kashmir problem and although I followed each word he said, and although Parliament approved his arguments with a hurricane of banged desk tops, I did not comprehend a word of his reasoning. Nehru had pled law and justice when Hindu

Hyderabad was forcibly taken into Pakistan by its chance Muslim ruler. Quite properly Nehru pointed out that this was a gross betrayal and he used arms to correct it. But when Kashmir, which is predominantly Muslim, was brought into India by a chance Hindu ruler, Nehru said that was all right. He argued that there was a higher law, but I could not understand his logic.

Sohan Lal prays for a peaceful solution to Indian-Pakistan relations. More than most he has suffered from the great troubles. He says, "All of us in India must work on our immediate problems. Our illiteracy is appalling. If we want to catch up with the world we must have more technical schools."

Of caste he says, "I am a Hindu and I understand the old bases for caste organization. It grew out of our belief in rebirth, which implies that at each successive birth the soul comes equipped with certain inherent mental abilities. Therefore each newborn individual is best able to perform certain jobs. This placed our caste system into a philosophical, metaphysical, social and religious framework. It was like the guild system in England or the specialization by family in Europe. But now the system is crumbling and outmoded.

"Mahatma Ghandi speeded its death by maintaining that so long as Hindu society was stratified no one could attain political maturity. I myself have long had the opinion that caste does not deserve to continue. Look at our Constitution. All distinctions of caste have been abolished. And great efforts are being made to bring the backward classes up to the level of the rest. Of course, the same thing is happening all over the world so we are merely part of a universal movement."

To be with Sohan Lal is a rare privilege. He is intelligent and charming. He owed me nothing yet he put his car and chauffeur at my disposal, he arranged meetings for me, he fed me, he answered some very prying questions, and he introduced me to his friends. He said he did these things because when he was in America, people had gone out of their way to help him.

Men like Sohan Lal know what is wrong with India. They recognize the immense poverty, the illiteracy, the oligarchy, the wrongs of partition and the scars of ancient social customs. But in his bouncing eager way Lal tries to do something about them.

Oh, yes. About everyone in India's being a crook. I crossed all of Asia with nine scattered pieces of luggage and never lost an item. But when I returned to America I found that thieves had completely ransacked my home.

In each Indian village—and more than 85 per cent of Indians live in tiny villages—the water supply is apt to be a hole dug in the earth. Such holes are about the size of a cellar to an average house and about as deep. In the rainy season, which comes in summer, the hole fills to the brim with clean fresh rain water. Then the drinking is good.

But as the dry season comes on, and as the winter months pass with no rain, the water level sinks toward the muddy bottom. Then the drinking is no good at all.

For the waterhole is all things to all people. They bathe in it, swim in it, urinate in it, keep their ducks there and pasture their cattle along the edges. Housewives clean their food in it or grow water lilies in a corner. A thick green scum forms. And everybody drinks the water.

It is a miracle that anyone lives. But old men laugh and say, "I've been drinking that water for seventy years. I'm sound and healthy."

Such men were the lucky ones, for in the average village life expectancy is only twenty-six years as compared with sixty-nine in America. Furthermore, villagers are so continually assaulted by disease that when any unusual sickness comes, death is likely to be epidemic.

This constant poisoning at the waterhole is not necessary. One simple trick would eliminate it. Dig deep wells. Over much of India the water level is within easy striking distance, say 70 feet. (Hundreds of American farmers go down 300 or 400 feet.) And the cost of digging a community well is not great. But Indian villagers are so poor that they cannot even scrape together enough common funds to save their own lives.

If you were all-wealthy and all-powerful, the four best things you could do for India would be these: a deep well for each village; enough cloth for each villager; a new system of agriculture; schools. Everything else is secondary to these primitive needs.

I spent some time at the edge of an Indian waterhole, playing with a group of delightful children. We spent an entire morning there and I recorded just what went into the waterhole and what came out. It was sickening, but the children enjoyed the water and they had lived through it. Now they might live to be old men.

They were great comedians, these children, and spent hours looking at one another through my colored camera filters. Then one of them brought to the waterhole his father, who had been working in the fields. His name was Ram and although he was only forty he seemed like an old man. We tried vainly to talk across our language barrier and he finally sent for another man who spoke English.

Ram said, "I have three little fields in which I grow rice. But my money goes to the *zamindar* and the *baniya*."

These were new words to me but by patient questioning and much later study I discovered what infamous terms they are. Because if America guesses wrong about the words *zamindar* and *baniya* we may invite tragedy in Asia.

"The *zamindar*," Ram explained, "owns the land. I pay him taxes. There are many kinds of taxes. Regular government taxes. And wedding taxes."

"What are they?"

"If the *zamindar's* daughter gets married he gives a big feast. This costs money, so he comes to all his tenants and collects a wedding tax. Then there is the automobile tax, too."

"Have you an automobile?"

"Heavens, no! But the *zamindar* does and that costs money too."

"So he collects it from you."

"Yes."

"Are such taxes passed by the Government?"

"I suppose so. Anyway, I have to pay them."

The *zamindar* is one of the most curious mistakes of history. When the British invaded India they sought only trade and honestly did not intend subduing the nation. But India was in such turmoil that the British could not trade unless they controlled a narrow strip of territory surrounding their establishments, and they could not control the narrow strips unless they controlled the land that touched those strips, and so one inevitable step drew them on to another until they had an excuse to control everything.

Unprepared for the massive job they had stumbled into, they had to devise some way of making India pay for the cost of the new Government—and for the astronomical fortunes shipped back home to England. So, groping in the dark, the British stumbled upon a recent innovation of their Muslim predecessors, who had inserted tax farmers between the Government and the people. This was the *zamindary* system, whereby rich men bid for the right to collect taxes and then milked the peasant to the absolute poverty level.

It was a bad system when the Muslims invented it. It was a bad system when the British found it. And it has remained intolerably bad right down to the present. It was one of the worst mistakes white men ever made overseas.

Americans find a special interest in how the accident happened. In 1759 the British were spending their own money to provide a government for India and drew up three alternatives whereby they might throw the burden onto the Indians: (1) collect revenues directly from the peasants; (2) collect it through appointed agents responsible to the Government; (3) farm it out to rich men as a form of speculation. Because they needed the money in a hurry, the British chose the third alternative, purely as a temporary expedient. The system worked, so it was extended from year to year, always as an expedient.

At the conclusion of the American Revolution, stubborn, self-righteous, and incorruptible Lord Cornwallis went from his defeat at Yorktown to the government of Bengal. It fell to him to make a final, binding decision on taxes. After thoughtful and protracted study of the three alternatives that had faced his predecessors, he decided firmly that the best way to keep revenue coming in with the least trouble was give all agricultural land outright to the *zamindars*!

Legally the *zamindars* had no claim to the land. Time out of mind it had belonged to the peasants. But Cornwallis' judgment comfirmed in ownership a gang of grasping, venal, contemptible tax collectors, whose icy hand upon the heart of India has well-nigh killed the country. Cornwallis' reasoning is instructive: "In case of a foreign invasion, it is a matter of the last importance, considering the means by which we keep possession of India, that the proprietors of the lands should be attached to us from motives of self-interest. A landholder who is secured in the quiet enjoyment of a profitable estate could have no motive for wishing a change."

Today there is violent agitation for the abolishment of *zamindars*. Laws have been passed expropriating their estates—with compensation— but the courts have held that since Cornwallis' time the *zamindars* have actually attained full title to the land of India through custom. Nehru and his followers have pledged themselves to new laws that will correct this old mistake.

But if India can blame the British for the *zamindars,* the Indians themselves are to blame for the *baniyas*. Ram says, "To pay taxes is difficult, so I borrow money from the *baniya*. In all my life I have never been out of debt to the *baniya*."

"Do you borrow only for taxes?" I ask.

"Oh, no! A wedding takes money. A funeral. Anything special."

"And the *baniya* always lets you have the money?"

"Yes. I have always paid my interest promptly."

"You never pay back the loan itself?"

"Who has enough money for that?"

Ram and the interpreter and I do some figuring and as nearly as we can work it out the interest is about 28 per cent per year. This is low compared to other *baniyas* who charge well over 36 per cent. But Ram's rate is high when contrasted to the areas where the Government has tried to stamp out the money-lending racket.

Ram says, "I also borrow to buy the gold and silver bracelets that my wife and daughters wear about their ankles. If I die, the *baniya* could use those bracelets to pay back what I owe him."

It is uncanny how a *baniya* can sell starving peasants trinkets which mortgage their entire lives. Ram has never been out of debt since his father died and he made his first loan to pay for the funeral. He cannot read. He cannot go to the movies. He knows nothing of politics. His life is the payment of interest to the *baniya* and taxes to the *zamindar*.

Between these two the Indian peasant is ground like a grain of wheat between two giant millstones. The simile is not good, for from the grinding of the wheat comes healthful food. From the grinding of the peasant has come the prostration of a great land.

Ram appears not to care. He laughs, knocks his bright-eyed son on the shoulder, and goes to the waterhole for a drink of the good cool water. Pushing aside the green scum, he scoops up a handful and is content.

Young men are beginning to move across India with slogans about *zamindars* and *baniyas* and waterholes. They are legitimate agrarian reformers in a nation that must start such reforms or perish. If Americans, scared by what happened in China when legitimate demands for agrarian reform slipped by default into communist hands, automatically brand all future agrarian reformers as communists we will lose India. These young men are not yet communists and there is no reason why they should become so. It is our job to help Nehru and those who will come after him to institute real agrarian reform. If this does not happen within ten years India will inevitably go communist.

In a major American city an intelligent woman called on me and said she had been worrying about India and had read something that made a lot of sense to her. "Why should we give India wheat while her princes and maharajahs have so much money?"

I said, "Lots of Indians are asking the same question. There is already talk of heavier taxation on the rich to provide money for digging the deep wells and building the roads that will be needed for agricultural reform."

She said, "Taxing the rich? That sounds like socialism!"

I continued, "And the Government will probably have to borrow money from abroad to build certain key factories."

She cried, "Government ownership! That sounds like state socialism."

I asked, "How else can the wells be dug? Or the roads built?"

She replied, "We mustn't have any more state socialism in the world. You would agree with that, wouldn't you?"

I replied, "I'm so strongly against state socialism in America that my wife calls me a reactionary. But now we're talking about deep wells and land reforms in India. Could you tax the villagers we've been talking about enough to pay for those improvements?"

She said, "I know they haven't the money. But we mustn't tolerate any more state socialism."

I asked, "Then would you leave the land in control of the *zamindars?*"

She said, "The one thing we mustn't have is expropriation. That's how England started."

I asked, "Then what would you do?"

She thought for a long while and replied, "That's what I've been wondering about. But the one thing we mustn't permit is any more socialism."

I simply had not the courage to tell her what the alternative was.

THE

FIGHT

FOR

FOOD

India must produce more food or she will starve. On the dry upland plains around Delhi, the national capital, experiments are taking place which may teach Indian farmers how to coax more nourishment from the soil.

These plains remind one of Kansas and Nebraska. In the dry season they seem barren but wherever water reaches a farm, yields are abundant. But the agricultural procedures are almost exactly what they were in prehistoric India some 4000 years ago. The plows are the same, the crops are identical and the yield is just about what it was then.

But within the past few years the Indian Government has lined off a tract of 17,000 acres where experiments are taking place in revising village life. In charge is a forty-five-year-old college graduate who has an indefatigable optimism, a love of the soil and eight children.

"I'm a typical peasant," he laughs. "More mouths than I can feed." M. B. Singh dips his hand into a sack of new gram seed, after wheat the most important grain produced on the plains.

"Lots of people call the Indian peasant stupid, but actually he's one of the cleverest farmers on earth. With his outdated tools he performs wonders.

"True he's conservative and suspicious, but if I can demonstrate a principle, and if it works and saves him money, he'll adopt it right away. Take the case of our new plows."

Mr. Singh runs back to his shed and throws open the doors which hide eleven new types of plow. He indicates one and says, "This is the one that was chosen. It does good work plowing a furrow four inches deep. And it costs $2.10."

You wouldn't recognize it as a plow. A long section of tree trunk has been pierced with three holes for yoking oxen. At the other end a cross beam has been lashed, and to its bottom end has been fixed a tiny steel plow. No screws or bolts are used and the plow will last the average farmer's lifetime.

"We've also invented a machine for threshing wheat. It's pulled by one ox and sells for $32. It takes the place of four oxen that used to walk around a stake all day.

"We've introduced only one expensive implement and it's the most popular of all. A five-row seed drill for $130. Now one pair of oxen replaces ten pair.

"It was amusing about this drill. The peasants looked at it and said it would never work. So we used it on only one farm. The gram came up in rows, properly spaced and easier to cultivate. It yielded more and was easier to reap. This year nearly every farmer has applied for use of the drill, but we can't handle them all. So the peasants are banding together to buy drills co-operatively."

Mr. Singh's experiment involves 18,000 villagers, which means 1.5 to the acre of tillable land. They are not forced to abide by the new procedures, and they retain full ownership and control of their land.

"In these fields you can see India choosing her future. The farm plots are so small that they must be combined. When 1/16th of an acre is shared by five different families, something must be done. Either it will be co-operatively, in this pattern, or by force in the Russian way.

"We keep our objectives very simple, so as not to frighten the peasants. So far we've tried only five experiments. 1. We've introduced improved seed. Punjab 591 is a wonderful new wheat that will yield, if they cultivate it the way we say, up to 60 per cent more wheat then we're now getting.

"2. We demonstrate improved cultivation techniques. For example, how many of those new plows do you suppose we sold in one year? 460.

"3. We uncover new markets for new crops. Later on I'll show you the milk shed which has made it possible for us to capture all the big hotels in Delhi.

"4. We've had sensational success with a fish scheme. All through history the village tanks have been used only for storing water. We found an average tank that covered exactly an acre and stocked it with a hard-flesh carp. From that acre, which had always been wasted and forgotten, we took in one year $86 worth of fish. An acre of wheat will yield $60 for the grain and $26 for the straw. In other words, from an acre of fish tank you earn exactly as much as you do from an acre of wheat, and you don't have to manure, cultivate or thresh. And fish is better for you."

Mr. Singh's fifth experiment leaves the non-Hindu baffled. Fine new bulls have been introduced to improve the cattle. But all the agricultural propaganda posters from England and America have to be redesigned. Because American signs feature cows that yield fine beef, whereas in India the cow is absolutely sacred. Therefore the Indian posters stress handsome appearance, increased milk yield and freedom from disease. But never a word about steaks or veal.

"In one way the flight of Muslims from this region to Pakistan has hurt us. In the old days Muslims, who like beef, used to sneak out at night and round up stray young bulls. Today the extra bulls roam wild and have become a serious problem. Obviously they can't be killed."

Now Mr. Singh leads us down the village path to see his milk shed, and we stumble by chance upon a rare sight. An Indian husband is bringing his thirteen-year-old wife home to live with him after her four years spent with her own parents while she was still too young to have children. Two lumbering bullocks haul a flower-strewn cart through the narrow streets. Scores of women shuffle through the dust chanting lovely marriage songs. The bride herself sits very erect, completely smothered in a heavy red blanket. On her head a clay flowerpot supports a silver bowl out of which grow mystical flowers and leaves signifying marriage.

At the door of a miserable hut the husband appears, trembling nervously. The songs increase in joyousness, the village children scream with joy, and slowly the red blanket is removed from the face of the trembling wife. She is a winsome little girl and the old women shout suggestive ideas at her so that she blushes. Now her husband leads her to her new

home, while Mr. Singh draws enormous cheers by shouting something
to the old women.

"I asked them when they would bring me some of the marriage food.
They were happy and proud that I would eat with them, for the husband
is dhoti caste, a washerman, and while he's not exactly an untouchable,
he must never touch any food a Hindu eats. I ignore caste and they like
me for it."

But now we reach the veritable untouchables. They live in a tragic,
filthy community outside the village walls. Here, in bitter squalor, in
huts that almost collapse from the wind, live the untouchables, the Harijans, as Gandhi called them, the children of God.

They are a boisterous and free lot. Their women do not hide their
faces but stare boldly at us. The children romp and riot while the grown
men chase a litter of fat pigs and proudly display them. "A new strain
we've introduced," Mr. Singh says proudly. "Yield lots more food."

And then, not fifty yards from the untouchables, we come upon the
new milk shed. It's spotless. "We built it here and said we'd buy milk at a
premium from anyone who brought his cows here to be milked. At first
nobody came. Then one man tried it. He actually did get more for his
milk. Now they all come and we do a brisk trade."

Who keeps the shed immaculate? "The untouchables over there. You
wouldn't believe it. I can teach them to keep their cows clean, but they
would never think of cleaning themselves. They're the untouchables.
Later on, perhaps . . ."

THE

NEW

MEM-

SAHIBS

Noel Coward, who can be extremely cruel when in the mood, made
the wry comment after meeting the British matrons of Singapore that
now he understood why it was so difficult to hire upstairs maids in London.

I could not agree to this libel, for I found the matrons of Singapore
both intelligent and attractive, and one night at the super-posh Tanglin
Club I saw several who were downright beautiful.

But I would agree heartily with the French cavalry officer who said
that in his lifetime only three things had really terrified him, a tiger in

the Malay jungles, a cobra in Mysore and almost any Englishwoman in the tropics.

What happens to perfectly decent women after they live in India or Java or Malaya is impossible to explain. At home they were not the sort to lord it over servants, for most of them had none. Nor were they self-appointed paragons of social virtue, for many English towns have an enviable freedom in social relations. But once put them in the tropics, and these same gentle girls become unbearable.

It would be unreasonable to expect women suddenly surrounded by twenty servants, when they had none before, to retain their balance, and few do. Quickly they succumb to delusions of grandeur and consider it inevitable that white women should order about almost any of the 1,500,-000,000 yellow and brown and black men of Asia. As one French priest-sociologist explained it, only the lowest-caste natives would hire out as servants because the others bitterly resented being kicked by white women.

It would also be unreasonable to expect that white women in the tropics should remember much about the democracy they knew at home. Almost alone and submerged in an alien sea of strange colors, strange foods and strange inhabitants, it is instinctive for them to clutch at the silliest rules for protecting their cherished social life. For real, archaic and oppressive social patterns you have got to go to the tropics and watch white societies protecting themselves from brown.

But it is not unreasonable to demand that from now on the mem-sahibs accept the citizens of Asia as human beings or stop coming to Asia. Proud Indians and Indonesians and Filipinos will no longer tolerate the social nonsense of past generations, for they know that the white men and his mem-sahib are no longer gods.

It must be quickly admitted that Englishwomen were not the only offenders in establishing insufferable social systems which ridiculed and insulted Asians. The Dutch in Java were as bad. Australians in Rabaul were worse. And although the French behaved a little better, they made up for it by excessively harsh economic exploitation. All the Europeans were alike.

But it was reserved for the Englishwomen to lead the pack. All across Asia you meet local citizens who speak with venomous hatred of the British social system as it affected them. Today many Indians frankly acknowledge the debt they owe to England, but they add that the social persecutions they experienced in English society were unbearable. Usu-ally they place the blame for this upon the women, holding that Eng-

lishmen were often prepared to accept Asians as human beings, but that
their women would never relent.

The desire for revenge that such behavior generated in Asia is incalculable, yet it must be taken into consideration when judging Asia's
future. There is a memory of social ignominy that this crop of political
leaders will never forgive, and many of their actions are obviously motivated by a desire to prove that Asian society will no longer accept white
domination in any particular.

Although Englishwomen were largely responsible for the hateful
policy of arrogant supremacy, it was left to their men to express this
policy in its most ridiculous form. A recent letter from such a gentleman
has had wide circulation in Asia, always to the accompaniment of hoots
of ribald laughter. A last-gasp Englishman explains to the public how
white people should govern Asia. The letter was written, believe it or not,
in 1951.

"Psychological propaganda and an outward show of authority are
worth dozens of committee meetings. Leading officials should wear colorful uniforms as often as possible.

"When the High Commissioner leaves King's House in his Rolls-
Royce, fine example of the world's finest motor car, he should be preceded and followed by traffic police outriders on motorcycles.

"The traffic police all over town should be warned of his journey and
should control and direct traffic accordingly to allow him free and swift
passage.

"His convoy should be ostentatious so that people will know when it
passes that it is the High Commissioner.

"All major officials should conduct themselves in the same way, so as
to impress the population. A suitable uniform should also be designed
for soldiers who are on leave, so that their presence will invariably be
noted.

"Lesser officials should be officials. When the secretariat empties itself
at tiffin time you cannot tell if the people coming out are officials or
junior assistants in a commercial undertaking.

"Newspapers, too, should give prominent display to the photographs
of highly respected citizens and accompany the photographs with suitable captions.

"High officials should also address the population frequently by radio
to remind the country that it is being well governed."

Such a letter, accompanied by the mem-sahib point of view, represents
such a discredited theory of colonial government as to be tragic in the
light of today's events. One might grudgingly admit that in governing a

totally ignorant and savage land such pompous nonsense might be necessary for a few decades. But the poison of such empty forms is that they remain as pleasant games long after their usefulness is past. And into the emptiness someone like Ho Chi Minh or Sukarno or Mao Tsetung injects a real, life-size revolution.

Contrast this bankruptcy of ideas with what Russia offers Asian people today. Leadership of their own lands. Increased crops. More food. Ownership by local people of local industries. It is true that most of the Russian promises are not fulfilled, but when opposed to Rolls-Royces and uniforms and police on motorcycles the Russian theory is going to win every time.

It is disturbing, therefore, to find that today in the first flush of America's world responsibilities, many American women fresh from two-room apartments have picked up the mem-sahib racket right where the Englishwomen left off. I have heard half a dozen American women sipping tea and saying, in self-pity, "If we Americans pulled out of here tomorrow, within six months these characters would be back in trees."

I am sure Englishwomen thought the same way right up to the minute they were being kicked out of one establishment after another. Surely the Dutchwomen were convinced that without them Java would collapse. And if Americans persist in such ideas, if they persist in playing the role of great white father and mem-sahib, our efforts to win Asia to our side are absolutely doomed.

All American firms sending employees to Asia, all governmental agencies having business there, and all friends seeing vacationists off should see to it that the women who go along are given a pamphlet explaining what happened to the English and Dutch and French and Australian societies that were built upon the tacit assumption that all people who are not white are feeble-minded.

There is much that is wrong with Asia. Some things are terribly wrong. And by and large sensible Asians want our help in correcting them. But they will not tolerate our ridicule.

It is good, therefore, to remark that in numerous instances white women have done great things in creating friendly respect between Americans and Asians. I think they have done a better job, sometimes, than their husbands, and it is such women that should represent America.

This is terribly important because Red China and Communist Russia are sending extremely powerful and impressive women to other parts of Asia. The results are impressive, for they are undoing the damages done by the mem-sahib. We must not leave the field of social victories entirely to the enemy. Let some other nation become the new mem-sahibs. Let us be the nation of democratic equality.

OBSERVATIONS

When I think of India I think of the Kashmiri Gate. It stands in the western wall of Delhi and through it have passed conquerors, new religions, old beggars and the princely viceroys of British India.

But I remember the Kashmiri Gate because of a somewhat different traveler. There was a young woman who haunted this gate and in some ways she spoke for India. I could pass through the gate to Sohan Lal's for a fine evening and I could think that India was a land of brilliant philosophy. I passed through the gate for dinner at the expensive hotels and I could imagine that India was a center of great wealth. And I drove in the countryside where the prolific growth of the soil impressed me, but when I came back through the Kashmiri Gate I would see this strange woman and I could never forget that she was India, too.

For she was naked. She was completely naked and once I saw a policeman gently advise her that she really must go home and put some clothes on. She pulled away and walked on through the Kashmiri Gate where the conquerors had marched.

She was about twenty-two, most attractive in appearance, very wild-eyed. She carried a few filthy belongings in a rotting cloth and was either a madwoman or someone protesting the bitterly high price of cloth. We looked at each other whenever we passed and she seemed to be a living protest. Actually she was merely a naked woman walking through the Kashmiri Gate. No one thought to arrest her.

There is much in India that no American can understand. It is a different land requiring different approaches. We hear about the cities, but it is a land of tiny villages. We develop high regard for Indians of superior education, but India is a land of illiteracy. We hear of princes and maharajahs, but here is a land of gnawing poverty. Most important, we hear of India's temporary problems, but fundamentally this is a land of immense stability with a permanent urge toward self-preservation and projection into the future.

I had in India the oppressive sense of history that has frightened many Western visitors traveling there: What happens in the next few decades is of almost no consequence to India. It will go on pretty much as before. Land reforms will take place. Strange new conquerors may march through the Kashmiri Gate, but India will remain. Its population will multiply and a thousand years from now India will be there, timelessly struggling with such new problems as will have arisen.

But for America the next few decades are of immense importance. We are clinging to a less fundamental perch, and that is why I have felt that it is more important for us to hold India's friendship than it is for India to worry too much about America. This may not seem obvious now, but as we go on I think it will become apparent.

I wish that some way could have been worked out for India, Great Britain and America to have combined as a team. That was impossible, so now I hope that America and India will co-operate on common problems. If that proves impossible—as evil-intentioned people in both America and India seem determined to prove—then all we can do is retreat to a tenuous friendship with Japan and pray to God that the rest of Asia does not blow up in our face.

I do not believe that Indian-American friendship has been lost. It has, however, reached the testing stage. Our handling of wheat for India was ridiculous and calculated to do us the most possible harm. Perhaps we should not have said at first that we would give them the wheat free. Involved are economic problems which I do not understand; but once having said we would, we were then committed, and our subsequent backing and filling and debating dissipated whatever good will we might originally have created.

The people of Asia are not stupid. One day they will stand in the world as our absolute equals. At that time they must be able to look back at a long history of constructive American-Asian relations. We started a good history with China. We continued with the Philippines and Japan. Right now the crucial chapters are being written in India.

PAKISTAN

PAKISTAN DEFIES THE LAW OF POLITICAL GRAVITY. IT SHOULD HAVE collapsed long ago but has become instead one of the most vital nations in Asia. Its accomplishments are unbelievable and its future assured. In the space of a few years—1940–1951—this seventh largest nation on earth was conceived, created, organized and placed on a firm foundation. As late as 1939 the eventual creators of Pakistan were protesting that under no circumstances should India be partitioned. Seven years later they had torn Pakistan from the body of India, had witnessed the mass slaughter of perhaps a million people, had arranged for the shifting about of six million more and had miraculously launched a great nation. The first years of Pakistan's history are without parallel.

First, Pakistan is a geographical absurdity. Organized solely on religious criteria it is as if one religious group in the United States felt there was no place for it within our republic. So New England withdraws from the Union and so does California. They form one new nation. There is absolutely no land connection between the two parts, no railroad that runs from Boston to San Francisco, no airline that is free to put down at Kansas City or Chicago. The only practical communication is via the Panama Canal, and there is no major seaport in New England! That is an exact analogy. For New England substitute East Pakistan near the Burma border. For California read West Pakistan on the Iranian border.

Second, Pakistan is an ethnic absurdity. Throughout most of the nation there is no racial or cultural difference—other than religious—between a Pakistani and an Indian. They are of one stock, of one inheritance. Most Pakistanis, except a few in West Pakistan of distant Persian or Arabian ancestry, are clear-cut Hindus who a few generations ago turned Muslim. There is no ethnical basis for Pakistan, especially in the eastern section.

Third, Pakistan is an economic absurdity. The bulk of the population is jammed into small East Pakistan (42,000,000 in an area the size of Wisconsin) while vast West Pakistan has only 28,000,000. The density of population in West Pakistan is 92 to the square mile, in East Pakistan 775. At a time when nations need industry to succeed, East Pakistan is the most rural major area on earth, only 1 per cent of its population living in cities of more than 50,000. Furthermore, East Pakistan's major cash crop is jute, of which she produces a large portion of the world crop, but almost all jute mills were left in India at partition; and West Pakistan produces a surplus of wheat and cotton but cannot trade with India, whose people are starving and naked.

Fourth, Pakistan is a military absurdity. Its two portions are 1200 miles apart and are separated by the armies of a mortal enemy. East Pakistan is nearly surrounded by India, and West Pakistan is threatened not only by India but also by Afghanistan, whose Pathan border tribes are agitating for Pakistan's Pathan border states to break away and join them. It is understandable why more than 65 per cent of Pakistan's yearly revenue goes to the military, but it is not understandable why this proud and fierce young land of 74,000,000 people says it will fight India's 346,-000,000 at the first sign of trouble, especially if India tries to hold onto Kashmir.

Fifth, Pakistan is an administrative absurdity. When the British came to India the Muslim conquerors of India had only recently lost their thousand-year rule of the sub-continent. They stayed aloof from the British and it was the Hindus, for generations virtual slaves, who co-operated with the new conquerors. The proud and once-superior Muslims petulantly ignored both the upstart British and the parvenu Hindu bureaucracy. Muslims would not learn English. They would not attend school. They would not apply for civil service jobs. Nor would they learn either a skilled trade or a business. As a result Hindus became the leading citizens, the wealthy merchants, the craftsmen and the petty government officials. Not until it was too late did the Muslims realize that they were sentencing themselves to a perpetually inferior status. An excellent young Pakistani scholar told me, "My family did not consider it a crime when I learned to speak English, but they did think it a sin." By 1940 Muslims knew that if Britain withdrew from India they would simply be engulfed by the better-trained Hindus. The partition of India was demanded primarily as a religious measure, but also because Muslims needed time to catch up. When they did finally form their own nation they discovered that all the learning they had spurned in the preceding 200 years had to be acquired at once. I have never seen so hardworking a government as Pakistan's. It is literally picking itself up by its own intellectual boot straps.

Sixth, Pakistan is a grammatical absurdity. The name was composed by a poet who took the first letters of various territories he thought ought to be included in a Muslim nation—P for Punjab; K for Kashmir—but he guessed badly. Pakistan didn't get all the initials in its name. However, there is even more objection to the name of India. Accurately, the word denotes the entire sub-continent and Pakistanis feel outraged that their enemy should have appropriated the name of the land they live in. They laugh about it, though, for the name India comes from the Indus River. Under partition almost the entire river is in Pakistan. So Pakistan editors never call their neighbor India. They call it by its ancient name Bharat.

Finally, Pakistan is in some ways a religious absurdity. More than 35,000,000 Muslims still remain in India and millions of Hindus have been left behind in Pakistan. These minorities are hostages who may be liquidated if riots start or who may form fifth columns if war begins. Since Hinduism and Islam are diametrically opposed religions—Hindus worship the cow, eat pork, cherish idols, whereas Muslims eat cows, shudder at pork, destroy idols—there is little chance that any large-scale conversion will take place. The religious problem will remain an exacerbation for many years.

Having logically proved that Pakistan cannot exist another day, I have, illogically, overlooked the one determining factor: religious patriotism. The people of Pakistan have ignored probabilities and difficulties. They wanted a state in which their religion would be protected and now they have it. Anyone who doubts the importance of religion in the modern world should visit Pakistan.

Casual visitors immediately think of several glib and presumptuous solutions to the problems facing India and Pakistan: (1) Avoid a Kashmir war by ceding Kashmir and surrounding territories to Pakistan and uniting East Pakistan to India. (2) Divide Kashmir so that Pakistan gets most of the territory while India gets enough to save face, (3) Forget Kashmir, submerge differences, and reunite India and Pakistan.

A Pakistani's reaction to such proposals is indignation and shock. Most Pakistanis would surrender their lives rather than their independence or their claim to all of Kashmir. I have talked with more than a hundred Pakistanis of all stations, and I have never met a single one who would even discuss any of the above proposals. There is much less likelihood that Pakistan and India will submerge their differences than there is that the United States and Russia will submerge theirs. Between capitalism and communism there is not the gulf that there is between Hinduism and Islam.

What is the likelihood of war? Every Pakistani I met said that if India refused to abide by a Kashmiri plebiscite (which would certainly favor Pakistan) war was inevitable. Furthermore, the presence of religious minorities in each country presents a terrible temptation. The outrages that followed partition could be duplicated whenever some fanatic calls for a religious war. Irresponsible leaders in both India and Pakistan have taken ghoulish joy in threatening civil riots if the Kashmir decision goes against them. Finally, two large armies with fairly immature leadership stand facing each other along remote boundaries. The likelihood of war is great.

At the same time, men of good will in both Pakistan and India recall the terrors of partition. The entire sub-continent was shocked by the massacres. People everywhere are determined that such madness shall not be repeated. Actual overtures of peace are being offered. Recently a Pakistan-Indian trade agreement was negotiated on sensible terms that three months earlier had seemed unattainable. The peaceable ideals of Mahatma Gandhi seem more desirable each day. Therefore, although the aggravations leading to war remain constant, the possibility of peace seems to be increasing slowly. Once more the world can observe the grimly fascinating race between common sense and disaster.

But to think of Pakistan only in terms of a Kashmiri war is like thinking of atomic power only in terms of atom bombs. Politically, economically and socially Pakistan is one of the most hopeful portents in Asia. Here is a nation that started absolutely from scratch with all odds against her, and in a time of world travail attained stability. In this respect Pakistan is a miracle.

In Karachi, the capital of Pakistan, there is a sacred tomb which proves that Quaid-i-Azam is dead. Under a desert tent, pitched in the middle of the city, stands a simple marble sarcophagus, and to this shrine comes a constant procession of weeping men and women to place flowers upon the grave of Quaid-i-Azam, the Great Leader. They stand in silent groups to pray for Pakistan, the country this great man built.

Quaid-i-Azam is dead, and yet as you walk the crowded streets of Karachi you are convinced that he must be alive, for probably never in history has one man so dominated the hearts of an entire nation. From a hundred billboards the Great Leader's face looks down compassionately, imploring his Pakistanis to buy government bonds. He instructs them in their duties as citizens. He assures them of the destiny of Pakistan.

In life the Quaid-i-Azam was a razor-sharp Bombay lawyer, Muhammad Ali Jinnah. He spent his life trying to do two things: win independence for India and devise a plan whereby Hindus and Muslims could live together harmoniously in the new nation.

Then, dramatically in 1940, Jinnah renounced the possibility of Hindu-Muslim co-operation and cried boldly that his Muslims must have their own free nation. In the brief space of seven years, unparalleled in history, Jinnah started from nothing and built a great nation, the fifth largest in the world. (Pakistanis claim their nation to be larger than either Japan or Indonesia. This is probably an error.)

Pakistan is the most important Muslim nation. It is the key country in the fight of Muslimism against communism. It is extremely wealthy. It has an enormous capacity for growth, and its future may determine the future of much of Asia. The credit for such an accomplishment is Jinnah's.

He was a very wealthy man, married to a wealthy wife. As a lawyer he was a ruthless and clever adversary. As a politician he was remorseless in exposing puffed-up emptiness. In private life he was an enigma, a tall, emaciated man renowned as the most impeccable gentleman in India.

His life was one of many contradictions. Despising the crowd, he was ultimately deified by the masses as their savior. Forswearing personal advancement in politics, he became the most powerful man in Asia. Working endlessly for Hindu-Muslim fraternity, he saw his acts help to kindle a civil war that called forth perhaps a million murders. Ignoring religion as beyond his province, he became in death the rallying cry for a world religious revival of Muslim hopes.

In order to understand something more of this remarkable man, I called upon his sister Fatima, revered throughout Pakistan as Miss Jinnah. She lives quietly in Karachi, her home marked by a perpetual honor guard. Tall, imperially thin like her brother, beautiful with her unruly head of bobbed gray hair, she wears the flowing chiffon robes of Muslim society and is extraordinarily graceful.

Her face is vividly alert. Her eyes dart eagerly until they fix themselves upon someone with whom she wishes to argue. Then, like her brother, she becomes a formidable adversary, puncturing false ideas with relentless vigor.

"Me try to tell you in an hour anything about my brother? Ridiculous. Impossible. He achieved so much that I could not even begin the story."

I asked if Mr. Jinnah would have approved Pakistan's present tendency to become leader of the Muslim world. "Why not? The big seem always to rule the rest. America's the biggest democracy, so she leads the democracies. It's the rule of power. The big get leadership thrust upon them. Pakistan is no exception to that rule."

Miss Jinnah, surrounded by photographs and paintings of her dead brother, whom she usually refers to as Quaid-i-Azam, seemed the impersonation of his ideals: loyalty, honesty, dedication to the state. She will accept no formal job with the Government, preferring to remain a free critic, and it is probable that if she were to denounce a cabinet, it would have to resign. She uses her position for the advancement of liberal ideas and is the special darling of students, whose grievances she works to correct. She always wears white, and when she moves about Karachi, the first lady of the nation, it is in a white convertible Packard. On the day I met her she had released a one-paragraph letter to the Government questioning the legality of an act which censored opposition newspapers. By nightfall the censorship was modified.

I felt the sting of Miss Jinnah's criticism when I remarked that it was curious that Mr. Jinnah, who was not essentially a religious man, should have founded a theocracy. She exploded, "What do you mean, a theocracy? We are a Muslim state. That doesn't mean a religious state. It means a state for Muslims. What would you have us be? A state for Christians? A state for Hindus?

"We are not a state run by priests or a hierarchy. We are a state organized according to Muslim principles. And I may say they are very fine principles for organizaing a state."

I tried to recover by saying, "What I meant was that your Government officially recognizes Muslimism as the state religion."

The previous flood of criticism had been only a summer shower. Speaking with the acid scorn that had characterized her brother's defense of

Pakistan, Miss Jinnah laughed. "Don't tell me that. All governments recognized one religion as paramount. In America Christianity is the state religion."

I tried to say that I didn't think this was entirely true, but Miss Jinnah laughed again. "You may have some subtle explanation whereby Christianity is not the state religion, but why have you sent thousands of missionaries to this part of the world? Why has America tried to change us from our state religion to yours? And if we don't change willingly, your governments intervene. On behalf of the missionaries."

I said, "I don't believe that's true, but even if it were, our Government still does not support these missionaries."

Miss Jinnah cut me short. "A likely story. Where does the money come from that missionaries spend trying to convert Indians and Pakistanis? You say from private individuals. All right. Why do they give the money? Because they feel drawn to the religion of their country. I cannot object to that. But in return you must not object if Pakistan feels drawn to Muslimism and supports it. We do so from exactly the same motives as you."

I argued, "But your country is run by only one party, Mr. Jinnah's party. And it's called the Muslim League. And if anyone tries to start another party he's cried down as disloyal to Pakistan."

Miss Jinnah became very patient. "You've been in the country less than a week and you are talking about things you don't understand. The Muslim League is the name of a political party. Nothing more. It has no connection with any church. It is not run by priests. Believers and nonbelievers both can belong. Even in the Government we have some who are not practicing Muslims. Pakistan is a Muslim country for two reasons. Most Pakistanis are Muslims. And the Muslim religion happens to include in its beliefs a complete social system which is the best yet discovered for governing a state."

I pointed out that only the day before the leaders of the Muslim world meeting in Karachi, at Pakistan's expense, had announced that an attack on one part of the Muslim was an attack upon all parts, that the time had come when all men of Muslim faith must stand together. "What," I asked, "would Mr. Jinnah have said about that?"

The beautiful gray-and-white lady leaned forward and smiled at me with great compassion. "How dare I guess what Quaid-i-Azam would have thought? He was a very great leader. No one could ever guess his mind. But on the question of a theocratic state let me assure you that Pakistan will not become that.

"I remember when the top leader of the Muslim religion came to my brother and said, 'Quaid-i-Azam, you have accomplished what not even the Prophet and the Koran could achieve. You have united the Muslim loyalties in the person of one man.' Quaid-i-Azam was like that. It was as the Great Leader, not as a religious fanatic, that he drew the Muslim world together."

During our talk Miss Jinnah sat in a deep chair, and when she wanted to emphasize a point her exquisite chiffon veils trembled in the air. She was a magnificent woman, almost overpowering in argument. Watching her brilliant and aggressive mind at work, it was not difficult to understand how her brother had been able to wear Britain down in debate and then wrench from Gandhi and Nehru a separate Muslim state. It has been said that Pakistan was born in the incorruptible fury of Muhammad Ali Jinnah's logic. I believe it.

THE

SHEIKH'S

WOMEN

The word *sheikh* has been so misused that I am going to describe Sheikh Sadiq Hasan with unusual care. He is a distinguished-looking man in his mid-fifties, about five feet six, of slight build and military carriage. His hair is graying and he covers it with an expensive caracul Jinnah-cap, named after the founder of his native Pakistan.

Sheikh Hasan wears Muslim clothes, a trim long coat with stiff buttoned collar. His white cotton trousers fit snugly about the ankles but bag enormously at the knees so that they appear to be a skirt. English shoes complete the outfit.

Hasan's face is unforgettable. His nose is big and sharp. His lips are finely drawn and his moustache is closely clipped. His eyes are the distinguishing characteristic of his face. Normally they are cold and competent, yet they often light up with sparkling fun when something witty is said. He has a habit of fixing you with his eyes, so that you see they are dark brown rimmed with blue.

His very good English is marked by two phrases which he uses almost as punctuation marks. "Well, you see . . ." and "I may say . . . ."

In addition to English the sheikh speaks Urdu, Hindustani, Kashmiri and Persian. He tells you, in his clipped way, that like the sheikhs of fiction he has just ridden in from the desert. On a stallion shod with fire? No, in a jeep.

But nothing Sheikh Hasan says is quite so surprising as his offhand remark that he has been to New York seven times. Before partition he lived in Hindu India, where he owned five choice carpet factories. His entire product was sold to a swanky New York store and he handled the contracts. Hasan says he liked New York.

"But I won't be going there again. When partition came I stuck by my Muslim religion. My five factories were lost, my family fortune, and even my clothes.

"I was wealthy in the old days, for we made the finest Kashmiri carpets, but now I get along with a small income. I don't weep about my losses. For Pakistan to have been born as a Muslim state is worth whatever we have had to suffer. I've forgotten my other days and gone to work. I was economic adviser to the Government and a member of Parliament. I've also helped start a college and I serve on a high-school board. I've also launched an orphanage. I keep busy.

"My reward is to see Pakistan flourishing. I may say we're a surplus state in everything. Very rich. Very promising."

He laughs and this is a good time to ask him what a sheikh really is. "A sheikh? To tell you the truth I don't know. I'm one. But the man who sweeps my gutter is, too. I think it was an old honorary title, but now everyone uses it. If you wanted to, you could be a sheikh, too."

But there is one thing about which Sheikh Sadiq Hasan never jokes. He spends most of his time now trying to find the thousands of women who were abducted during the riots and who are now kept as brothel slaves in remote districts.

"Americans don't understand the terrible things that accompanied the birth of Pakistan. More than 500,000 people were massacred. Hundreds of trains were ambushed by maniacs with swords and guns. More than 12,000,000 people became refugees.

"I may say that no part of this terror was worse than the way women were abducted. Gangs of men would swoop down on refugee trains, shoot the men and drag away the young women. I may say most of the girls were used for immoral purposes and now live hidden away in dark cellars, absolute slaves. I may say there were thousands of them, many thousands. On both sides.

"Four years have now passed and most of these girls are still held in slavery. There was a girl we found in Pakistan. She refused our efforts of help. Refused to go home. I may say she was afraid her family would revile her. Almost no girl wants to go home, and they'll hide from the committee. But I talked with her and sent her back to India. Her family was blessed when she returned. She sent word that she had never been so happy and that life was starting over again.

"Not all stories end so well. We track down some girls who have been so tortured and misused that they cannot remember home. We can't make them go back.

"I've been working on this problem for three years. It is a blot on the reputation of both Pakistan and India that these girls have not been exchanged. I don't insist upon this for the sake of good government, however. I don't even do the work for the sake of the girls. I insist upon it for what the Muslim calls God and the Hindu, Kharma. God would will that strong nations do the right thing.

"Four tasks remain. First, every girl must be returned or the man holding her must be jailed. Second, police must be given extraordinary powers and bonuses for recovering these girls. Third, we must double or treble the number of hired searchers. Fourth, as a gesture of humility let Pandit Nehru himself seek out one of the slaves held in India. Let Liaquat Ali Khan do the same and let there be a ceremonial exchange to symbolize how ashamed of ourselves we are."

Sheikh Hasan, with the aid of his committee, has already located 7,175 Hindu girls in Pakistan, while the Indian Government has returned 14,070. But on one point Hasan grows violently angry. Indian newspapers claim that every one of the 2,000 Pakistani army officers has a Hindu girl locked up in his barracks.

"By heaven, if a single such case is brought to my attention I'll haunt that man out of Pakistan. I'll ruin his honor and destroy his reputation. I may say that I've investigated this charge and up to now have not found it to be true."

When his anger subsides Sheikh Hasan asks that one point be made clear. "Pakistan and India broke away from one another with the greatest violence. I may say the tragedies of partition will never even be recorded in our generation. But today the two countries have forgotten the terror and look forward to years of friendship. You might ask how two countries can forget 500,000 murders. We have to forget. That's why, when I go to India today, I move about without police escorts. I get hearty cooperation from the Indian Government. On this small problem of enslaved women we've been able to co-operate. That's why I have hope for the future."

MOTAMAR

Motamar is a word that will be used a great deal in the future. It stands for Motamar-e-Alam-e-Islami, which means World Muslim Conference. The movement was launched quietly in 1948 as an aftermath of the shock caused by the loss of the Israeli-Arab war. Motamar now represents thirty-six Muslim nations with a reputed Muslim population of 661,000,000.

The handsome young secretary of Motamar is Inamullah Khan, a Burma-born Muslim of thirty who now lives permanently in the spiritual capital of Muslimism, Karachi.

Mr. Khan speaks excellent English, learned at an American missionary college, and says, "Motamar is a vast peoples' organization. We started with a yearly dues of $3.30 but now we've dropped the charge to almost nothing in order to enlist every Muslim in the world.

"The thing to remember about Motamar is that it is not a political organization. We are not backed by any government. We have no candidates running for office. And we support no one political party.

"Motamar is a revivalist movement. Our cry is, 'Back to Mohammed. Back to the Koran.' This means that we are not related to the hierarchy of Muslimism. In fact, we would like to eliminate the priesthood altogether. Muslims do not need priests. We can be married and buried without priests. They merely exist to take advantage of poor people who do not know that marriage is merely a civil contract requiring only two witnesses. We claim that God does not ask that a human soul be introduced to Him by a priest.

"Our motto comes from the Koran. 'Verily, all Muslims are brethren.' We believe this and we teach it. That is why the entire Muslim world is combining to insist that four grave injustices be corrected. Kashmir must be given to Muslim Pakistan. Western New Guinea must be given to Indonesia. The French must set free the North African Muslim colonies, which they now enslave. And sooner or later something will probably have to be done about Palestine."

While Mr. Khan spoke, Motamar was holding a world conference of Muslims in Karachi and the 128 delegates gave united proof that they were tired of being kicked around by non-Muslim powers. Newspapers carried banner headlines on the first unanimously adopted resolution: "Aggression against any Muslim state is an attack upon all Muslim countries."

Mr. Khan is not by any means a fiery radical. He's a successful businessman—heavy building—whose partners encourage him to serve Motamar as unpaid organizer. With careful reasoning and with constant quotation from the Koran, he identifies the exact mission of his organization. "Our message to the people of Islam is taken from the Koran: 'Cling ye to the cord of Allah and be united.' Let me be very frank about this. Obviously Motamar will lead to some kind of Pan-Islamic unity.

But what form it will take we do not predict, nor do we care. It might be like the British Commonwealth of Nations with the binding factor not the King but the Koran. Or it might be a federation with an over-all federal government. Most likely it will be a loose bloc of states with common interests and trade agreements. But whatever the form, all Muslim nations must move closer together. We hope that Motamar will show the way.

"That's why we've chosen for our guiding principle a saying of the Prophet: 'The whole Muslim world is one body.' We are going to show Muslims that they can live best by living in one great nation that abides by the Koran in all things. Our primary interest is cultural. How do people live? They live best when they abide by the Koran. That is the kind of brotherhood we speak of, and not brotherhood on the narrow political level.

"But inevitably we will be drawn into politics. We do not believe in watertight compartments, any more than Mohammed did. That's why Muslimism is a complete religious and social system. Orthodox priests have always stressed the narrow religious aspect. Motamar is going to stress the social program, for the Koran is the best single guide yet devised for the government of a nation.

"By our spiritual force Motamar will insist that the government of each Muslim nation establish what the Prophet visualized as the ideal government. It will be a state socialism, benevolent in character, religious in spirit and Pan-Islamic in world affairs.

"Motamar insists that every Muslim state provide the bare necessities of life for all people. Thus there will be no need for communism in Muslim countries. Pan-Islam will represent a great world force, socialistic in nature, keeping a middle course between communism and capitalism."

In an article published some time before, Mr. Khan had made this point more forcefully. He wrote, "Muslims of today are wide awake. The bluffs of the big powers fail to impress. The tall talks of the United Nations gods are before them. They know how capitalist America and communist Russia embraced each other in Palestine. They know that Sudan is still in imperial clutches, and how Muslim Africa still remains crushed under the 'civilizing' heel of one colonial power or the other. The Muslims are fully aware that their future is safe neither with godless Russia—nor with the dollar god of America."

Mr. Khan insists that a Pan-Islamic league would be a threat to no one. "Consider my own country, Burma. I lived there happily in a devout Muslim family. When I reached twenty-two I realized that if I wanted to live at the center of Muslim life I would have to move to what was then

Muslim India, where the great battles of Muslimism were being waged. I gave up my home and a rich income and a chance to win position in the Burma Government. I chose Islam, and I have been happy ever since.

"But I do not go around shouting that the few Muslims in Burma ought to have a separate state. All Motamar insists is that Muslims everywhere have the right to all basic liberties and a proportionate share in the government.

"I don't know enough yet about the separatist movement in Siam. If the Muslims there have a legitimate grievance, something ought to be done. But all Motamar says is that the Siamese Muslims must be allowed the right to develop a Muslim way of life. We think that applies even to the 50,000,000 Muslims now living in Russia."

It is apparent to the outside observer that sooner or later moderates like Mr. Khan are going to have their hands full. In a surge of zeal Motamar, at its first world-wide meeting, elected as spiritual leader of the movement one of the savage old war horses of Muslimism, the Grand Mufti of Jerusalem. Younger members of Motamar were astonished when the leaders of the movement filed past the Grand Mufti, bowed and kissed his hand. In fact, there is a branch of Muslimism which keeps reminding Muslims of the basic paths to salvation. Only recently the permanent Muslim Conference resolved: "The path of our salvation lies in praying, *zakat*, fasting, pilgrimage, and *Jihad*, the Holy War. We must not underestimate the importance of *Jihad*, which, involving as it does the supreme sacrifice of self, is an expression of one's complete trust in God."

Mr. Khan would have none of this violence, except possibly in the case of Kashmir. "I must honestly admit that if the Pakistan Government accepts any compromise on Kashmir, Motamar will have to unite the Muslim world in defense of brother Muslims who have been so betrayed.

"But we pray that India will be sensible and that Kashmir will soon be ours. Then we shall attend to other problems. We want to bring Muslimism up to date. Not more Western, but more alert to social problems. If the West has a good workable idea, we should borrow it. But the judge of what is good or bad must be the Koran."

Unconsciously and with no political insinuations, Mr. Khan concludes with what could prove to be one of the Prophet's more far-seeing judgments: "Take learning wherever you find it, even if it be in China."

OBSERVATIONS

Perhaps more than in any other part of the world, events in Asia are modified by religion. Certain nations have become so committed to their religions that any deviation is unthinkable.

There are two striking exceptions. In China, Confucianism signifies no formal religion but rather an ethical system uncomplicated by metaphysics or theology. The matter-of-fact Chinese seemed to prefer this unadorned religion; but recent decades have witnessed a decline in allegiance to Confucianism. Now that communism has swept China with such a virulent fever, perhaps it will become the new religion.

Korea, the second exception, is unique in the world. It has never had a prevailing religion. A 1945 census revealed that in a population of 25,000,000 more than 24,000,000 reported themselves as adhering to no religion. Since Christianity's mere 500,000 followers constituted the biggest single sect, Korea becomes by default the only Christian nation in Asia. (Tiny Lebanon shifts between Christian and Muslim from one census to the other.)

The oldest continuing civilized religion in the world is Hinduism. No analogy can be used to describe this curious and powerful religion. It resembles no other. It probably covers a wider range of human experience than any other religion and automatically provides a haven for almost any level of intelligence. In its basest manifestations it seems merely a sexual orgy. In its sublimest, especially in the god-man dialogue of the *Bhagavad-Gita,* it equals in compassionate wisdom the holy books of any other religion. Hinduism has been tried in various other countries— Indo-China and Indonesia, for example—but it has never flourished outside of India and has always been quickly supplanted. But within India it has had an astonishing vitality, withstanding assaults by Buddhism, Islam and Christianity. Ultimately it will probably form a barrier isolating India from the rest of Asia. This has already happened with Pakistan, for rightly or wrongly India's Muslims came to believe that no minority could possibly live freely within a Hindu state. In fact, there is grave apprehension in India right now over the likelihood that orthodox Hinduism will gradually strangle the democracy and force a theocratic fascism upon the nation. There is a great possibility that this might happen. If it does, India will regress into a true dark age and any hope of contact with the rest of Asia will be forlorn. On the other hand, if the spiritual values of Hinduism illuminate a true popular democracy, India would probably find her leadership increasing, for the teachings of the *Bhagavad-Gita* concerning good citizenship are among the most profound on earth.

Buddhism started as a reform movement within Hinduism (about 525 B.C.) and with lightning rapidity became one of the world's master reli-

gions. It swept India and was even adopted by Emperor Asoka as the state
religion. But Hinduism tenaciously re-established itself and Buddhism
disappeared from India to become at one time or another the principal
religion of China, Tibet, Burma, Ceylon, Thailand and Indo-China and
the leading non-political religion of Japan. A warm and generous religion, neither nationalistic nor imperialistic, it has little chance of becoming a major force in unifying Asia, for it is fragmented into many
sects. It is, however, politically vital today because of its repeated, resolute
hostility to communism. It may be the ultimate factor that keeps Thailand, Burma and Ceylon from turning communist.

Christianity is in retreat in Asia. It is being thrown out of many
countries as alien and inappropriate. Its material fortunes have rarely
been so low. But at the same time it represents the dominant religious
influence on the present leaders of Asia. Few of them would subscribe
publicly to Christianity, but in private they acknowledge with astonishing frequency that they owe much of their education, their attitude
toward law and their knowledge of the world at large to this alien
religion. It is thus an enormously potent legacy that Christian missionaries and Christian teachers have left behind. There is still, in every
country—almost in every town—some important Asian leader who can be
counted on to understand the West. This tragic and wonderful contradiction—low estate but exalted power—reminds one of the early days of
Christianity when the essence of its message changed nations.

The most vital religion in Asia today is Islam. Pakistan, Indonesia,
Malaya and all the nations from Iran westward across Africa to Morocco
are literally followers of the Prophet. Shocked to their heels by their
military defeat in Israel and humiliated by centuries of domination by
other religions, Muslims have belatedly determined that their lands must
unite in one formidable union. For the next half-century attempts to
achieve this union will be a dominant factor in Asian politics. As success
is attained it is to be expected that Islam will force many nations to make
difficult decisions. Fanatics already claim the Southern Philippines,
Northern Burma and Southern Thailand. Reasonable Muslims insist
that the French colonies of Northern Africa be set free. Grimly determined radicals are pressing the Indonesian Government to declare a
theocracy, while extremists in Iran murder political opponents. And in
all Muslim countries there is a minority which is determined to invade
Israel and expel the Jews.

On the other hand, Islam is a major constructive force in Asia. If the
laudable ideals of Motamar could be attained, life in Islamic Asia would
be much improved. If Miss Jinnah is correct, and if nations like Pakistan

and Indonesia can avoid degenerating into rabid theocracies—and there is enormous pressure to make them so—the Islamic nations could become what they dream of becoming: a third force in the world going their own way without transgressing the rights or interests of others.

But ultimately any Pan-Islamic movement must come into conflict with Hindu India. If Motamar says resolutely that its members will have to go to war if Kashmir is not delivered to Pakistan, this can only mean that all the nations of Islam will exert moral pressure on India in seeking the cession of Kashmir. And that will crystallize Hindu-Muslim antagonisms into a kind of perpetual enmity. (Even if war comes it is doubtful if the Islamic countries could offer Pakistan much military support now. In the future, however, when they have become stronger, they might effect a coalition that would strangle India.)

The nation which will face the most difficult decisions will be Indonesia. Traditionally this nation is a friend of India in almost exactly the relationship that exists between England and America. Indonesian life, customs, literature and art were greatly influenced by India, which indeed brought an advanced civilization to the islands. Therefore when, in the first days of both Indian and Indonesian national existence, Pandit Nehru visited Indonesia the effect was electric. It was as if brothers had met again after long years of absence and most Indonesians looked to India in those days as the leader of Asia with whom they wanted their smaller nation to co-operate.

This honeymoon cannot last long. Indonesia is a Muslim nation and bit by bit she will find that her interests coincide with those of the other Muslim lands. She will be forced to make extremely difficult choices and although the present Indonesian leaders—Sukarno, Hatt, Natsir and Sjahrir in particular—will continue to incline toward India, it is almost certain that a more religiously nationalistic group will ultimately take over. Their interests and sympathies will incline toward Pakistan.

In the meantime Pakistan is one of the thrilling nations of Asia. It is literally being born in front of your eyes. Karachi, once a sleepy, unimportant seaport of 200,000 exploded overnight into a national capital of 1,500,000. On its flat plains Karachi encompasses many little cities: clusters of mud refugee shacks, tent cities, lean-to cities, cave cities and a bright new modern city. Daily for the past five years caravans have arrived at Karachi bringing refugees, enterprising young men from the hinterlands, and keen would-be politicians. Through the streets great lumbering camels haul the produce of this new nation down to the harbor. In fragile temporary huts government officials work long, dedicated hours to get their new nation started right. In ancient mosques devout Muslims pray five times each day, offering thanks that they have been given to see the creation of the world's foremost religious state. Karachi is one of the few cities in Asia that has enough food, enough jobs and enough dedicated young men to construct a new society.

Even so, it is a true miracle that Pakistan exists at all. If it can survive the next ten years, its ultimate prosperity should be assured. The venture is one of the most exciting dramas of our time and Americans should applaud the attempt.

But we face a serious temptation in Pakistan. Paradoxically, we may get into trouble because we like Pakistan too much for anybody's good. Let me first explain why almost all Americans who visit both Pakistan and India much prefer the former. (1) Pakistan, having watched what happened to her Muslim neighbors when they lost world support in their war against Israel, is determined that the world shall understand her legitimate aspirations. (2) Pakistan has mastered the techniques of modern public relations and employs them in getting her story to the world. (3) The simple logic of her stand on Kashmir is immediately appealing when contrasted to India's turgid reasoning. (4) India, having opposed the United States on several points, has been severely criticized by Americans, whereas Pakistan has consistently sided with us. (5) It appears to be easier, for what reasons I do not know, for Americans to understand Islam than to understand Hinduism. (6) Americans also find it easier to identify themselves with Pakistan, a young and virile nation, than with India, a proud and ancient land.

The result is that nineteen out of every twenty American newsmen seem to prefer Pakistan. That is permissible so long as personal prejudices do not obscure basic truths. But it would be mere petulance for America to brand either Pakistan or India as all villain or all hero merely because one or the other happens to agree with us at the moment. If we find that Kashmir should be ceded to Pakistan, then in support of international justice we should recommend such a cession. But, in agreeing with Pakistan on the one specific problem, we must not condemn India permanently. Long after this present contention has been settled, the facts of geography will remain. Pakistan and India will still share their subcontinent and part of Pakistan will still be surrounded by India. If in a moment of self-righteousness we alienate ourselves from either of these two great powers, we shall in the future be unable to co-operate with them on possibly greater problems.

AMERICA AND ASIA

SO FAR I HAVE REPORTED MAINLY ON THE QUESTIONS I ASKED A LARGE
number of Asians. But while I probed their opinions, they were doing a little investigating of their own. Almost every educated Asian asked
me some question or other about the United States, and certain interroga-
tions became so inevitable that I could predict exactly how they would be
phrased.

I shall now give those persistent questions plus my answers.

The first question was asked by everyone. It was asked yesterday and
will surely be asked tomorrow: "How can you justify your treatment of
the Negro?"

I: I can't. I can only say that millions of us treat Negroes decently.
Your papers report the few who don't.

Asian: But what about the lynchings? Not even the British or Japs
lynched us, and we were their enemies. The Negroes are your friends.

I: The evil is dying out. You must believe me.

Asian: But it still continues.

I: All savage customs die slowly.

Asian: So as mob lynchings die out, legal lynchings take their place.

What about the mass electrocution of seven Negroes for a crime which did not even involve murder?

I: This question has been asked me so often that all I can do is refer you to the official explanation published by our State Department. There was a foul crime. Due process of law was followed. Judgment was passed, and the men were executed.

Asian: Yes, I know that. But Russian papers say that if seven white men had committed the crime there would have been no death sentences. Is that right?

I: How can I say what might happen?

Asian: But do you think seven white men would have been electrocuted for such a crime?

I: No.

Asian: Would the case even have come to trial?

I: In my state, absolutely yes.

Asian: But in other states, no?

I: Perhaps not.

Asian: Is what our papers say correct? That if white men had been involved the whole case would have been hushed up?

I: Haven't we argued this case long enough?

Asian: It can never be discussed enough when our papers use it as proof that America will always be the enemy of everything African and Asiatic.

I: Do you believe propaganda, or what your own judgment tells you is true about America?

Asian: On this point you cannot convince me. Has any Negro stood up and defended America for its treatment of Negroes?

I: Yes, a famous ballplayer named Jackie Robinson did. And some musicians. And I think Ralph Bunche would.

Asian: Oh, no! Ralph Bunche refused a good job in Washington because you don't allow Negroes to live there.

I: Your facts are not entirely correct, and I do think we've talked about this too long.

Asian: But to me the one single important fact about America is that you despise all people of color.

I: Oh, no! The bulk of Americans don't despise anyone. Did you hear about the friendly ovation we gave the Japanese swimmers who came to California?

Asian: But don't the F.B.I., when they investigate you, ask if you have ever entertained colored people in your home?

I: I don't believe that's true. The F.B.I. have been to see me several times. They've never asked me that question.

Asian: But the F.B.I. is pretty much like the Gestapo, isn't it?

I: Certainly not.

Asian: But they have investigated you, haven't they? They investigate all writers, don't they?

I: You misunderstand. I said they'd been by to see me. About men who had applied for very important government jobs.

Asian: But the F.B.I. and the Gestapo are after the same thing, aren't they? Crushing all liberal ideas.

I: Will you try to understand what I am going to say? We have reason to think that communist Russia is determined to destroy us. We have found spies hiding among us. In high places. We have asked the F.B.I. to protect us.

Asian: But the F.B.I. is a Gestapo. That's what I'm asking.

I: No. There is a fine line between a policeman and an oppressor. Our policemen haven't crossed that line yet.

Asian: But if you were to talk as liberally at home as you do here, the Un-American Activities Committee would arrest you, wouldn't they?

I: They have no power to arrest.

Asian: They threw Howard Fast in jail. Because he wrote books defending Negroes.

I: I think you have your facts wrong, but even so there was due process of law.

Asian: You quibble. Isn't it a fact that as a liberal you are in danger in America?

I: Not at all. On many points I'm a liberal and I haven't been prosecuted.

Asian: But Owen Lattimore was. That case worried us desperately. Did you know that most Asians thought highly of him? They considered him one of the few Americans who knew anything about Asia. He had just finished a speaking tour here when he was arrested.

I: He wasn't arrested.

Asian: I thought he was. Anyway, Senator McCarthy ruined him and he's been run out of American life. Because he was liberal.

I: As a matter of fact, Lattimore wasn't ruined. He still has his job. His university classes are bigger than ever. He's sold many copies of his book. And he's a popular lecturer.

Asian: But he was destroyed in Congress. I read about it.

I: Not at all. Our Congress has exactly the same rule that yours does. No member may be sued for libel because of what he says in Congress.

Asian: But isn't the difference that our Parliament protects human liberties whereas yours is totally reactionary?

I: You're entirely wrong. Have you ever heard of Senator Douglas? Or Ives? Or Vandenberg?

Asian: What I mean is, aren't your senators determined to put down popular movements wherever they appear?

I: I don't believe that's true. In South America, in Europe, in India and in Indonesia we backed popular liberal movements.

Asian: But you are determined to restore Chiang Kai-shek and Bao Dai and Syngman Rhee. Let me explain what worries me. We think that from now on any popular reform movement that arises in Asia will have to fight America.

I: Absolutely not. America has always been the champion of freedom.

Asian: But not here in Asia. Never where yellow people are involved. What about Chiang Kai-shek?

I: I'm willing to discuss Chiang. I happen not to like him for China because I think most Chinese don't like him. But if we are forced into a war with Russia, and if Red China helps Russia against us, then it would be morally criminal for us not to use Chiang's help to subdue Red China.

Asian: Then you admit that popular leaders like Mao are your enemy?

I: If they insist upon fighting us, yes.

Asian: Then you admit that all young Asians with new ideas of reform will have to look to Russia for leadership and support?

I: I didn't say that. I said that if such young leaders feel there is no hope for them in American friendship and if they insist upon attacking us, then we'll defend ourselves.

Asian: And to save yourself you'd throw Chiang back on Chinese soil?

I: If a general war developed, and if Mao supported Russia, yes, I would advocate using Chiang's help.

Asian: So America will align itself with reactionaries everywhere? And when you win, you'll support those reactionaries in control of the world? So that an American victory means world reaction? Isn't that right?

I: Not at all. You must believe that even if we are forced to associate with reactionaries to preserve freedom, when the crisis is past we will not install those reactionaries in control of aspiring peoples.

Asian: You are proposing the impossible.

I: That's right. The impossible. But that's what we must work for.

Asian: And I for one don't believe it can be done.

I: If it isn't, if America lines up permanently against all reform, then obviously we are finished as a great nation. That's why I insist we can support freedom.

Asian: I'm afraid the better gamble for Asiatic liberals is to side with Russia.

I: Apparently you don't know what Russia does to liberals. I'll admit that right now the Russian way looks easy. The American way looks hard. But you know that our way is the one you can trust. In the long run.

Asian: But there's still the critical question. Can we trust you? You lynch Negroes. You despise everyone with color. And you persecute liberals. How can we trust you?

I: Let me reply by asking one question. You said you'd known about two hundred Americans. Were they the kind of people you describe?

Asian: No, they were not. But what do you expect me to believe? The fine people we see visiting Asia? Good and generous? Or the people we read about who lynch Negroes? And who hate all liberal movements? If you were an Asian, would you trust Americans?

I: You've got to.

Many times I went through this argument and only rarely did I go away thinking that I had won. For no matter what an American says, the Asian keeps drifting back to a few terrible questions that are indeed almost unanswerable. If we could assure him on these points—1. that we do not lynch Negroes; 2. that we do not despise people with color; 3. that we do not persecute liberals—then I think we might win his support. If we can prove that we are not irretrievably opposed to legitimate reform, then other Americans who follow me will win some of their arguments with Asia.

BASIC

FACTS

FOR

AMERICANS

America has an honorable place in Asia, not as the new imperialist, for Asia will not tolerate that; nor as the perpetual Santa Claus, for the American taxpayer will not condone that; but as a co-operating friend working on problems of mutual concern and no doubt mutual profit. As we formulate our program for co-operation we should keep several basic facts in mind. Some of these have been discussed in preceding pages.

(1) *Asia is the foremost land mass in the world and comprises the largest assembly of people.* (Pages 5–6)

(2) *Asia, plus Europe and Africa, completely encircles the United States.* (Pages 5–6)

(3) *Asia is barely able to feed its people.* (Pages 40–41)

(4) *Population pressures will probably become increasingly severe.* One of the most paralyzing facts about Asia is that when food supply increases, population increases by exactly the number of people who can live at near starvation on the new food. Population figures in India and Indonesia prove this. When those areas were ravaged by pestilence and anarchy, population levels remained low, but when British and Dutch efficiency established some kind of order plus a secure food supply, population increased fantastically. Pessimists therefore reason that nothing can be done for Asia and that it is doomed to poverty, anarchy and starvation. I can't agree. It is true that India, Indonesia and China bred new millions whenever the food supply improved. But there were other areas such as Malaya, Thailand and Burma which have remained actually underpopulated. It is further true that the sexual emphasis in Hinduism has undoubtedly influenced India's and Indonesia's growth (the latter having imbibed Hinduism for a substantial period), but today Hindu leaders themselves are stressing the more spiritual aspects of their comprehensive religion. But the greatest hope lies in the fact that Asiatic leaders are aware of this terrifying problem. Some limitation of population is absolutely necessary. Perhaps Japan will demonstrate how this can be accomplished. As Asia assumes responsibility for its own destiny its leaders will not be able to escape the peril of a population that breeds itself into starvation. Pandit Nehru has already announced that India must learn to practice birth control. Other national leaders will unquestionably follow suit. But in spite of these hopeful signs I cannot forget the frightening potential of an Asiatic population increasing by 181,-000,000 every ten years! (This estimate is obtained by projection of India's demonstrated increase of 42,000,000 in the last decade.) If Asia continues to breed right up to the last grain of rice, sooner or later she must absorb the world. I cannot shake from my memory that foreboding statement of the American in India: "If we work to increase the life span of all Indians, then we are immoral if we do not at the same time make plans to give them Canada and all of the United States west of the Mississippi." Population increase and our attitude toward it should be considered in all our relations with Asia. During the next fifty years the present rate of increase will probably be maintained. After that, as education spreads, there should be a leveling off. But during that fifty-year

critical period America must do whatever possible to encourage voluntary population limitation, our goal and Asia's being a better life and
longer life for a population that can live comfortably on an available
food supply. The one thing we dare not do is to ignore the problem or its
logical consequences. (I am not reviving the cry, "Yellow Peril." Although
Asia's population increases each ten years by more than the total population of the United States, nearly half the increase is Aryan, as in India,
or Malayan, as in Indonesia. Nor is this inevitably a peril unless we
consciously alienate Asia and make her future billions our enemy.)

(5) *Religion is a prime moving force in Asia.* (Pages 228–32)

(6) *Much of Asia is more than 90 per cent illiterate.* (Pages 121–23
and 130–31)

(7) *Therefore of necessity Asia is an oligarchy.* (Pages 130–33)

(8) *For the present America must concern itself with convincing a
relatively few key Asians that it is in their countries' interest to remain
friends with us.* This is one of the salient facts about Asia. We are fighting for the understanding of a very few people. If we could convince this
handful that our way is better than the Russians', we would win Asia.
At the topmost level we are contending for the friendship of men like
Nehru, Sukarno, Liaquat Ali Khan and Chou En-lai. We have already
lost the last named to Russia. We must not lose the others. At the second
level we are fighting for the newspaper editors, the radio men, the industrial leaders and the college professors. We are doing good work in
bringing some of these men to America so that they can see for themselves
what our civilization is like. We should bring more, for Russia welcomes
them. We should also send from America counterparts of these Asiatic
leaders so that on all levels we will understand Asia. I am proud to say
we are accomplishing a good deal with this particular group. The third
level consists of the educated small businessmen and village farmers. So
far there are not many of this class who account for much in the counsels
of Asia, but as land reform gets under way they will become of paramount importance. We should have American experts working with
these men. At present we are not doing too badly: Fulbright Fellows,
medical and practical missionaries, agricultural specialists and some edu-
cators. It is on the fourth and most vital level that we have failed. College
students, recent graduates and young intellectuals tend to find Russia
much more alluring than America. Why is it that a young and vital
nation like the United States should suddenly lose its significant message
to young thinkers around the world? If you show a mature Indian businessman a General Motors plant he is bound to be impressed. But youthful students in Malaya or India surveying what America stands for

spiritually are apt to remain contemptuous. This is regrettable and we should do something about it. Exchange professors are helping. We should see that inexpensive American books are scattered through Asia. We should send good movies and keep the scabrous ones at home. We should continue to invite Asiatic students to America. Above all we should present ourselves throughout the world as a nation of some philosophical and moral depth. I know this sounds like fuzzy thinking but I remember that when Holland lost Indonesia, Holland was still a pretty considerable nation; but it so happened that all young Indonesians thought Holland was washed up. In this sweeping, swirling world what people think still determines history.

(9) *For the present it is the cities of Asia, not the countryside, that are important.* This is a temporary phenomenon, growing out of factors just reviewed. The pitch and purpose of Asiatic life are presently established by the cities. Here the oligarchs, the students and the business leaders converge. Here the policies of Asia are set. Cities like Tokyo, Shanghai, Manila and Bombay dominate life, even though more than 80 per cent of Asia lives in villages. This unbalanced importance of the city will disappear once the villagers learn to read and vote, but for the present we must watch the cities for those signs of social and political upheaval which will mark much future history. Especially spectacular are the newer cities of Asia. Djakarta, for example, had in 1940 a population of 800,000. Today, swollen by the tides of refugees fleeing internal disorders, it has almost 3,000,000. It is a vital center exercising an influence far out of proportion to its natural weight in Indonesian life. An official explained why: "If Washington were destroyed, wiping out your entire Government, you could go to a city like Des Moines or Denver and find a group of men quite capable of carrying on. Someone would know how to handle taxes, another foreign affairs, another national health. But here, if our capital of Djakarta were destroyed, Indonesia could have no government." A key contributor to the importance of cities like Calcutta, Karachi and Singapore is the peculiar concentration there of the unemployed intellectuals. They are key factors in Asiatic politics, contributing to both the importance and explosiveness of the crowded cities. What little education Asia has enjoyed has been classical, would-be Indian officials memorizing Latin and would-be Chinese officials memorizing Confucius. The result has been a plethora of philosophers and a dearth of bricklayers. Since Asians are naturally gifted in disputation, everyone who could became a lawyer. This was usually a prelude to unemployment which in turn led the young classical scholars right into the middle of some kind of revolution. Gandhi, Jinnah, Sukarno, Chou En-lai and

Madame Chiang Kai-shek represent the bright young men and women who won their revolutions. It is a dead cinch that their present counterparts—lacking an English or Dutch imperialism to connive against—are plotting against their own governments. These turbulent cities of Asia present the same political paradox as do the oligarchs. Today the cities and the oligarchs are important. Tomorrow it will be the countryside and the awakened people.

(10) *Sooner or later the people of Asia will govern themselves.* This is the only fact about the future of Asia of which I am reasonably sure. I don't know when the transfer of authority will take place. I can't foresee the tortured upheavals that will accompany the revolutions. Nor can I guess which fortunate countries will engineer the transfer peaceably. But it will take place. If we were to suppose otherwise we would have to rewrite all of history, we would have to modify man, and we would have to halt in mid-flight the aspirations of the human mind. Let us work upon the assumption that the present uneducated masses of Asia will one day become both educated and competent. What prospects for the future then emerge?

WE

WILL

HAVE

A SECOND

CHANCE

It is now generally admitted that between 1940–1950 we engineered a fiasco in our relations with China. Judged solely on the basis of that performance, we are so inept in dealing with Asia that we should abandon the continent to the Russians. But we are going to get a second chance, and if we mess things up this time we shall have no alternative but to scuttle back to North America and await the hurricanes.

Each problem we faced and fumbled in China we shall meet again in every other Asiatic nation. India, Indonesia, Burma, Ceylon, Pakistan, Indo-China, Malaya and Iran will present us with almost exactly the same choices we met in China. For these nations are going to recapitulate much of China's history.

In the 1920's the Chinese revolution completed the overthrow of an old feudal order. The new nation, faced by the same illiteracy problem that still plagues Asia, had perforce to adopt an oligarch who could give

China the best government then attainable. Chiang Kai-shek was that oligarch.

Then the United States made several fundamental errors, all springing from our unwillingness to face the facts of life. We did not acknowledge that Chiang was a logical development in this stage of China's growth. Nor did we recognize the ferment of new ideas among the younger Chinese. Vast political forces in China were moving to a crisis while we ignored the probable consequences. We dreamed and dallied. We meddled and muddled just long enough to defeat ourselves on all counts. We refused Chiang adequate coherent support to enable him and China to progress, but we did ambiguously offer just enough to ensure that his communist enemies would smear him as a tool of American imperialism. We created a classic example of diplomatic frustration. And into the midst of that frustration stepped Russia.

Within the decade it is likely that the United States will meet each of these problems again—in each Asiatic country. Consider India. Following her successful and peaceful revolution she had no alternative but to give her government to enlightened oligarchs, many of whom were very great men, but all of whose ideals had been formulated in the 1920's during the battle against the British. They were good men to lead a revolution or to become the political saints of a new nation. But they were not the right men—as no men could be—to govern the nation indefinitely. Their oligarchy too will shudder before the attack of young new leaders with radical ideas of land reform, industrialization and popular democracy.

At that time the United States will face two alluring courses, either of which will ensure our defeat. The first will be to brand indiscriminately all new leaders as communists, thus driving them into alliance with real reds. The second will be to abandon the present leaders of India whenever real disruptive communism starts to erode and undermine the state.

The course which will save us in all of Asia is to support substantial governments wherever they exist and to back forever and forever the ultimate masses of the people as they grow toward responsibility and the control of their own political existence. Thus the timing of our decisions in Asia will be one of the most difficult jobs we have ever tried as a nation. This must not be construed as power politics. Nor is it crass and immoral realism. It is the task of an intelligent and moral nation trying to find its way.

(1) Let us keep our normal wits about us. Asia is not a continent of barbarian hordes or inscrutable evil. It would be a most healthy step if the word *Asia* were never again in American print to be prefaced by adjectives like *inscrutable* or *mysterious*. They are only fuzzy wraps we throw around our minds when we feel the unpleasant chill of ignorance. The political, social and economic motives which make Asians behave as they do are the same that make Texans or Frenchmen behave as they do.

(2) Let us apply our keenest brains to the problems of Asia. Although the embassies of Paris or London offer more glitter and publicity, Asia cries out for the attention and intelligence of our ablest minds: diplomats, merchants, technicians, writers and military advisers. Our political reporting from Asia should shine with precision and glow with humanity.

(3) Let us banish from our minds the commonest clichés about Asia. Three good ones to start with are these: "Asia is bound to overrun the world." (I have given several reasons why this is not inevitable and we must work to alleviate the forces which might seem to make it so.) "Asiatic religions are barbarous." (I have yet to study one at close hand that did not contain deep spiritual beauties.) "You can't fight the whole Chinese people." (I am particularly afraid of inhibiting untruths, and although I am devoutly attached to peace, if war is forced upon my nation I won't want it to be hamstrung by psychological fears which are not well founded.)

(4) Let us especially purge our thoughts of any lingering illusion that whenever things get tough, or whenever we lose a battle or a friend, we can abandon Asia. If trouble or unfavorable temporary decisions soften us rather than stiffen our resolve, then we certainly should stay out of Asia. That is to say, we should make immediate plans to resign from the world.

(5) Let us anticipate normal disappointments and greet them with patience and persistence. We cannot afford to be thrown off balance by mere irritation, damaging ourselves and our friends through petulance. It does not matter if some Indian leaders rail wildly against us in public; if it is a good and wise thing to send wheat to India (and it was) we should send it. We know it is unfair for Asia to hate us today merely because Europe mistreated her in the past. We have inherited Europe's

role in many worthy particulars and will have to take the automatic hatreds, too. This is no time to argue nineteenth-century history; we have got to make the best of the present. Therefore if our missionaries are thrown out of China, we must transfer their hospitals and schools and churches elsewhere—in Asia. If we must close our banks in Hong Kong, we must reopen them in Saigon. And if communism has wrecked Korea, we must help to rebuild it.

(6) Let us not scorn our European allies in Asia. The costly folly of their colonialism is only part of the truth. The other is that Great Britain, because of her far-sightedness in working out peaceful Indian, Pakistanian and Burmese settlements, is today widely and deeply respected in many parts of Asia. As a learned Indian remarked to me, "After England was kicked out the front door, she appeared at the kitchen offering to help us with the dishes." Thanks to this, British thought and philosophy underlie much Asiatic law, most Asiatic business procedures and almost all Asiatic attitudes toward the sanctity of parliamentary government. Asians today ridicule Americans and remember the English as fairly decent men.

(7) Let us not, even as we practice the wisdom of forbearance, be beguiled into appeasement. To grovel before Peking's communist junta as British diplomats found themselves doing is as futile as it is humiliating. It banishes from those it seeks to placate the last vestige of respect for the supplicant. No Asiatic ally worth the having can be bought that way. We work with Asia, we conciliate, we help, we even at times contribute outright—but we do not appease.

(8) Let us remember our numerous friends in Asia. Every man who was educated in a missionary college, every woman who was treated in an American hospital, every Asian who visited America is a potential friend. Even in communist China there must still be hundreds of thousands of men and women who would welcome us back. Our policies should be built around these people who know us, and they include most of the present rulers of Asia. We must succor those now governed by the enemy and we must support those who are learning to govern themselves.

(9) Let us proclaim that we are a democracy and that we, like almost all Asiatic nations, won our independence through revolting against our own alien masters. Let us remind the new countries of Asia that we too were once a struggling nation with all the problems that beset the newborn: our credit was no good, our central government was impotent, our enemies pounced upon us, and we had to abandon one form of government and later withstand a great civil war before we were successfully launched. Let us assure Asiatic nations now teetering between our way and Russia's that we are closer to the spirit of democratic nationalism

than Russia can ever be. America, not Russia, is the natural friend of youthful nations. Of course, to make such claims we must believe them. I was mortified when an Indian leader told me, "Every self-respecting Indian, Burman or Pakistani renounced his British titles as unbecoming a democracy. But we encouraged Sir Benegal Rau to keep his because we know that American newspapers and dowagers just love titles." Let us not be ashamed that we were born in revolution.

The future of the West in Asia is in terrible doubt, for we inherit the legacy of hatred built up by careless white men who preceded us. But the cost of failure is too staggering for us to hesitate, for when we have solved our problems in Asia we shall meet each one all over again in Africa.

PERSPECTIVE

One way to understand Asia is to study South American history. The great revolution which swept that continent in the nineteenth century has belatedly reached Asia. Had there been Russian communists in 1850 it is likely that Bolívar, O'Higgins and San Martín would have been so labeled, and if Russian support had been available against reactionary governments, these reformers might have indeed become communists. Left to themselves, they constructed free nations. It is to be hoped that Asian leaders will do the same. But whether they do or not, the revolution is under way.

Only a short time ago Holland was a leading imperial nation. She held dominion over parts of India, Ceylon and all the swarming islands east of Singapore. Her fleets drove Britain's from the sea and even threatened the Thames. Today Holland is a lovable and restricted little land while great Indonesia has become a focal point of world history.

It is possible that within fifty years we shall remember Great Britain with affectionate reverence as a group of relatively inconsequential is- lands with a glorious past, while India becomes one of the three or four major nations of the earth.

It is also possible—I think probable if we continue to make basic mistakes—for the United States to become a museum relic like Greece, honored in memory for having brought to the world a fresh clean version of freedom; while Asia becomes the effective center of the world.

Such a decline is not inevitable, but we can avert it only through intelligence, tolerance and hard work.